An Archive of Taste

An Archive of Taste

Race and Eating in the Early United States

Lauren F. Klein

University of Minnesota Press
Minneapolis
London

This book is freely available in an open access edition thanks to TOME (Toward an Open Monograph Ecosystem)—a collaboration of the Association of American Universities, the Association of University Presses, and the Association of Research Libraries—and the generous support of Emory University and the Andrew W. Mellon Foundation. Learn more at the TOME website, available at: openmonographs.org.

A different version of chapter 1 was published as "Dinner-Table Bargains: Thomas Jefferson, James Madison, and the Senses of Taste," *Early American Literature* 49, no. 2 (Spring 2014): 403–33; copyright 2014 by the University of North Carolina Press, reprinted by permission of the publisher, www.uncpress.org. Different versions of portions of chapter 3 were published in "Speculative Aesthetics," *Early American Literature* 51, no. 2 (Spring 2016): 437–45; copyright 2016 University of North Carolina Press, reprinted by permission of the publisher, www.uncpress.org. A different version of a portion of chapter 4 was published in "The Matter of Early American Taste," in *The Cambridge Companion to Food and Literature,* ed. J. Michelle Coughlan (Cambridge University Press, 2020); copyright 2020, Cambridge University Press, reprinted with permission. A different version of chapter 5 was published as "The Image of Absence: Archival Silence, Data Visualization, and James Hemings," *American Literature* 85, no. 4 (Winter 2013): 661–88; copyright 2013, Duke University Press, reprinted by permission, www.dukeupress.edu.

Published by the University of Minnesota Press
111 Third Avenue South, Suite 290
Minneapolis, MN 55401-2520
http://www.upress.umn.edu

ISBN 978-1-5179-0508-8 (hc)
ISBN 978-1-5179-0509-5 (pb)

A Cataloging-in-Publication record for this book is available from the Library of Congress.

Printed in the United States of America on acid-free paper

The University of Minnesota is an equal-opportunity educator and employer.

UMP BmB 2020

To my parents

Contents

Acknowledgments

This book began nearly a decade ago as a dissertation at the Graduate Center of the City University of New York. It seems only fitting that I should begin these acknowledgments by thanking my dissertation committee members, David S. Reynolds, Duncan Faherty, Ammiel Alcalay, and Joshua Wilner, who helped to shape the project in its initial stages. David Reynolds has remained a steadfast supporter of my work, and Duncan Faherty has become a trusted mentor, colleague, and friend. I owe a debt of gratitude to Jenny Davidson, who joined my committee as an outside reader, and has since become a dear friend. At several key phases of this project, as she has throughout my career, Jenny generously offered her expert intellectual guidance and professional advice. I would not be writing these words of thanks without the gift of her friendship.

I should also thank Joe Ugoretz, who directed the Instructional Technology Fellowship (ITF) program where I worked during my final years of graduate school. He remains an exemplar of graduate-student mentorship and advocacy. My colleagues in the ITF program, especially Jeff Drouin, Lisa Brundage, John Sorrentino, and Helen Davis, provided solidarity and support during the dissertation-writing process. Several colleagues in my cohort at the Grad Center, as well as several friends at other institutions, read and commented on early drafts of this work. Anton Borst, Rebekah Rutkoff, Karen Weingarten, Karen Weiser, Nora Morrison, and Tim Alborn deserve particular mention for their input during those years, as does Sari Altschuler, whose path has fortuitously continued to intersect with my own. I am grateful for her friendship as well as her disciplinary expertise, which has significantly enriched this book.

I could not have known that the writing group that Sarah Blackwood, Kyla Schuller, Karen Weingarten, and I convened in my final year in New York would continue into the present, nor could I have imagined how much I would come to rely on it as a source of intellectual engagement and emotional support. Time and time again, these three kind, generous, and razor-sharp scholars read over these pages, commenting at the levels of argument, structure, sentence, and tone. This book is so much better for their contributions, as I am for their friendship.

In my first year in Atlanta, Nihad Farooq and Natalia Cecire quickly became trusted colleagues and treasured friends. Nihad and Natalia are also among those who read numerous chapter drafts, enriching this book with their keen insights. Additional friends read and offered feedback on sections of this book: Matt Gold, Dawn Peterson, and Yanni Loukissas. My thanks goes to them as well.

I thank the anonymous readers at the University of Minnesota Press, whose generous and generative comments greatly improved this book. I also thank the anonymous readers at *Early American Literature* and *American Literature* for their feedback on the essays that would become chapters 1 and 5, respectively. Ed Larkin and Ed Cahill offered valuable feedback on the essay in *Early American Literature* that would form the conceptual basis for chapter 3. J. Michelle Coghlan provided thoughtful commentary on the previously published book chapter from which portions of chapter 4 are drawn.

As I prepared this book for publication, David Lobenstine's expert editorial eye helped me to refine the book's argument and structure and pushed me to clarify each and every claim. I remain so appreciative of the time he invested in this project. Thanks are owed also to Paul Vincent, who copyedited the manuscript, and David Martinez, who indexed the book.

Although I moved to Emory University in fall 2019, this book was written during my time at Georgia Tech, where I worked between 2011 and 2019. In the School of Literature, Media, and Communication, my colleagues Nihad Farooq, Yanni Loukissas, Carl DiSalvo, Anne Pollock, Aaron Santesso, Narin Hassan, Chris LeDantec, Nassim Parvin, Joycelyn Wilson, Janet Murray, Hugh Crawford, Carol Colatrella, Susana Morris, and André Brock all provided crucial grounding and moral support as I completed the book manuscript. My department chair during that time, Richard Utz, was steadfast in support of my scholarship. A research fellowship from the New York Public Library (NYPL) in fall 2013 also enabled me to conduct crucial archival work for this project. I thank Thomas Lannon, of the NYPL Manuscripts and Archives Division, for his invaluable assistance and expertise.

At the University of Minnesota Press, deep thanks are owed to Danielle Kasprzak, who acquired the project and guided me through the initial review process; and to Pieter Martin, who saw the book through publication, providing reassurance and support. Throughout the process, Anne Carter remained a constant source of information and expertise. In the production department, Mike Stoffel and Ana Bichanich also provided invaluable assistance.

Over the decade that it has taken to usher this book into the world, I have been buoyed by my friendships: Aileen Brophy, Nora Morrison, Mike Epstein, Sarah Madigan, Toby Moore, Mary Beth Kennedy, Sloan Johnston, Eamon Johnson, Frances Wall Jha, Saurabh Wall Jha, Jess Daniels, Gaylen Moore, JC Dwyer, Jenny Davidson, Jen Liu, Luca Marinelli, Ian Loew, Loren Hough, Meredith Betterton, Nihad Farooq, Todd Michney, Jacob Eisenstein, Shawn Ramirez, Yanni Loukissas, Kate Diedrick, Lauren Wilcox, Richard Patterson, Carl DiSalvo, Betsy DiSalvo, Chris LeDantec, Renata LeDantec, Miriam Posner, Natalia Cecire, Sari Altschuler, Sarah Blackwood, Lauren Waterman, Karen Weingarten, Kyla Schuller, Leora Bersohn, Carrie Weber, Catherine D'Ignazio, and many more I could continue to name. Among my extended family, Jon Zinman and Mary Coffey, Beth and Dick Zinman, and Rand Niederhoffer and Adam Lapidus deserve special thanks for their interest in the project, and their support along the way.

Among the first conversations I had with my partner, Greg Zinman, were about this project, and it is not an understatement to say that this book would not exist without him. For over a decade, I have turned to him in my moments of greatest doubt and greatest inspiration. He has always been ready to listen and to affirm, and in the process he has read countless versions of every chapter of this book. His own scholarship continues to inspire me, as does the love that he shows to our two daughters, Loie and Aurora. Greg: I love you, and I could not have completed this project without you.

It is not everyone who can claim three generations of family involvement in the making of a book. But I can do so, proudly. My grandmother, Elaine Niederhoffer, herself an author, copyedited the seminar paper that would become chapter 1 of this book. I will always feel her influence on these pages. My sister, Amy Klein, a poet and musician, offered a final read of the Introduction on the morning before I submitted it as part of my tenure dossier. My parents, Diane and Francis Klein, also read, commented upon, and line-edited many parts of this book. That they did so with such eagerness was not a surprise, as they were the ones who taught me to read and write as a scholar. Among my strongest grade school memories is of my mother sitting next to me in front of our family's Macintosh computer as I completed each writing assignment, reading over each line as I wrote, suggesting more nuanced words to use and more sophisticated ways to express my ideas. And it was my father who would offer suggestions of how I could enhance my interpretations, pointing out valences of the language and themes that I had overlooked, often supplementing my classroom notes with his own annotations of each novel or short story or poem that I had been assigned. It is to my parents that I owe my love of learning, and it is to them that I dedicate this book.

No Eating in the Archive

There is no eating in the archive.

This is not only a practical admonition, extended to any would-be researcher. It is also a methodological challenge: there is, quite literally, no eating—or at least no food—preserved among the books, letters, newspapers, manuscripts, and other documents that constitute the archival record of the early United States. Although eating is among the most universal of human activities, the traces of the culinary habits of that era are scant. Even cookbooks, that most basic bastion of our contemporary culinary lives, contain only lists of ingredients, as detailed preparation instructions were not typically included until the second half of the nineteenth century. Personal receipt books, as recipe books were known at the time, contain family names and the occasional address, but rarely offer sufficient detail about the lives of those who inscribed the recipes in pen and ink. Documents such as shipping inventories and ledger books suggest certain foodstuffs that might have been consumed, but offer little additional information. Letters from the era provide tantalizing, but often fleeting, mention of meals consumed. Even the novels of the time, which one might assume would serve up a trove of fictive cuisine, rarely discuss food or eating in more than a single line of prose.

How, then, are we to approach the study of eating—of the many and multiple meanings of our appetites and pleasures—in the early United States? How are we to conceive of its archive, where we would otherwise locate the material basis of the stories that we seek to tell? Scholars from across the disciplines have long possessed methods for preserving, compiling, describing, and interpreting the artifacts of everyday life in the new republic. And yet the artifacts associated with eating, which most embodied and were immediate of everyday experiences, remain perishable in the most literal sense. What's more, the experiences they might record—like the succulent crunch of a Newtown Pippin, the variety of apple that Thomas Jefferson requested be crated and sent to him from

Virginia while he served as minister to France—can at times pose a threat to archival preservation itself.[1]

I have spent the past decade thinking about these constraints: about the food that I cannot taste; about an understanding of eating that is far removed from our present food culture; and about the methods that might allow me, along with other scholars and students of early American literature and culture, to recover, and at times reimagine, the experiences of eating embedded in the archive of the nation's founding. In the process, I have been drawn to the conceptual paths by which eating came to matter in that particular temporal moment. By exploring contemporaneous aesthetic philosophies in concert with contemporary interpretive techniques, I have arrived at a view of how eating exposes a range of theories and tensions at play in the early United States. As I argue in the pages to come, eating emerged as form of aesthetic expression over the course of the eighteenth century, and subsequently transformed into a means of expressing both allegiance and resistance to the dominant Enlightenment worldview. Imported from Europe and incorporated into the ideological framework of the United States largely intact, this view authorized certain individuals—namely, the white, property-owning men who served as the nation's prototypical citizens—to derive heightened social and political significance from the sense of taste. At the same time, those excluded from this narrow conception of citizenship recognized in eating an accessible means of demonstrating their own sense of national belonging, as well as additional and, at times, explicitly oppositional aesthetic theories.

But we—as both students and scholars of the nation's founding—cannot fully appreciate the force or depth of this aesthetic mode by relying on the archive as it is currently conceived. We must of course first account for the evidence that is preserved in the archival record, however scattered or scant. But we must then account for the experiences of eating that resist preservation, and therefore remain undisclosed. My own method of accounting for these evidentiary gaps involves interweaving textual artifacts with accounts, both real and fictive, of foods harvested, dishes prepared, and meals consumed. Into these reconstituted narratives, not unlike a reconstituted stock, I infuse the additional aspects of eating that remain bound to the bodies of those who performed the harvesting, preparing, and consuming. In doing so, I reveal how figures ranging from the nation's first presidents to their enslaved cooks employed eating in order to elaborate—or, alternatively, in order to challenge—received ideas about the nature of sensory experience and subjective judgment. *An Archive of Taste* thus demonstrates how an attention to eating allows us to identify additional actors and agents who were directly involved in establishing the nation's cultural foundation, as well as additional methodological techniques for acknowledging, if not ever fully recovering, the range of experiences that remain conscribed to the past.

A "Most Celebrated" Account of Eating

As an initial example of the application of these techniques, as well as of their impact on our understanding of the nation's cultural foundation, consider what at least one culinary historian describes as the "most celebrated" account of eating of that time. It is not a contemporaneous account, since none are known to exist, but a scene that appears in the final pages of the *Recollections and Private Memoirs of the Life of Washington,* written by Washington's grandson, George Washington Parke Custis, and published in 1860, sixty years after the first president's death (Adrian Miller, *Cabinet,* 39). Washington, we are told, "was remarkably fond of fish," and, one February morning, "it happened that a single shad was caught in the Delaware" (Custis, 421). Samuel Fraunces, Washington's steward and "a man of talent and considerable taste," acting on his epicurean impulses, snatched the fish from the fishmonger "with the speed of an osprey" (421). After nearly forty years of experience as an innkeeper, caterer, and chef—including a previous stint as Washington's steward in New York—Fraunces was convinced that his quick action "had secured a delicacy that, above all others, . . . would be agreeable to the palate of his chief" (421).[2] When the dish was served, however, Washington did not respond as expected: "'Take it away,' thundered the chief; 'take it away, sir; it shall never be said that my table sets such an example of luxury and extravagance.' Poor Fraunces tremblingly obeyed, and the first shad of the season was removed untouched, to be speedily discussed by the gourmands of the servants' hall" (422).

Washington's emphatic rejection of an otherwise "agreeable" fish demonstrates how food functioned as an emblem of both personal and political values. Just fifteen years after the nation had declared independence, decisions about what to eat and how to eat had already become more than mere reflections of one's dietary preferences; food was employed to express a very particular culinary ideology, what I term in these pages *republican taste*. This sense of taste courses through many narratives of the nation's founding, even if it is not named as such. It is characterized by a commitment to the virtues of simplicity, temperance, and moderation, which themselves derive from fundamental republican political ideals.[3] And this sense of taste, I contend, has a crucial and as-yet-unacknowledged source: the dining table. Indeed, in certain respects, these virtues were first cultivated at the table, and only then transposed to the civic sphere. In response to the "luxury and extravagance" that came to be associated with the British Crown (and, evidently, with a plate of fresh fish) Washington and the other "founders" consistently worked to establish plain living as a core quality of U.S. citizens.[4] In this particular account, Washington's anger seems to derive from his frustration at Fraunces's failure to recognize how, in Washington's new role as national figurehead, the "example" of tasteful and temperate consumption must always be placed ahead of the immediate gratification of his personal palate.

The full significance of accounts of eating such as these, interspersed throughout the archival record of the nation's founding, comes into focus when situated within the larger discourse of taste and the multiple meanings that the term "taste" contains. These meanings span from the sensory experience of eating, to personal preferences for certain flavors, to more general inclinations toward (or against) certain cultural expressions.[5] From this conceptual vantage, we can begin to identify how such instances of eating, however anecdotal or otherwise incomplete, help to expose the larger significance of food and eating in establishing a cultural foundation for the United States. At the same time, we must also attend to the sensory and material dimensions of aesthetic taste, and its evolution as a philosophical and political concept, over the course of that era. To do so can help to affirm the importance of considering lived experience and culinary expertise alongside the range of artifacts that traditionally constitute the archive of the early United States—indeed, those that constitute the American archive as a whole.[6] By attending to that interplay between texts and bodies, and between subjective experience and acculturated response, we come to see the archive of taste in a new light: one that illuminates the intellectual work, as well as the labor, involved in the cultivation, preparation, and consumption of food.

For behind the story of Washington's ill-fated fish, and the other accounts of eating in the early republic that can be surfaced, are the stories of the men and women who labored to produce the edible matter of republican taste. In this case, we are prompted to consider the stories of the "gourmands of the servants' hall," those who ultimately consumed—and, we are led to believe, delighted in devouring—the "delicacy" intended for the commander in chief. What were their experiences as "servants" to the first president of the United States? And how did they contribute, along with Washington, to the image of the republic that he sought to create?

Custis identifies one of these "gourmands" as an enslaved man by the name of Hercules, the "chief cook" at Mount Vernon, who, in the summer of 1790, was summoned to Philadelphia to serve the "masters of the republic" as the president's chef (422, 423). According to Custis, Hercules's culinary skill was so "highly accomplished," and his command over the kitchen so adept, that he "would have been termed in modern parlance, a celebrated *artiste*" (422). Confirmation of his "elegant" cookery comes from several secondhand accounts, as well as from Washington's own hand, disclosing how tightly matters of taste were bound to the culinary knowledge of individual cooks, as well as to the broader institution of slavery (qtd. in Adrian Miller, *Cabinet*, 64).[7]

Washington's personal correspondence also discloses something else: on the morning of February 22, 1797, the date of the president's sixty-fifth birthday, Hercules escaped from Washington's Mount Vernon estate.[8] In a letter to his nephew, George Lewis, Washington describes his cook's escape as the "most inconvenient thing" ever experienced by himself and his family, for both practical and philosophical reasons (469). As was the case with many of the nation's founders, Washington's ideological commitment to ensuring the liberty and equality of all Americans was directly impeded as he pursued his personal pleasures and tastes. Stated once again: this pursuit depended both practically and philosophically on the enslavement of others.

In his letter to Lewis, Washington makes this conflict explicit: "What renders it more disagreeable," he states, referring to Hercules's escape, "is, that I had resolved never to become the Master of another Slave by purchase; but this resolution I fear I must break" (469). Washington's words offer a profound reminder of how any form of cultural expression,

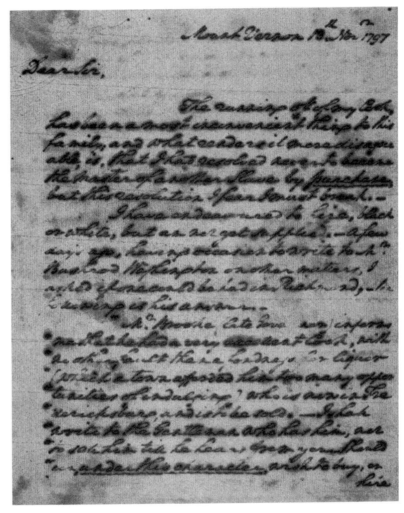

Figure 1. This letter, written by George Washington to George Lewis on November 13, 1797, reveals how Washington's desire for tasteful food was practically and philosophically dependent on the enslavement of others. Courtesy of the Manuscripts and Archives Division, New York Public Library.

including but not limited to eating, is inextricably linked to the larger relationships—among individuals, and among individuals and institutions—that give rise to it. In other words, in this single line, penned in Washington's own hand, we glimpse not only the extent to which he relied on Hercules in his daily life, but also the extent to which this daily reliance involved—indeed, was fundamentally premised upon—that most abhorrent institution in the nation's history.

This seemingly self-contained episode points to the two major analytical aims of this book. The first is to expose the imbrications of politics and taste, especially as they relate to issues of slavery and race. As Kyla Wazana Tompkins has established, eating functioned as a "trope and technology of racial formation during the first 130 years of the U.S. republic" both before and after slavery (*Indigestion*, 2). In support of this thesis, and against the essentializing claims of the time, I offer an array of new evidence that documents the tastefulness of figures such as Hercules, who were forcibly excluded from the republican project, even as their knowledge and labor directly underwrote it.[9] The second aim builds on the first, and it is to model how a sustained attention to taste as both formal philosophy and everyday experience allows additional theories of aesthetics, of agency, and of the people who exemplified both, to enter into the stories we tell about the nation's founding. These stories, often rooted in the lives of the enslaved, enrich our understanding in the present, demonstrating by whom and by what means that cultural foundation was composed.

To achieve this latter aim requires that we come to see the archive of the early United States as a site of embodied philosophical thinking as well as a collection of historically significant artifacts. This more capacious critical stance enables us to consider how meals such as the "first shad of the season," cooked for the pleasure of the commander in chief, might be interpreted in terms of the theoretical work that they perform.[10] For acts of cooking and eating, in their synthesis of the sensory, the cerebral, and the social, offer what Lauren Berlant, in conversation with Jordan Alexander Stein, has identified as an underexplored set of "practices and registers for theorizing life" (20). Eating, in other words, offers an untrafficked entry point into a better understanding of an individual, a community, or a culture, while also helping to conjure a sense of what our distance from the past will forever occlude from view.[11] By focusing on cooking and eating in the early United States—the era that gave rise to many of our current ideas about the human, about race, and about the archives that inscribe such beliefs and structures into history—I show how meaning is inherently mediated by the materials of its conveyance. By offering an account of how taste came to matter as both a sensory experience and a political act, I demonstrate how the embodied cultural practices thought to be consigned to history might instead advance an expanded conception of the early American archive. In so doing, *An Archive of Taste* advances an expanded conception of the archive itself, one constituted through the body and the senses as much as through the written record, and one that must be reconstituted—and reinterpreted—long after the fact.

An Expanded Archive of Eating

It has long been a basic tenet of food studies scholarship that, as Roland Barthes has averred, "information about food must be gathered wherever it can be found" (24). And for at least as long, it has been the ground truth of early American literary studies, the primary disciplinary field in which I place this work, that information about that era is similarly diffuse.[12] As a locus classicus for the cultural heritage industry in the United States, the nation's first decades, in particular, often seem overstudied. As evidence of this claim, one need look no further than the regular churn of best-selling biographies of the "founding fathers," Washington among them. Yet these well-known histories rest on many unknown ones, to which scholars have only (relatively) recently begun to attend. Household inventories, receipt books, shipping logs, and even relatively rich texts such as Washington's response to Hercules's escape, remain what Susan Scott Parrish describes as "underdetermined" documents, most often scanned for contextual information, and rarely plumbed for their depths (265).[13] Yet for scholars of the early United States, and of early America more broadly conceived, these fragments constitute our primary texts; there are rarely others that can provide a narrative frame. Thus, like the archive of eating, the archive of the early United States is an archive of necessity. It is one that, to paraphrase Barthes, consists of any and all documents that can be found. Aside from the handful of texts that, over time, have been elevated to the level of canon—and, in the case of certain records of the nation's founding, encased in bulletproof glass—this archive is similarly comprised of texts otherwise set to the side.

Consider the sources that contribute to the account of Hercules that I have just provided: a series of reminiscences by George Washington's grandson, first published in a Washington, D.C., newspaper and only later collected, expanded, and reprinted as a book; a letter from an otherwise unmemorable single-term congressman describing a dinner with the president, made accessible to the public only when it was printed in the *Pennsylvania Magazine of History and Biography* in 1884; and another nineteenth-century account, a biography of Martha Washington, authored by a woman, Margaret Conkling, about whom little is known.[14] None of these sources center on Hercules, for neither his life experience nor his cooking was considered a valid subject of scholarship in his own time. But rethinking the archival status of eating allows us to infuse new meaning into these records, and others like them, more than two centuries after the meals that they reference were cleared from the tables on which they were served.

Of course, information about eating can be gleaned from other sources as well. In addition to narratives and letters, relevant information is embedded in recipes and cookbooks, and sometimes *on* them, as food spots and cooking stains often endure longer than ink. Information about eating can also be found in farmers' almanacs and seed catalogs, receipts for purchases and packing lists, as well as in the flavors and histories of the foodstuffs themselves.[15] The taste of a heritage grain, for example, can signal the agricultural environment that gave rise to it, and in some cases point more precisely to the knowledge and labor of those who cultivated it over generations, allowing it to achieve its most flavorful form.[16] The path of a particular foodstuff, like squash or okra, which traveled from Africa to North America via the Caribbean, can also point to the peoples who brought it with them, and who brought it to new life in new locales.[17] The "elegant" presentation of Hercules's fresh-caught shad can indicate the taste preferences of both the people who prepared the dish, and the people who consumed it.[18] Yet these details are insufficient on their own; they function as placeholders for the stories we yearn to hear, but cannot be told without significant scholarly intervention. Their original richness, which today might be documented through a single Instagram shot, an episode of a cooking show, or an entry on a food blog, can only be approximated through the partial accounts that remain.[19]

In assembling the accounts that serve as the basis for this book, I also aim to illustrate how the archive of eating is best constituted by a heterogeneous set of documents and sources, and read through a commensurately heterogeneous set of interpretive techniques. These span from more familiar methods of close reading and historical synthesis to more speculative methods for theorizing and even visualizing large amounts of text. I will elaborate on this mixed methodology in the pages to come.

Here, the key point is that I place these methods alongside each other not in spite of their differences, but precisely because of them. This approach is one that, I believe, will allow scholars who seek to study food and eating in the early United States, as in all eras conscribed to the past, to go beyond gathering "information" about their objects of study, as Barthes first proposed, so as to imbue those objects with additional richness and depth.[20]

This mixture of methods is essential to assembling the archive that I rely upon for evidence of my historical claims, as well as for my theorization of the concept of an expanded archive of eating. This expanded archive is one that must be first constituted by a range of sources "gathered" together and then reconstituted by each scholar through their own critical and creative processes. For the knowledge that is conveyed through this expanded archive is significant both for how it augments our overall understanding of the early United States and for how it offers additional insight into the individual lives of those, such as Hercules, who conceived and executed each dish that is documented therein.

"One man's meat is another man's poison," as the saying goes, and it is hard to disagree: individual tastes and preferences are the result of a complex set of physiological, psychological, and social factors that are often difficult to disentangle, let alone document on the page. Grant Achatz, the pioneering molecular gastronomist and executive chef at Alinea, the Michelin three-star restaurant in Chicago, is not the first to observe that "flavor is memory"; one need only recall the tea-soaked madeleine that begins Marcel Proust's *In Search of Lost Time*; or, as a more recent example, the transcendent spoonful of ratatouille in the eponymous Disney/Pixar film that at last restores the jaded food critic's childhood love of food (qtd. in Max, 91; Proust, 48). One might reference any number of additional examples that cut across literary and popular culture, but the connections between the sense of taste and the stories it evokes are not limited to the imagination alone. A recent brain-imaging study compared the neurological response during the act of eating to what happens when the flavor of that particular food is only recalled: the two experiences are visually indistinguishable (Max, 91).[21] Physiology, psychology, and evidently neurology, all contribute to our understanding of the imaginative richness of the sense of taste.

The results of this particular brain-imaging study, or of anyone's personal Proustian madeleine, do not suggest that the sense of taste is wholly cerebral, however. A person's taste for certain foods and his or her memories of them are also influenced by social and economic factors, as Pierre Bourdieu has shown: "The antithesis between quantity and quality, substance and form," he explains, "corresponds to the opposition—linked to different distances from necessity—between the taste of necessity, which favors the most 'filling' and most economic foods, and the taste of liberty—or luxury—which shifts the emphasis to the manner (of presentation, serving, eating etc.) and tends to use stylized forms to deny function" (xxix). We truly are what we eat, not only in terms of individual identity, but also in terms of socioeconomic status. Our sense of taste thus reveals and reflects how circumstances outside of our control also shape our sense of who we are. For this reason, as well, it becomes a scholarly imperative to look beyond the standard places we might expect to find information about eating. To elaborate upon Barthes's opening claim: information about food must indeed be gathered wherever it can be found. But it is only by bringing together this full range of information—as well as the information that resists recovery—that we can get our fullest sense, so to speak, of the matter of taste.

The Philosophical Significance of the Sense of Taste

The complex synthesis of the sensory, the cerebral, and the social that is engaged each time we take a bite of food and then determine whether or not we like it was intuited by countless thinkers, as well as home cooks, long before it was proven by either sociology or neuroscience. But how is it that the descriptor of this synthesis—that is, the sense of taste—has come to serve as the primary metaphor used to describe a much wider range of processes for passing judgment on art and other forms of culture?

For example, we might praise a friend for having "good taste" in food or in fashion; or a newspaper article might credit an internet "taste-maker" with popularizing a new restaurant or nightspot. In these cases, the term "taste" serves as shorthand for the more abstract concept of aesthetic judgment, the ability to assess an object's artistic or cultural merit according to an unspecified set of subjective standards and objective rules. One might assume that the casual term supplanted the more formal one, as is often the case with philosophical jargon. But that assumption would be incorrect. In fact, the idea of "aesthetic judgment" has a surprisingly short history in relation to the much longer lineage of taste. In the Western philosophical tradition, this lineage can be traced as far back as the fifteenth century, but, as Carolyn Korsmeyer has documented, "it was in the seventeenth century that the usage" of taste to describe what we now describe as aesthetic judgment began to "spread" (41). And while the notion of aesthetic judgment would soon supplant the metaphor of taste as the primary philosophical model of what is sometimes also described as "evaluative assessment," there exists a distinct period of time, coincident with the long eighteenth century, during which taste provides "the chief analogy by which the apprehension of the beautiful and of fine artistic qualities and even social style is explicated" (40).

Indeed, the eighteenth century has been called the "Century of Taste," and those who lived in North America in the late colonial era and into the early republic discussed matters of taste in abundance.[22] Edward Cahill has demonstrated how such discussions "permeated [the] literary culture" of the early United States (2). And yet, they, too, employed only the metaphor of the sense of taste in order to do so. The word "aesthetic" as a "rubric for philosophical questions of taste had no currency in English until the nineteenth century," Cahill states (3). It was not until 1750, when the German philosopher Alexander Baumgarten appropriated the word "aesthetic," which had previously been employed to describe sensation in general, to refer to the study of subjective experience and judgment, that the term acquired anything like its current meaning.[23] It would then take several more decades—well into the nineteenth century—for the word to attain widespread usage in English in any form.[24] Cahill dates the first use of the term in the United States to an 1812–13 essay on fine arts published in *The Halcyon Luminary,* a literary magazine (33). And as late as 1849, nearly a century after Baumgarten's initial formulation, American intellectuals such as Elizabeth Palmer Peabody puzzled over the precise meaning of "this vague, this comprehensive, but undefined word" (1). Instead, U.S. citizens continued to employ the metaphor of the sense of taste—the actual, gustatory sense—through which to formulate and articulate their ideas about how aesthetic judgments were made.

In order to fully understand the social and political valences of this term as it was taken up in the early United States, it is important to consider the developments in the philosophical discourse of taste that had transpired in England and Scotland over the previous century. These developments began in London, in 1711, with the publication of Anthony Ashley Cooper, the third Earl of Shaftesbury's *Characteristics of Men,*

Manners, Opinions, Times. Almost immediately engaged by the English cultural critics Joseph Addison and Richard Steele in the pages of their journal, the *Spectator* (ca. 1712), these ideas soon traveled to Scotland through the work of Francis Hutcheson, whose *Inquiry into the Original of Our Ideas of Beauty and Virtue* (1725) engaged the thinking of that original group in a more formal philosophical register. One generation later, in the early 1750s, the Scottish moral sense philosophers—a group that included David Hume and Henry Home, Lord Kames, among other notables—extended the ideas expressed in those early works into a set of fully formed theories of taste. To these thinkers, the metaphor of taste seemed to offer the most compelling conceptual model of how we process our every encounter with the world: each single experience, aesthetic or otherwise, is first registered through the senses; and then, and only then, is it evaluated by the mind.[25]

The evaluative nature of this process of passing judgment was important to the moral sense philosophers for two key reasons. First, it pointed to the existence of an innate sense that guided individuals in their subjective judgments; and second, it suggested how that sense could be cultivated and refined.[26] Each of the famed philosophers named above identified a close correspondence between the process of cultivating a taste for certain foods and cultivating a taste for various forms of culture. They recognized how, in both contexts, individuals possess an innate sense of their likes and dislikes, and yet they also possess the ability to shape their tastes according to additional external social and cultural standards. These external standards, in turn, can be—and, as Bourdieu would later claim, are in fact—internalized and assimilated back into that internal sense.

This model of an instinctual sense of taste nevertheless influenced by external factors was embraced by another influential group of thinkers: those who plotted the political structure of the fledgling U.S. government. For in spite of their theoretical belief in the value of representative democracy, these men—Thomas Jefferson, James Madison, and Benjamin Franklin chief among them—were deeply concerned about the true capacity of U.S. citizens to make their own political decisions. What if, they worried, the people who had fought to secure their freedom from monarchal rule could not be trusted, in the end, to govern the new democracy? Could they be counted on to vote on behalf of the public good? Could they be expected to behave with benevolence and virtue? In these regards, the possibility that each person's sense of taste could be refined offered a degree of reassurance; with the proper guidance, even the least "civilized" of the nation's citizenry could perhaps be cultivated so as to perform their civic duties in a morally appropriate manner.[27]

This view represented no vague aspiration. The founders were quite clear, following the moral sense philosophers, in their belief that the capacity for making tasteful decisions about the arts had a direct and causal relation to the capacity for passing moral judgments.[28] For instance, Benjamin Franklin wrote to Kames in 1762, a few months after his *Elements of Criticism* was published: "I am convinc'd of your Position, new as it was to me, that a good Taste in the Arts contributes to the Improvement of Morals" (*Papers,* 10:147).[29] This aspect of Scottish Enlightenment thought has long been recognized as foundational to the notion of "civic virtue" that undergirds American democracy; but the idea at the heart of this thinking, which is rooted in the act of eating, has yet to be sufficiently acknowledged or explored.[30] By reasserting the connection between good taste and good citizenship—a connection that has always existed, yet has remained overlooked—we can expand our own sense, in the present, of the people who exemplified this tasteful citizenship.

Independent of politics, the good taste of the "founders" has in fact long been established. Franklin, Jefferson, and Madison, along with Washington, are often among the first names invoked in accounts of the emergence of an American cuisine: Franklin for his obsession with turkey (among a multitude of culinary pleasures); Jefferson for his reputation as a great gastronome; and Madison for his legitimate horticultural skill (he was once observed in retirement, at work in his garden, "wearing Pantaloons patched at the knees") (qtd. in Ketchum, 621).[31] But a new understanding of eating as equal to the "Arts" that contributed to the cultivation of civic virtue does more than breathe new life into these dusty anecdotes; it expands the basic story we are able to tell about the nation's founding by incorporating the contributions of those directly responsible for preparing and presenting the food that the founders ate. More specifically, it reveals how figures such as Hercules, along with James Hemings, Jefferson's enslaved cook (and Sally Hemings's older brother), whom we will meet in chapter 1, along with many others whose culinary lives and legacies are explored in this book, directly contributed to the cultural foundation of the United States alongside the founders and their abstracted ideals.

Impossibility and Necessity in the Archive of Eating

Hercules worked with twenty-three other men and women in the President's House, eight of whom were, like Hercules, enslaved. But aside from a few biographical details, such as first names, job titles, and (only in some cases) dates of birth and death, little else is known about the nature of the men and women's lives.[32] For unlike figures such as Washington, whose contributions are recorded in the nation's most valorized documents, the records of those who labored at their tables, in their kitchens, and in their fields, are far more difficult to assemble—if they exist at all. Theirs is an archive "predicated upon impossibility," to invoke Saidiya Hartman's description of the records that constitute the archive of slavery as a whole ("Venus," 2). Hartman characterizes her own efforts to animate this archive as a composite process: "Listening for the unsaid, translating misconstrued words, and refashioning disfigured lives" (2). Throughout, she remains "intent on achieving an impossible goal: redressing the violence that produced numbers, ciphers, and fragments of discourse, which is as close as we come to a biography of the captive and the enslaved" (2–3). As Hartman observes, "redressing the violence" of the archive of slavery is a fundamentally "impossible" task. But in the years since her foundational work, scholars of Atlantic-world slavery have sought to develop new critical methods that can allow us to come closer to, if not to ever fully access, the ghostly lives of the enslaved.[33] Hartman's own method of "critical fabulation," for example, involves an interweaving of archival information with fictionalized narrative, enabling her to "mime[] the figurative dimensions of history" ("Venus," 11). More recently, Marisa Fuentes, in her study of the enslaved women of eighteenth-century Barbados, describes a related method of "reading along the bias grain" of archival fragments so as to "create more elasticity" within them, thereby expanding their scholarly significance (78).

Called by these methods, both ethically and intellectually, *An Archive of Taste* in turn calls upon fellow scholars of food studies, and of the early United States, to consider how our work might be similarly enriched by a renewed attention to the gaps in our archives, and, in particular, to the gaps left by unrecorded acts of eating, and the voices of those who, often through the conscripted preparation and presentation of food, made those acts possible. In this book I consider how an assemblage of critical and creative methods, including the interpretive techniques most familiar to scholars of early American literature and culture, such as close reading and historical synthesis, as well as several more speculative methods, including a version of Fuentes's technique of reading "along the bias grain," might be trained on the fragments that constitute the expanded archive of eating. These speculative methods also include a set of computational techniques for analyzing and visualizing large amounts of text, as I discuss in chapter 5. When employed together, this range of methods works to expand the significance of the archival fragments and the gaps between them—gaps that, in spite of any amount of elasticity, we cannot hope to ever fully close.

The unanswered questions left by these gaps help to underscore how the archive that enables arguments about the importance of food and eating in the early United States intersects, both materially and conceptually, with the archive that enables arguments about the violence of slavery and its aftermath in the present. Each is an archive of necessity, constituted by an incomplete set of artifacts that can never offer full access to the lived experience of the past. Each is also an archive of necessity in that, in its incompleteness, it cannot but reify the social and political hierarchies of the era in which it was first compiled.[34] For this reason, these archives require careful and creative approaches to the information they do contain. Because these archives, however incomplete, are also necessary; they are what enable us to identify—in kitchens and at tables, on plantations and in stores—new forms of cultural expression. And from these forms we can develop new theories of their significance for how we understand ideas about aesthetics, agency, and the human itself.

In the chapters that follow, I draw from these intersecting archives of necessity in order to explore how food came to matter in the early United States. The chapters proceed in roughly chronological order, although each reaches backward to the eighteenth-century origins of the discourse of taste that forms the book's philosophical basis, while also engaging texts through the mid-nineteenth century. Because of this spiraling progression, I have chosen to center each chapter not on a particular period or text, but instead on a particular aspect of eating, one that gains additional theoretical significance when considered in the context of the dominant discourse of taste. I thus explore matters of taste, as well as matters of embodiment, satisfaction, imagination, and absence. In each chapter, I elaborate upon one of these matters in order to challenge the assumptions embedded in the dominant discourse of taste in important ways. In the process, I also elaborate a set of methods for drawing knowledge from incomplete archives, disclosing additional information about the food culture of the early United States.

To these intertwined theoretical and methodological ends, the first chapter, "Taste," is set at the table, specifically the dinner table of Thomas Jefferson as it was apportioned by his enslaved chef, James Hemings. The chapter explores how Jefferson employed the table as a literal and figurative platform for his republican political ideology. I demonstrate how, as I have begun to explore, in the late colonial era and into the early republic America's cultural and political leaders—Jefferson among them—identified a causal relation between the cultivation of the American palate and the cultivation of a democratic citizenry. But because these men relied upon their enslaved chefs and servants to enact their vision, what they encouraged was not a furthering of their enforced hierarchy of racial difference, as they so strongly desired, but, instead, a performance of republican citizenship that was made possible as much through the lived experience and culinary expertise of figures such as Hemings as by any political expression of the founders' sense of taste. Chapter 1 thus carries an argument about the archive of the early United States, as well as about the politics of that archive. To this latter end, I employ mediated documents such as the emancipation agreement requested by Hemings, but signed only by Jefferson and his white maître d'hôtel, and the firsthand account of Paul Jennings, the federal pension office clerk who was once enslaved by James Madison and served as his valet. Jennings's account, which was recorded by a white amanuensis "almost in his own language," enables me to confirm who was directly responsible for the production of republican taste (iii).

Chapter 2, "Appetite," centers on two great gourmands: the French food writer Alexandre Balthazar Grimod de la Reynière and the American polymath Benjamin Franklin. These men help to show how an attention to the eating body confirms the functional limits of both the sense of taste and its aesthetic and political applications. Franklin serves as my primary example of the contradictory ideological uses of the discourse of taste. But Franklin, unlike Jefferson or Madison, remains more aware of his failures to subject his appetite to reason, even as he still cannot connect those personal failures to his more profound failure to take a strong political stance against slavery. This lack of connection is not coincidental, I contend. Rather, it confirms the limits of a political philosophy that rests on an unstable human base. To supplement my argument about the limits of the sense of taste as a guiding political force, I turn from Franklin to Grimod, the flamboyant French epicure, and then to an additional figure, Phillis Wheatley, the enslaved African American poet. I argue that their literary works, produced in full knowledge of how their bodies—marked by disability in the case of Grimod and race in the case of Wheatley—were excluded from the dominant Enlightenment project, offer stronger indictments of the sense of taste than do Franklin's satirical musings. I also show how they issue critiques of the narrowness of what I term the *tasteful subject*. This is a subject who exemplifies good taste to the highest degree. By directly engaging with the irrepressible force of appetite, as it alternately compels and conscripts, Grimod and Wheatley help to reconfigure the idea of this tasteful subject, with broader implications for the Enlightenment subject more generally conceived.

Chapter 3, "Satisfaction," takes as its point of departure Malinda Russell's *A Domestic Cookbook* (1866), discovered only in the past decade and now recognized as the earliest known cookbook written by an African American cook of any gender. The introduction to that volume weaves together information about Russell's culinary training with an account of an armed robbery that she experienced en route to Liberia many years before. Connecting Russell's cookbook to its culinary antecedents—Amelia Simmons's *American Cookery* (1796) and Mary Randolph's *The Virginia House-Wife* (1824)—I consider how cookbooks can be read as narratives, narratives can be read as cookbooks, and how both can be read as aesthetic theory. I argue that before the word "aesthetic" achieved widespread use, any attempt to make sense of taste entailed the adoption of a speculative philosophical mode. I employ the term "speculation" in its basic sense: exploratory and provisional, enabling a capacious understanding of what theory entails. By proposing a speculative approach to the theory of taste, I demonstrate how a range of generic modes, including cookbooks, might be understood for the theoretical work that they perform. Through these works, I elaborate an alternative theory of aesthetics that, in focusing on the satisfaction of others rather than the gratification of personal taste, exposes the practical limits of republican taste. This theory opens up additional possibilities for expressing personal agency that reside in the economic rather than the political sphere. While this sense of satisfaction closely tracks the emergence of liberal capitalism and the role that black citizens would play in it, it also points to an additional revolutionary register, one at that point fully imagined but not yet achieved.

In chapter 4, "Imagination," I analyze several more demonstrably literary works written as the pressure to abolish slavery continued to mount. More specifically, I compare the works of Harriet Jacobs, the author and formerly enslaved woman, and of Lydia Maria Child, the author, abolitionist, and editor of Jacobs's work. Jacobs's characterization, in *Incidents in the Life of a Slave Girl* (1861), of the man who enslaves her as an "epicure," sets the stage for the comparison with Child, who, in addition to her antislavery fiction, nonfiction writing, and editorial work, also wrote a best-selling cookbook. Child's explicit endorsement of the interdependence of eating and aesthetics, and her belief in how both of these informed political opinion, prompt a closer consideration of the imagined space of nineteenth-century social reform (Jacobs, 12). From this perspective, Jacobs's *Incidents* acquires as-yet-unacknowledged significance for its exploration of the limits of both taste and fiction. In markedly different ways, Jacobs and Child reimagine past events and envision possible futures. By considering the range of registers through which eating operates for each writer—as sensory experience, as embodied aesthetics, and as social act—I show how we can see the hopeful futures imagined in abolitionist fiction, even as we acknowledge the potential worlds that, because of diminished social or political agency, dispossession, or enslavement, remained out of reach, regardless of the defiance with which they were imagined.

The final chapter, "Absence," returns to the story of James Hemings, first explored in chapter 1, in order to show how a set of computational methods—in particular, social network analysis and data visualization—offer additional possibilities for addressing the absences in the intersecting archives of slavery and of eating. I also describe how the demands of these archives pose productive challenges to the archive of the United States overall. A contrast between a set of data visualizations of Hemings's archival trace with Jefferson's own charts and tables demonstrates how we must tread carefully when continuing to employ interpretive methods rooted in Enlightenment philosophy. For the underlying premise of the dominant discourse of taste—that what can be sensed can always be known—does not account for the experiences that, either by nature or by intent, resist knowing altogether. In this chapter, the connections that are forged between past and present are intended to prompt readers to consider the ways in which matters of taste can cross multiple disciplinary registers and temporal zones.

The Epilogue reinforces the central role of enslaved cooks in producing republican taste by considering a final archival fragment associated with Hercules, whose "first shad of the season" began this Introduction. More specifically, I consider the portrait that graces the cover of this book and that, until recently, was believed to be of Hercules.[35] I explore how, in contrast to formal philosophies enshrined in print, vernacular expressions of taste continue to resist preservation and circulation. This remains true even with the advent of digital techniques, and here I refer not only to more sophisticated techniques of computational analysis employed in chapter 5, but also more basic methods of online research. After a discussion of how the portrait of Hercules entered the contemporary imagination via digitization and then, as a result of its deauthentication, disappeared from the digital archive in which it was housed, I consider a second portrait that has recently captivated the public imagination: *Scipio Moorhead, Portrait of Himself, 1776*, painted by Kerry James Marshall in 2007. (Scipio Moorhead was the enslaved black artist who is credited with creating the frontispiece for Phillis Wheatley's *Poems on Various Subjects, Religious and Moral*, discussed in chapter 2.) I posit Marshall's portrait as a visual analogue of Hartman's aforementioned method of critical fabulation, as well as of the methods that I discuss and demonstrate throughout this book.

Indeed, the issue of gaps in the archive—in the archive of eating, in the archive of slavery, and in other archives of necessity—is one that persists into the present, even as increasing amounts of archival material are being digitized and made available online. Marshall's fabulated portrait, Russell's tantalizing cookbook, Grimod's performative dinners, and Hemings's artful cookery, among the other acts of cooking and eating that are explored in this book, join Hercules's fresh fish in revealing the richness of the archive of eating, as well as the range of methods that are required to coax flavor from the fragments that the archive contains. These methods might be visual as much as textual, created with an artist's brush as much as keyboard or a line of code. And it is together that they are able to elicit knowledge about the persons, communities, and cultures that would otherwise recede from view.

1

Taste

Eating and Aesthetics in the Early United States

Thomas Jefferson and James Madison sat at the table together in late spring, 1790, while James Hemings—Jefferson's enslaved cook and Sally Hemings's older brother—prepared the meal "which was to save the Union" (Jefferson, *Writings*, 1:275). The North and the South had been unable to come to an agreement on the issue of states' debts, and Jefferson, seeking "to find some temperament for the present fever," had invited the opposing sides to a "little dinner" at his house (*Papers*, 17:206, 27:782). As he later recalled in his autobiographical *Anas*, "I thought it impossible that reasonable men, consulting together coolly, could fail, by some mutual sacrifices of opinion, to form a compromise" (*Writings*, 1:275). The "compromise" worked out over the meal—that the South would support the federal assumption of states' debts in exchange for the promise of relocating the nation's capital from its temporary home in New York City to the shores of the Potomac—would become known as the Dinner-Table Bargain, what historian Jacob Cooke has called "one of the most important bargains in American history" (523). However, scant evidence for the famous dinner, other than Jefferson's retroactive account, can be found. Madison makes no note of the meal in his journals or letters, and if James Hemings ever recalled aspects of its preparation, for he could write and read well, his account was certainly not preserved. Several twentieth-century analyses of the congressional record have determined that the North had already obtained sufficient votes to support debt assumption by the time that the dinner supposedly took place.[1] In light of this research, it is almost certain that the Dinner-Table Bargain, as described in the *Anas,* did not take place in the way that Jefferson so precisely recalled.

But Jefferson's retroactive refashioning of the order of events is not surprising in the context of his ideas about eating. Indeed, Jefferson viewed the act of eating as emblematic of his republican ideals.[2] Early in his tenure as minister to France, in 1785, Jefferson acknowledged the "pleasures of the table" as a set of experiences, both gustatory and aesthetic, that could "unite good taste with temperance" (*Papers*, 8:569). In this he anticipated the formulation of the great gastronome Jean Anthelme Brillat-Savarin, who, writing a half century later in *The Physiology of Taste* (1835), would distinguish between the "pleasure of eating [as] the actual and direct sensation of satisfying a need," and the "pleasures of the table [as] a reflected sensation which is born from the various circumstances of place, time, things, and people who make up the surroundings of the meal" (182). Brillat-Savarin, like Jefferson, drew from the philosophy that elevated "reflected sensation" over "direct sensation," with the former serving as an indicator of the individual ability to pass judgment upon the latter. The ability to pass appropriate judgment was, of course, determined by the sense of taste, and Jefferson consistently identified the table as a key site for its cultivation.

Thus when circumstances—namely, the fracturing of aristocratic rule that would culminate in the French Revolution—required that Jefferson author his own declaration of culinary independence, he sought to infuse the "pleasures of the table" that he had learned to appreciate from the French with additional aspects of a distinctly American sensibility.[3] He began to cultivate, in his garden in Paris, a variety of indigenous American ingredients "for the use of my own table" (*Papers*, 12:135).[4] He also developed a serving style "after the American manner," in which plates were placed directly on the table and guests served themselves, reflecting the virtuous simplicity of the republic's citizenry (*Writings*, 1:156). His use of a round or oval table, and his insistence on seating his guests "pell-mell," were intended both to express the egalitarianism inherent in the nation's founding and to foster the respectful exchange of ideas that would sustain its future growth.[5] The "good taste and abundance" for which Jefferson's table would soon become renowned—what I term Jefferson's *republican taste*—was thus on full display during the "little dinner" that resulted in the famous Compromise (qtd. in Fowler, 19).[6] But the more complex bargain brokered at that table, and at every meal that Jefferson served, remained unrecognized: his own attempt to reconcile a sense of taste that expressed the ideals of the republic with a taste for food prepared by the people he enslaved.

In the past decade or so, scholars of eighteenth-century British literature have begun to acknowledge the influence of the gustatory sense of taste on that era's cultural output.[7] Citing the philosophers who helped forge the connection between the gustatory and aesthetic senses of the term, including Lord Shaftesbury and David Hume, among others discussed in the Introduction, Denise Gigante, for example, argues that "taste became the most vivid strand of a complex civilizing process in which individuals were taught to regulate themselves, and their motivating appetites, from within" (*Taste*, 7). While focusing on the philosophies of Edmund Burke and Adam Smith, a set of theorists who engaged the gustatory sense of taste less directly, Simon Gikandi nevertheless also acknowledges how their ideas about aesthetic taste "were haunted by the materiality of social life, especially the excessive values generated by luxurious living" (17). Scholars of eighteenth-century America often make recourse to similar arguments about the need to regulate excess, and about the role of the body in that process of regulation, when explaining the appeal of the discourse of taste on the nation's founders, including Jefferson.[8] But none have commented on the close correspondence between the cultivation of the aesthetic sense and the cultivation of the American palate.

I propose that, in the late colonial era and into the early republic, America's cultural and political leaders identified a causal relation between the cultivation of the American palate and the cultivation of a republican citizenry. Thomas Jefferson and James Madison, among the men most directly involved in articulating a political ideology for the United States, each understood the ability to make tasteful decisions about literature and other forms of culture as reflective of a greater capacity for moral judgment, and consequently for appropriate political behavior. The cultivation of good taste, as Elizabeth Maddock Dillon explains, "ideally produced subjects who enacted their freedom in a moral and lawful manner, thereby creating the ground for a new political community—a community of taste—united by individual consent and judgment rather than by constraint and subordination" (498). More recently, Edward Cahill has exposed the "dialectic of liberty" at the core of this theory, evident in a discourse of aesthetic taste that not only addresses the issues of "individuality, autonomy, and agency but also their necessary limits" (5). Cahill shows how contemporaneous literary and artistic works dramatize the "tensions between liberty and constraint that structure eighteenth-century aesthetic theory's main concepts and debates" (8).

By introducing the idea of eating into this expanding body of scholarship, I aim to illuminate the sensory and material dimensions of aesthetic taste in the early United States. More specifically, I place this composite conception of taste within the "political horizon of interpretation" that Cindy Weinstein and Christopher Looby, following Fredric Jameson, seek to associate with the aesthetic (29).[9] In so doing, I aim to explore the ways that eating provided an example, three times a day, for colonists, and later citizens, to think through their political, moral, and social concerns. In addition, I show how the shared experience of eating "formaliz[ed] a practice of good fellowship," as David S. Shields has argued about the analogous experiences that took place in literary salons, coffeehouses, and social clubs (*Civil Tongues*, 196).[10] This fellowship expressed the virtuous, republican citizenship that Jefferson and Madison envisaged for the new nation. In short, it is my contention that expressions of gustatory taste—by which I mean acts of eating that indicated an ability to subjugate appetite to reason, and consequently to elevate the cause of the public good over personal interest—were understood as expressions of civic virtue.

Indeed, an attention to eating, and to the related process of cultivating taste, is present throughout the writings of Jefferson and Madison, and is further accentuated in the material traces of their relationships with their enslaved chefs and servants. This chapter will focus on these intertwined pairs of relationships: between Jefferson and James Hemings, who has already been introduced; between Madison and Paul Jennings, the enslaved man who served as Madison's lifelong valet and, in 1863, recorded his memories in *A Colored Man's Reminiscences of James Madison*; and between Jefferson and Madison, who were lifelong friends. The two founders have long been considered in concert, for they shared most political views and intellectual influences, as well as a Virginia address. But it is only through a consideration of these four men together—two enslavers and two enslaved—that we come to see how Jefferson and Madison's heightened attention to the sense of taste affected their vision for an agrarian American republic, and ultimately shaped the government they together helped to create.

More specifically, a new analysis of Jefferson's most famous (and infamous) statements about slavery demonstrates the centrality of this composite notion of taste in his opinions about national identity and racial difference, while an examination of Madison's less considered writings on the same subject illustrates how his own emphasis on the cultivation of taste forces him to confront evidence of black as well as white tastefulness. The men's shared response to this evidence of black taste was to attempt to distance the cultivation of taste from its gustatory origins. But what this distancing ultimately exposes is not a clear hierarchy of racial or sensory difference, as Madison and Jefferson hoped to enforce through their words and actions. Rather, through their insistence on the significance of the sense of taste, the founders reveal a sense of republican citizenship that is constituted as much through the lived experience and culinary expertise of enslaved men and women, such as James Hemings and Paul Jennings, as by any political expression of their own cultivated taste.

Taste, Temperance, and the Issue of Slavery

Thomas Jefferson and James Hemings shared a history, and not simply because of the link to Hemings's sister Sally. When Jefferson traveled to Paris to assume the position of minister to France, in 1785, he took James Hemings with him, and there apprenticed him to the chef of a prince. Hemings learned to cook in the high French style, and later became the chef de cuisine at Jefferson's Parisian residence. As noted by Annette Gordon-Reed in her monumental biography of the Hemings family, James Hemings's role as chef "made him responsible for every success and failure regarding a critical component in that diplomatic household" (*Hemings,* 227).[11] This statement makes clear that Jefferson's dinner-table diplomacy—and, in all likelihood, the eventual popularization of his particular version of republican taste—would have been impossible without Hemings's gastronomical skill. In his reliance on Hemings, Jefferson also demonstrates the contradiction at the core of republican identity, one brought about by the persistence of slavery in a country defined by its republican ideals. Jefferson's elevated attention to issues of taste, placed in the context of his acquiescence to the institution of slavery, accentuates the ways in which his personal actions undermine his vision of a national identity for all residents of the United States.

In September 1793, several years after Jefferson and Hemings had returned from France, Jefferson penned a short paragraph that established the conditions for Hemings's eventual emancipation. The resultant document was witnessed and signed by Adrien Petite, Jefferson's white maître d'hôtel, even as Hemings could write in both English and French. In its single sentence, the agreement exposes the conflict between Jefferson's desire to reward Hemings for his exemplary service in the form of his freedom, and his awareness of the immediate and profound impact that Hemings's emancipation would have on his table. The agreement, in its entirety, reads:

> Having been at great expence [*sic*] in having James Hemings taught the art of cookery, desiring to befriend him, and to require from him as little in return as possible, I do hereby promise and declare, that if the said James shall go with me to Monticello in the course of the ensuing winter, when I go to reside there myself, and shall there continue until he shall have taught such person as I shall place under him for that purpose to be a good cook, this previous condition being performed, he shall be thereupon made free, and I will thereupon execute all proper instruments to make him free. (*Papers*, 27:119)

The implications of slavery on the development of Jefferson's republican taste are here laid bare. According to the terms of the agreement, Hemings must exchange his culinary knowledge for his personal liberty. Jefferson's agreement—for in truth, Hemings had no choice but to consent—exemplifies what Saidiya Hartman has identified as a form of "barbarism" unique to slavery, one made manifest not only in the "constitution of slave as object but also in the forms of subjectivity and circumscribed humanity imputed to the enslaved" (6). To be sure, Jefferson's measured tone and offer of friendship illustrate, in stark relief, the incontrovertible authority of Jefferson as enslaver, and the resultant subjection of Hemings as enslaved. In the agreement, Jefferson characterizes himself as a benevolent force of freedom, but his concern with the practical implications of Hemings's release reveals the ways in which his heightened valuation of the "art of cookery" takes precedence over the foundational rights of the republic. By stipulating that Hemings instruct a replacement cook before he can be freed, Jefferson ensures that Hemings's absence will be neither felt, nor tasted, at Monticello. At the same time, Jefferson's insistence that Hemings train another man "to be a good cook" before he can be freed offers incontrovertible evidence of his awareness of Hemings's skill. The prospect of losing James Hemings as his chef requires Jefferson to articulate, for the first time in writing, the larger social and political impact—not to mention the monetary value—of Hemings's cultivated culinary expertise.[12]

Jefferson's approach to the emancipation of James Hemings, indicative of the gradualist theory of emancipation that he endorsed through-

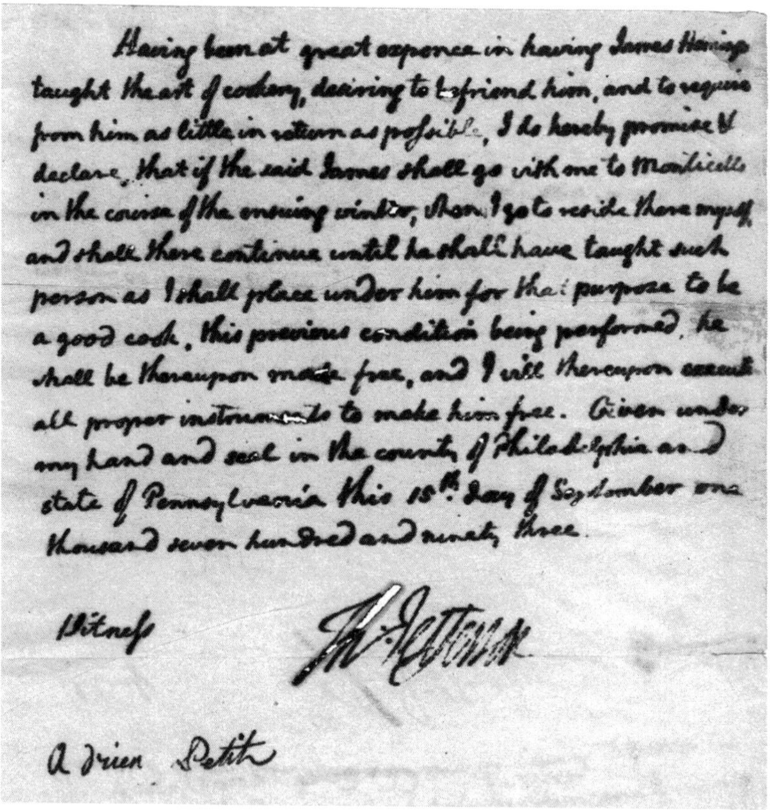

Figure 2. This document, dated September 15, 1793, was written by Thomas Jefferson and witnessed by his white maître d'hôtel. It outlines the conditions for James Hemings's eventual emancipation. Collection of the Massachusetts Historical Society.

out his life, demonstrates how his consistent attention to the sense of taste interferes with his ability, and his willingness, to address the issue of slavery in the United States. In *Notes on the State of Virginia* (1785), Jefferson's longest publication and his only book-length endeavor, he inveighs against the "unhappy influence on the manners of our people produced by the existence of slavery," although he does not implicate his own manners—or his tastes—in this assessment (*Writings*, 1:225). He nevertheless actively impugns the manners and tastes of black people as he asserts that they "participate more of sensation than reflection" (2:194). This language derives from the moral sense philosophers, who theorized judgments of taste as involving an immediate sensory experience followed by an assessment of, or a "reflection" about, that experience. As the emancipation agreement strongly underscores, Hemings, a black person, demonstrated the ability to make appropriate judgments of taste in abundance. But as Jefferson continued to insist upon his exclusionary version of republican taste as a model for the nation's, he contributed to what Eric Sundquist identifies as the "state of unresolved crisis" of American identity that endures to this day (30). Sundquist locates the origin of this conflict in the incompatibility between the constitutional legitimization of slavery in the United States and the "overarching ideology of liberty" that "authorized its cultural independence, territorial expansion, and rise to world power" (30). Certainly, Jefferson's incorporation of the "ideology of liberty" into his conception of republican taste at the same time that he employs this sense of taste as a justification for the continued enslavement of James Hemings, and all other black Americans, perpetuates this "crisis" of national identity.

Less immediately evident is how Jefferson's insistence on the need for a shared national sense of taste underlies his construction of a hierarchy of racial difference. This hierarchy, in turn, subtends his philosophical arguments both for the continued enslavement of black Americans as a group and for the eventual expatriation of formerly enslaved black Americans to the western coast of Africa. It also reveals the complexities of the sense of taste itself. Indeed, Jefferson's assessment, in the infamous Query XIV of the *Notes,* that black people are "dull, tasteless, and anomalous" reproduces the phenomenon that David Kazanjian, following Etienne Balibar, identifies as the "rise of numerous, hierarchically codified, particularistic differences" that accompany the movement of any group toward equality (*Writings,* 1:194; Kazanjian, 2). Kazanjian's analysis emphasizes Jefferson's "codification" of race in terms of quantifiable physical qualities and measurable population units—the influence, he contends, of Enlightenment empiricism. But taking into account the additional emphases on sensory experience and subjective judgment, it is my premise that Jefferson also develops his "indelible" racial categories by attending to qualitative assessments of black and white people's divergent tastes. Rather than ascribe the contradiction between Jefferson's republican ideology and his opinions about race to his own personal deficiencies, as many have argued, or to a generalized "crisis" of national identity, as Sundquist might claim, this theory of the interdependence of equality and difference provides a model for understanding Jefferson's ideas about taste, race, and nation as a single, albeit flawed, conceptual system.[13]

Jefferson's belief in the strong relationship between race and nation has, in fact, already generated significant critical attention. Peter Onuf, for instance, asserts that Jefferson perceived enslaved African Americans as "constitut[ing] a *distinct nation*," and for this reason, viewed the range of "crimes" committed against them—captivity, relocation, and bondage—"in national terms" (3). This conceptual link between race and nation helps to explain why, in the same Query in which he comments about the absence of taste in black people, Jefferson also criticizes one formerly enslaved man, Ignatius Sancho, for his extravagant writing style. Although Sancho's essays had been uniformly praised in Europe, Jefferson disparages his work for "escap[ing] incessantly from every restraint of reason and taste" (*Writings,* 1:196). Jefferson indicts Sancho's excess of taste much as he had previously reproached the inferior taste of black Americans as a group. Jefferson resists acknowledging any similarity in taste between black and white Americans, just as he refused to acknowledge the good taste of James Hemings, for this admission would challenge Jefferson's conception of national taste, and consequently his conception of the nation itself.

Jefferson's most famous published statement against slavery, included in Query XVIII, clarifies how he makes use of the notion of taste to define and defend his vision of a national identity for the United States. Evoking the tone and the moral force of a Puritan jeremiad, Jefferson expresses his fears about the future of a nation still dependent on slavery: "I tremble for my country when I reflect that God is just: that his justice cannot sleep forever: that considering numbers, nature and natural means only, a revolution of the wheel of fortune, an exchange of situation, is among possible events: that it may become probable by supernatural interference! The Almighty has no attribute which can take side with us in such a contest" (*Writings,* 1:227). As noted by many critics, Jefferson derives the basis of his philosophical argument from the Lockean formulation of slavery as a state of war. In these often-quoted lines, Jefferson conjures a "contest" of divine magnitude. His distress at the notion that God cannot "take side" with white America underlies his conviction about the fundamental differences between white and black people. He readily adapts his ideas about an association between race and nation to conform to Locke's critique of slavery. But by invoking both "numbers" and "nature," Jefferson again demonstrates how his belief in the inevitability of emancipation emerges from his view of black and white people as discrete populations and as qualitatively separate subjects. Jefferson is unable to envision a United States in which black and white people might live together as equals because of his perception of their distinct national affiliations, and because of his intractable ideas about their irreconcilable tastes.[14]

Jefferson's scrupulous attention to matters of taste is therefore among the major factors that lead him to condone the continued existence of slavery. Consider his conclusion to the passage quoted above: "But it is impossible to be temperate and to pursue this subject through the various considerations of policy, of morals, of history natural and civil. We must be contented to hope they will force their way into every one's mind" (*Writings*, 1:227). Jefferson's supposition that it is "impossible to be temperate" with respect to the subject of slavery, combined with the fact that the passage appears in the Query on manners, confirms his conviction about the crucial influence of taste in determining matters both "of morals" and "of policy." Jefferson's career as a politician, not to mention his own acts of enslavement, would have attuned him to the difficulty of resolving such an issue, one that encompassed economic and cultural as well as moral concerns. But it is also possible to read this statement as an affirmation of the temperate republican discourse that he sought to elevate to an art at his table. His language suggests that a discussion about slavery's abolition would necessarily entail a lack of temperance, and this intemperance would prove damaging to the nation's emergent sense of self. Because the United States' political institutions had not yet stabilized, and its (white) national identity had not yet sufficiently coalesced, Jefferson was unwilling to endorse any action that would detract from his project of producing tasteful, temperate citizens.

Throughout the *Notes*, Jefferson reinforces his argument for the importance of a shared sense of taste in shaping a national identity. He frequently employs the trope of temperance, that signal attribute of republican taste, in order to explain how political principles are affected by the exercise of subjective judgment. For example, in regard to the potential danger that immigrants might pose to the young nation, Jefferson states: "They will bring with them the principles of the governments they leave, imbibed in their early youth; or, if able to throw them off, it will be in exchange for an unbounded licentiousness, passing, as is usual, from one extreme to the other. It would be a miracle were they to stop precisely at the point of temperate liberty" (*Writings*, 1:120). Jefferson draws upon the philosophical discourse of taste, as a sense that is influenced both by individual experience and by culturally sanctioned rules, in order to convey his perception of the threat posed by foreigners seeking entrance to the United States. He also draws from the language of temperance, introduced into North America with the arrival of first Puritan settlers, and which would permeate Anglo-American discourse into the nineteenth century and beyond.[15] Connecting this Puritan concept with the more embodied idea of "eating and drinking too freely," as Benjamin Franklin would define it with respect to his own intemperate body, as discussed in chapter 2, Jefferson discloses his awareness of the dangers of excessive indulgence that can come with the cultivation of taste (Franklin, *Memoirs*, 3:327).[16] Here, Jefferson employs the verb "imbibe" in order to convey the delicate balance between temperance and pleasure that is required for the cultivation of appropriately republican taste. In addition, his use of the phrase "temperate liberty" provides an uncannily accurate description of his pragmatic political philosophy. As the primary author of the Declaration of Independence, Jefferson believed that all men were "endowed by their Creator" with the unalienable right to liberty, but evidently only if that liberty could be tastefully acquired (*Writings*, 1:29).

For Jefferson, the role of taste is essential both in determining qualitative aspects of U.S. identity and in supporting the nation's claim to cultural superiority. It is no surprise, then, that Jefferson identifies temperance as the virtue that will eventually guide the nation toward the abolition of slavery. Jefferson anticipated that the next generation of citizens, raised on American soil, nourished by native crops, and—significantly—impelled to action by the influence of American taste, would eventually address the issue of slavery. In a 1785 letter to a British correspondent, he explains: "These [young men and women] have sucked in the principles of liberty as it were with their mother's milk; and it is to them I look with anxiety to turn the fate of this question" of slavery (*Papers*, 8:356). Once again, liberty is something that is ingested. His metaphor suggests that the "principles of liberty" nourish the mind, just as a "mother's milk" fortifies the body.[17] He evokes the sense of taste in order to convey his confidence in the moral force of American culture and employs the idea of eating in order to reinforce his belief in the importance of each citizen's total incorporation of republican values. Here, Jefferson suggests that liberty can indeed be tasted; and that, in turn, a taste for liberty, acquired and cultivated in youth, will provide the impetus to confront and resolve the issue of slavery in the United States.

And yet, the trope also points back to the instinctual aspects of taste—what Jefferson himself would later describe in a letter to a friend, the philosopher Thomas Law, as an "innate sense" that is registered "through the eye in visible forms, as landscape, animal figure, dress, drapery, architecture, the composition of colors, &c., or to the imagination directly, as imagery, style, or measure in prose or poetry" (*Letters*, 1336). According to this statement—for it represents the clearest formulation of aesthetic taste Jefferson ever recorded—the "faculty" of what he called interchangeably "criticism or taste" is characterized by "visible" or mental forms, and registered by the sensorium "directly" before being processed by the mind. Here, again, is a conception of taste that looks ahead to Brillat-Savarin—in this case to the "analysis of the sensation of tasting" included in *The Physiology of Taste* (40). Brillat-Savarin's conception of taste encompasses three forms of sensation: "direct" and "complete" sensation, both closely tied to the physical experience of eating; and a "reflective" sensation, "the opinion which one's spirit forms from the impressions which have been transmitted to it by the mouth" (40). While Jefferson, in his letter to Law, derives his formulation of taste not in relation to eating, but in relation—and, at times, in opposition—to the moral sense, it shares certain key features with Brillat-Savarin's; both believe that the sense of taste originates in the sensory impressions of the body, about which assessments (Brillat-Savarin's "opinions") can then be cultivated and refined.[18]

With this formulation of taste, Jefferson finds himself in a bind: he can continue to insist upon the influence of society and culture in refining the reflective aspects of the sense of taste, which would allow him to continue to exclude black Americans from his project of cultivating taste in U.S. citizens. But that insistence would also require that he excise from the sense of taste its most potent force: its origin in instinctual appetite. While shaped by a national culture, Jefferson's republican taste still carries with it the power and pleasure of innate desire. As evident in Jefferson's vision for an end to slavery, motivated by principles "sucked in" from infancy, and therefore incapable of being overturned, the sense of taste is predicated on both immediate sensory experience *and* acculturated response. Even if

Jefferson was unwilling to explicitly acknowledge that black Americans could cultivate a sense of taste, his heightened valuation of the sense of taste—evident in his statements on slavery and its abolition, as well as at his dining table—demonstrates his awareness of the multipart process by which taste can be cultivated and refined by any and all people.

Agricultural Citizenship and the Cultivation of Taste

The process of cultivating taste, to which Jefferson was so deeply attuned, extends from his interest in cultivation more generally conceived. Well before Jefferson traveled to France and was exposed to the pleasures of the table, he invested significant time—and symbolic weight—in what he called the "art of agriculture." Indeed, Jefferson viewed agricultural cultivation, like tasteful consumption, as an acquired skill. The acquisition of this skill, he believed, would directly result in the refinement of those who participated in it. To wit: in 1784, Jefferson wrote to James Madison, who was by then a dear friend, inviting him to purchase a "little farm of 140 ac[res]" adjoining his own, where together they might establish "a society to our taste" (*Papers*, 6:550, 10:612). Framing his vision in terms of a conception of taste again steeped in Scottish Enlightenment theory, and characteristically infused with his own ideas about temperance and virtue, Jefferson explains, "The one here [i.e., Jefferson himself] supposed, we can regulate to our minds, and we may extend our regulations to the sumptuary department, so as to set a good example to a country which needs it, and to preserve our own happiness clear of embarrassment" (10:612). Although scholars strongly believe that Jefferson refers here to the "embarrassment" of slavery, it is Madison who, in mulling over the proposition, makes the reference explicit.[19] As he wrote to a friend two years later, still undecided as to whether to agree to Jefferson's plan, "My wish is if possible to provide a decent & independent subsistence . . . [and] to depend as little as possible on the labour of slaves" (*Papers*, Congressional Series [CS], 8:328). For Madison, the stakes of this "farm of experiment" were clear: if he and Jefferson were to model the "decent & independent" existence they envisioned for the United States, they could not set their "good example" while relying on a staff that was enslaved (Jefferson, *Papers*, 6:550).

Although Madison never matched Jefferson in the fervor of his remarks—recall Jefferson's famous proclamation, in the *Notes* that "those who labour in earth are the chosen people of God"—he shared Jefferson's conviction that a life of farming was most conducive to the cultivation of republican taste (*Writings*, 1:229). As early as 1792, in an essay for the *National Gazette*, Madison proclaimed farming to be "pre-eminently suited to the comfort and happiness of the individual *Health*," as well as to "*Virtue*, the health of the soul" (*Papers*, CS, 14:245). For Madison, as for Jefferson, the economic independence and self-sufficiency accorded by subsistence farming enhanced citizens' personal and physical well-being, as well as their benevolent participation in society: "The class of citizens who provide at once their own food and their own raiment may be viewed as the most truly independent and happy. They are more: they are the best basis of public liberty, and the strongest bulwark of public safety. It follows, that the greater the proportion of this class to the whole society, the more free, the more independent, and the more happy must be the society itself" (14:246). Echoing Jefferson's belief that he "kn[ew] of no condition happier than that of a Virginia farmer" whose "estate supplies a good table, [and] clothes himself and his family" (*Papers*, 11:682), the view expressed here—that the "class of citizens" who rely on no one but themselves for food and clothing are the "most truly independent and happy"—accentuates Madison's understanding of the link between the financial freedom facilitated by small-scale farming and the independence of thought required for republican citizenship. What is not acknowledged, of course, is that this idealized vision of farming was dependent upon the labor of people who were enslaved.

By the time of this essay's printing, Madison had already implicitly rejected Jefferson's proposal for a farming community of taste. In August 1784, Madison had accepted his father's gift of 560 acres from the family's Montpelier plantation, and along with it, a sizable staff of enslaved people. Twelve years later, in 1796, he divested himself of all other land holdings, including an arable tract of land in upstate New York, retaining ownership only of his plantation at Montpelier. Several historians have observed that this moment marked an ideological as well as a financial turning point. "Notwithstanding his best efforts," Drew McCoy asserts, Madison "thus found himself no less dependent on Montpelier and on slave labor" (233). Irving Brant's assessment is more severe: "For better or worse, [Madison] was yoked to the Virginia plantation for the rest of his life" (342). In the context of his beliefs about the virtues of farming, however, Madison's sale of his land in the free North marked a more specific shift. From this point on, Madison spoke less of "labour in the earth" as the ideal endeavor through which to sustain virtuous citizenship. Instead, he focused his attention more fully on the techniques and methods of agricultural cultivation as models—and metaphors—for the cultivation of taste. This conceptual shift from the labor of farming to the art of cultivation afforded southern plantation owners, including Madison himself, a means of continuing to extol the virtues instilled by agrarian life while avoiding a personal confrontation with the implications of slavery.

Madison's famed address to the Agricultural Society of Albemarle, the Virginia county in which he lived, delivered on May 12, 1818, emphasizes the virtues that can be derived from advanced techniques of cultivation. He first positions the "faculty of cultivating the earth . . . by which food is increased beyond the spontaneous supplies of nature" as the purview of "man alone," and asserts that "this peculiar faculty gives to man a pre-eminence over irrational animals" (*Papers*, Retirement Series [RS], 1:260). Using terms associated with the discourse of taste, he frames the art of agriculture as a reflection of man's capacity to subject "instinct" to reason, as well as an example of what separates the "enlightened and refined nations on some parts of the earth, and the rude and wretched tribes on the other." He posits a direct connection between advancements in agriculture and "improvements" in "civilized life." When he declares that "civilization is never seen without agriculture: nor has agriculture ever prevailed, where the civilized arts did not make their appearance," he implies that the cultivation of the land also contributes to the cultivation of those who participate in it.[20]

Madison's involvement in Jefferson's project to build a university for the state of Virginia, in 1818, the same year as the Albemarle address, offered him an additional opportunity to explore the interrelation of agricultural cultivation and the cultivation of taste. Jefferson frequently stated that his aim in designing the buildings for the University of Virginia was to provide "models of taste & good architecture" for the students (qtd. in Wagoner, 98). While in the *Notes*, Jefferson had defended U.S. artists against the claim that the nation had "not yet produced one good poet," he later concedes that Europe is "where genius is most cultivated, [and] where are the most excellent models for art" (*Writings*, 1:95). In a 1785 letter to Charles Bellini, a Florentine viticulturist who moved to Virginia in order to provide assistance in establishing a vineyard, Jefferson returns to extolling the state of the arts in Europe: "Were I to proceed to tell you how much I enjoy their architecture, sculpture, painting, music, I should want words. It is in these arts they shine" (*Papers*, 8:568). At home, Jefferson described being surrounded by "rude, mis-shapen piles, which, but that they have roofs, would be taken for brick-kilns" (*Writings*, 1:212). In proposing his Palladian design for the University of Virginia, Jefferson clearly intended to "cultivate" taste, and perhaps even genius, on campus.[21]

It should be noted that Charles Bellini failed in his experiments with grape growing. Thanks to a character reference from Jefferson, however, he was soon hired as professor of modern languages at the College of William and Mary. This easy transition, from agriculture to education, reflects Jefferson's presumption of the close relation between the two fields. The "Report of the Commissioners for the University of Virginia," signed in 1818 by both Jefferson and Madison, illustrates their mutual belief in the formative role of agriculture as an acquired skill, one that shapes citizens' taste. The report clarifies the mission of the school as one that will "harmonize and promote the interests of agriculture" on the grounds that knowledge of this "art" would help "form [students] to habits of reflection and correct action, rendering them examples of virtue to others, and of happiness within themselves" (*Papers*, RS, 1:327, 1:239). Again employing the language of Scottish moral sense philosophy— forming "habits of reflection" for themselves and providing "examples of virtue" to others—Madison and Jefferson reconfigure their discourse of agricultural citizenship so that it might apply to the plantation structure of the farms in the South. Most notably, they no longer express a belief in the necessity of participating in the actual tilling of the soil, or the harvesting of vegetables and grains, in order to reap the personal and public benefits of farming. (One might recall Jefferson's original vision of neighboring "little farm[s]" that they would work themselves.) Instead, they propose that a more refined engagement in the craft of cultivation is sufficient and even superior as a means of preparing students to become exemplars of taste.[22]

The language of the University of Virginia report confirms Madison and Jefferson's shared understanding of the importance of cultivation, as it applies to agriculture, to the process that will produce virtuous citizens. In the following lines, they rely on the metaphor of cultivation in their argument endorsing the benefits of education for all: "As well might it be urged that the wild and uncultivated tree, hitherto yielding sour and bitter fruit only, can never be made to yield better; yet we know that the grafting art implants a new tree on the savage stock, producing what is most estimable both in kind and degree. Education, in like manner, engrafts a new man on the native stock, and improves what in his nature was vicious and perverse into qualities of virtue and social worth" (*Papers*, RS, 1:330). Emphasizing the close connection between agriculture and the "civilized arts," they focus on a specific form of cultivation— the "grafting art"—as the dominant trope of this comparison. They also propose that the effects of grafting can be experienced by even the most "savage stock" (although, to be clear, their version of savagery here extends only to the "uncultivated" white men whom they would deign to admit into the university).[23] Several lines later, when Madison and Jefferson assert that advancements in agriculture have "rendered the [natural] elements themselves subservient to the purposes of man, have harnessed them to the yoke of his labors, and effected the great blessings of moderating his own," they further differentiate the cultural work of farming from the actual labor required to produce it. In so doing, they demonstrate how this rarefied form of cultivation, and by implication the sense of taste, functions not only as a controlling metaphor but also as a controlling regime; it allows U.S. citizens to cultivate their land, their minds, and their morals without having to account for the fact that those who produced their nation-sustaining food were, for the most part, still enslaved.

In 1822, acting in his capacity as president of the American Board of Agriculture, Madison wrote to a number of regional agricultural societies expressing his concern with the present "crisis in the agriculture of Virginia" (*Letters*, 285). Referring at once to the impoverishment of the soil, a result of more than a century of plantation farming, and to the recalcitrance of the farmers themselves, who refused to revise their methods of cultivation in accordance with modern techniques, Madison explains that this "crisis" could, in large part, be attributed to farmers "enslaved" to "ancient modes" of farming (285). Asserting that "in no instance . . . is habit more unyielding, or irrational practice more prevalent, than among those who cultivate the earth," Madison targets plantation farmers not for their enslavement of other people, but for their enslavement to old habits. He invokes the metaphor of slavery, which in an audience of plantation owners would be acutely felt, in order to illustrate the crucial importance of subjecting "unyielding" habit to rational thought. However, by urging plantation owners to examine the effects of enslavement while permitting them to avoid confronting the institution of slavery itself, Madison extends his own "crisis" into the U.S. psyche. Whereas the nation's originary "crisis," as theorized by Sundquist, derives from its constitutional legitimization of slavery, Madison's is more specific: a model of cultivated agricultural citizenship that advances republican virtue at the same time that it enforces—in lived experience as in symbolic language—this most glaring conceptual contradiction. Madison reveals, moreover, how his views about the virtues of cultivation, which would seem inherently and irreparably flawed, in fact incorporate into the body and mind the fundamental tension of the sense of taste.

This is the same tension that Jefferson confronted in his racial hierarchies, which Washington confronted at his table, and that we will see confronted, and at times challenged, throughout this book: the tension inherent in a sense of taste that relies on both immediate sensory experience and acquired cultural norms. For later aesthetic philosophers, those who allied themselves with the ideas of Immanuel Kant, this "both/and" formulation of the sense of taste threatened to destabilize their rigorous theories about aesthetic response. But for political figures such as Jefferson and Madison, it allowed them to retain a belief in the civilizing force of the sense of taste while minimizing the value of the embodied sensory experiences in which, as a result of their enslaved plantation staffs, they less often directly engaged.

Moderating the Political Body

By most accounts, James Madison inhabited the "eighteenth-century ideal of a republican statesman" (McCoy, 34).[24] According to one contemporaneous account, Madison displayed "a moderation, temperance, and virtue in every thing" (qtd. in McCoy, 34).[25] The personal narrative of Paul Jennings, Madison's valet, who was born into slavery at Montpelier, and in 1863, recorded his memories in *A Colored Man's Reminiscences of James Madison*, would seem to confirm the fourth president's moderate mien. "I never saw him in a passion, and never knew him to strike a slave," Jennings recalled, before continuing: "He was temperate in his habits. I don't think he drank a quart of brandy in his whole life. He ate light breakfasts and no suppers, but rather a hearty dinner, with which he took invariably but one glass of wine. When he had hard drink-ers at his table, who had put away his choice Madeira pretty freely, in response to their numerous toasts, he would just touch the glass to his lips, or dilute it with water, as they pushed about the decanters. For the last fifteen years of his life he drank no wine at all" (15-16). Among Jennings's daily responsibilities was to set the table for dinner, and as Madison became increasingly infirm, Jennings was also required to cut the food on Madison's plate into pieces small enough for him to eat.[26] Perhaps because of his intimacy with Madison's eating habits, or because of his own exposure to the discourse of taste, Jennings draws a direct link between the president's regulation of his physical "passion" and the tem-perance of his choices with respect to food.[27] In opposition to the domi-nant perception of Madison as a tasteful U.S. citizen, his dependence on Jennings, a man he enslaved, confirms the fundamental flaws in his per-sonal expression, as well as in his political application, of his republican taste.

As early as 1772, Madison noted in his commonplace book that "our Taste depends on the organization of our bodies & the dispositions or situations of our Minds" (*Papers, CS*, 1:21). This statement, copied from an English translation of the Abbé Du Bos's *Critical Reflections on Poetry, Painting, and Music* (1719), describes Madison's understanding of the sense of taste as comprised of physical and intellectual components, in keeping with Jefferson's and the Scottish Enlightenment view. A subsequent note—"when our Taste happens to change, it is not owing to Argument or to Persuasion, but to some Physical Alteration in our Bodies, or to some prevailing & aspiring Passion of the mind"—indicates his view of the body as the central site of aesthetic control. This formulation of taste, how it is developed, and how it is refined, points to why Madison could not conceive of a nation that included black citizens.

Madison's support for a moderating political body, and his belief in the "salutary" influence of personal taste, together contribute to his resis-tance to admit black Americans into the nation he helped to create.[28] His justification for the expatriation of all black people to the African coast, like Jefferson's, rests on a dual assessment of the "insuperable" nature of white prejudice and the "Physical & lasting peculiarities" of black Ameri-cans as a group (*Papers, RS*, 1:469). In her analysis of this statement, Gordon-Reed underscores the point that Madison does not identify "black skin" as the source of the "peculiarities," but rather, refers to "the *peculiarities* of the black people, as if more than skin color was at issue" ("Resonance," 188–89). However, she is unable to ascertain "what those other lasting peculiarities were." But in an 1819 letter to antislavery advocate Robert J. Evans, which was subsequently published in the *Daily National Intelligencer,* Madison writes that black people are "always . . . uncontroulled [*sic*] by some of the most cogent motives to moral and respectable conduct." This reprehensible assertion aligns with Jefferson's in the *Notes,* and suggests that Madison, like Jefferson, believed that one "peculiarity" of black people had to do with a "moral and respectable" core that, unlike that of their tasteful white compatriots, was somehow "uncontrolled" by an external guide.

Even when presented with irrefutable evidence of the tastefulness of black Americans, such as the "most gentleman-like manner" with which Paul Jennings was reported to have escorted a neighbor around Montpelier, Madison remained unwilling to admit that race did not play a factor in the cultivation of taste (Dolley Madison, *Papers,* 223). Here, his treatment of Jennings's predecessor William Gardner provides a revealing example. Gardner had served Madison in Washington in the early 1780s, and was thus exposed to the political debates that culminated in the *Federalist Papers.* As a result of this experience, Madison decided that Gardner's "mind [was] too thoroughly tainted to be a fit companion for his fellow slaves in Virg[ini]a," and consequently had Gardner sold (*Papers,* CS, 7:304).[29] Madison justified his decision to his father, explaining that he could not "think of punishing" Gardner by sending him back to Montpelier "merely for coveting that liberty for which we have paid the price of so much blood, and have proclaimed so often to be the right, & worthy the pursuit, of every human being." But the action that Madison took—selling Gardner rather than releasing him from bondage—illustrates his own unshakable belief that even a black man with an incontrovertible taste for liberty was considered unfit for self-governance.

The entrenchment of Madison's racialized conception of taste is further corroborated with the report provided by Christopher McPherson, a free black man once invited to dine at Madison's table. "I sat at Table Even[in]g & morn[in]g with Mr. M his Lady & Company & enjoyed a full share of the Convers[ation]," McPherson recalls (qtd. in Elizabeth Dowling Taylor, 14–15). While it is impossible to know "whether such encounters influenced Madison's opinion of the abilities of people of African descent, or if he read them only as exceptions to the rule," as Elizabeth

Dowling Taylor observes (15), McPherson's assessment of Madison's view is easily discerned in a subsequent letter, a note of thanks to Madison for lending him a horse. "This with the Family going off tomorrow on the Same Horses—and other Considerations—Stamps upon my mind an appropriate Sense of your goodness, that is not easily expressed," McPherson writes. "I shall however watch for an opportunity to Convince you how Sensible I am of it" (*Papers*, CS, 17:380). McPherson explicitly conveys an "appropriate" recognition of the Madisons' generosity, and continues to hope for an "opportunity" to demonstrate his sensibility. That he employs both the word "Sense" and the word "Sensible" in his letter is significant; as a free black man who could read and write, and as someone with significant experience interacting with prejudiced white people, McPherson would most likely have been familiar with the assumption, as articulated most ignominiously in Jefferson's *Notes,* that black people fail to exhibit that "tender mixture of sentiment and sensation" that characterizes the tasteful behavior of white folk (*Writings*, 2:194).[30] Here, McPherson takes an active step, one which he knew would be required, to disabuse Madison of his notion of black Americans' unreflective tastes.

It was the unreflective and insensible tastes of white Americans, however, that prevented the movement for general emancipation from gaining force. Madison, like Jefferson, placed his faith in the gradual emergence within the U.S. public of a "sensibility to human rights, and a sympathy with human sufferings, excited and cherished by the discussions preceding [Independence], and the spirit of the institutions growing out of that event"; as a result, he and others failed to advocate for the immediate abolition of slavery (*Papers*, RS, 1:428). And yet, his own actions accentuate the flaws in an approach to emancipation that depends on individual "sensibility." Madison, himself, refused to consider emancipating the people he enslaved. After his death, his wife, Dolley, continued to host extravagant parties "every Wednesday evening, at which," according to Paul Jennings, "wine, punch, coffee, ice-cream, &c, were liberally served" (16). In need of funds to support this demonstration of "taste of so high a tone," Dolley began the process of selling the people that the family had enslaved, one person by one (*Papers*, 265).

Although Madison had promised Paul Jennings his freedom, as he reported to a journalist in 1848, Jennings was required to travel with Dolley back to Washington, which separated him from his wife and children. There, nearly eleven years later, Jennings finally obtained his freedom through a purchase arrangement with Daniel Webster, the Massachusetts senator—himself a great gastronome—who valued Jennings for, among other qualities, his cultivated sense of taste. More specifically, Elizabeth Dowling Taylor reports that "one of the great draws at Webster's home was the culinary fare prepared by his African-American cook, Monica McCarty," and that Webster placed a high valuation on food that was tastefully prepared and presented to his guests (144). For this reason, he was likely already attuned to Jennings's masterful service as he had experienced it at the Madisons' table. What is certain is that, upon arranging to pay for Jennings's freedom, Webster appointed Jennings his butler and dining-room servant. Taylor provides a range of evidence to support the assertion that the "meals that McCarty cooked and Jennings served were appreciated," and cites one diner's report that, at the Webster home, "the table is capital" and "everything is given at the top of the heart" (164). In this way, Jennings's exemplary taste both confirms and contests Madison's intertwined assertions about the concept. Jennings's good taste confirms the general view that taste indeed matters; his good taste was the trait that first prompted Webster to take note of him in the Madison household, and that prompted Webster to extend his offer of assistance. But Jennings's good taste also strongly contests Madison's belief in it as a quality that only white people could possess; Jennings, a black man, employed his own exemplary sense of taste in order to enable himself to become free.

It thus seems fitting that Madison's death, as observed by Jennings, took place at the table—the actual as well as metaphorical site for the contradictory senses of republican taste. "I was present when he died," Jennings recalled: "That morning Sukey brought him his breakfast, as usual. He could not swallow. His niece, Mrs. Willis, said, 'What is the matter, Uncle Jeames?' [sic] 'Nothing more than a change of mind, my dear.' His head instantly dropped, and he ceased breathing as quietly as the snuff of a candle goes out. He was about eighty-four years old, and was followed to the grave by an immense procession of white and colored people. The pall-bearers were Governor Barbour, Philip P. Barbour, Charles P. Howard, and Reuben Conway; the two last were neighboring farmers" (18–19). It is impossible to know what Madison meant by the "change of mind" that he experienced in his final moments. But it is easier to interpret the "immense procession of white and colored people" who "followed [him] to the grave." Indeed, Madison's personal actions,

Figure 3. In 1847, shortly after obtaining his freedom, Paul Jennings sat for a portrait at the E. L. Perry Photograph Company. Courtesy of the Estate of Sylvia Jennings Alexander and Montpelier, a National Trust Historic Site.

in death and in life, affected U.S. residents of all races. His contributions to the *Federalist Papers* consolidated support for the Constitution, helping to "secure the Blessings of Liberty" for his fellow (white) American citizens. Indeed, the principles of temperance and moderation that comprise his vision of popular government continue to influence the creation and modification of representative democracies today. At the same time, by extending the notion of personal taste from the cultural realm to the political, Madison ensured that black Americans would be precluded from participating in his project of regulating the national body. That his final pallbearers were "neighboring farmers" signifies, moreover, how Madison's conception of agricultural citizenship, with its emphasis on the art of cultivation rather than the labor of farming itself, allowed him to justify the continuation of slavery in the free United States. The virtuous farmers who once supported Madison's vision of an independent and self-sustaining republic ultimately supported Madison's body itself.

The Archive and the Repertoire of Republican Taste

Paul Jennings went on to lead a long life, settling in Washington and finding employment first as a butler and dining-room servant in Daniel Webster's home, and later as a clerk in the federal pension office. When he died in 1874, he left a daughter, two sons, and numerous grandchildren. He also left the daguerreotype, pictured on the previous page, which, according to Elizabeth Dowling Taylor, he had taken as one of his first acts as a free man.[31] The daguerreotype contributes to our testament, in the present, of Jennings's contributions in the past. Taken along with his *Reminiscences,* which entered the archival record almost by chance—it was a colleague at the pension office who, upon hearing of Jennings's past life in such close proximity to a U.S. president, asked if he might commit his memories to paper—his archival record enables us, as scholars today, to develop a sense of how republican taste was exchanged and transacted in the early United States. Indeed, this notion of republican taste would soon be met by a range of additional aesthetic theories and forms of personal and political agency, evident throughout the Atlantic world.

There exists no analogous archival record for James Hemings, however. The sole surviving document authored in his own hand is an inventory of the kitchen utensils at Monticello, which dates to 1796, the year of his legal emancipation. The document was likely compiled as Hemings was preparing to complete the transfer of his culinary responsibilities to his younger brother Peter, the person whom Jefferson designated to serve as James's replacement as per the terms of the emancipation agreement that Jefferson had authored several years before.[32] And while Hemings could have himself authored a more personal account of this most profound of life transitions, it would not come to pass. In 1801, five years after he penned his kitchen inventory, he took his own life. The final archival reference to Jefferson's skillful chef is a letter composed by an innkeeper friend, several months after Hemings's death, confirming the "melancholy circumstance" of his suicide (*Papers*, 34:569–70).

If James Hemings, in the summer of 1801, found himself enmeshed in this most profound of personal crises, the rest of the country, at that same time, saw itself absorbed by international affairs: in July of that year, Toussaint Louverture signed and then summarily sent to France a constitution for the colony of Saint Domingue. The Constitution of 1801, as the document is now known, abolished slavery in that colony, declaring that "there was to exist no other distinction [among men] than that of virtues and talents, and no other superiority than that which the law gives in the exercise of a public function" (qtd. in James, 263). Prompted by Susan Buck-Morss's influential essay "Hegel and Haiti" (2000), scholars now point to that moment, and to the events that ensued, as evidence for an argument about the emergence of modernity—the era in which the ideological tensions between personal and political liberty at last began to be addressed.

More recently, however, scholars including Sibylle Fischer and Monique Allewaert have offered perspectives that complicate that tidy summary, seeking to excavate both aesthetic modes (Fischer) and unexplored spaces (Allewaert) that "offer ways to build stories about places and actors that archives documenting the citizen-subjects of print cannot" (Allewaert, 50). For even as the Constitution of 1801 may be recognized today as the event that allowed the nation of Haiti, the first black republic, to enter the archival register, it was not true that it performed that inscriptive function at the time. Jefferson, for one, reversed course from his initial (if tepid) support for the revolutionary movement. As president, he chose not to respond to a letter from Toussaint's successor Jean-Jacques Dessalines asking for a closer alliance on the basis of their nations' shared ideological underpinnings. Working closely with Madison, then secretary of state, Jefferson instead asked Congress to ban trade with the nation, and severed all diplomatic ties.[33]

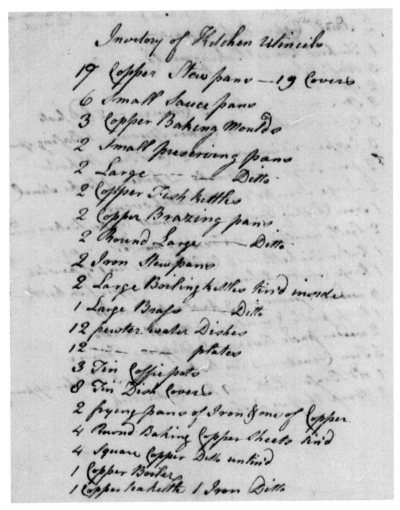

Figure 4. This inventory of kitchen utensils was penned by James Hemings on February 20, 1796, as he prepared for his emancipation and departure from Monticello. Courtesy of the Library of Congress, Manuscript Division.

But if the aim of the Jefferson administration was to "reduce Toussaint to starvation," depriving him, along with the people of Haiti, of actual as well as ideological food, others recognized that Toussaint's taste for liberty, temporarily sated by slavery's abolition in that place, could no longer be suppressed.[34] As rumors spread that Toussaint was planning to incite additional uprisings across the Caribbean, Jefferson wrote to the governor of Cuba explicitly attributing Toussaint's motivation to a failure to regulate his personal taste: "Appetite comes with eating, my friend, and Toussaint, who before did not desire more than the Ysland of Santo Domingo for his rule, is now planning to successively incorporate the neighboring Ysland of Jamaica . . . then Cuba, then Puerto-Rico, and finally the whole Globe" (qtd. in Fischer, 6). Toussaint's desire for liberty—the same desire that Jefferson and Madison had, not thirty years earlier, extolled as a marker of their sense of taste—is here reframed by an unnamed white interlocutor as an instance of unrestrained "appetite." By this account, the impulses of Toussaint's (black) body cannot be cultivated into a version of taste that conforms to the Scottish Enlightenment view. Instead, his taste for liberty becomes evidence of how bodily appetite interferes with, rather than contributes to, the cultivation and expression of republican taste.

In her work on the history of aesthetics, less known to scholars of the Atlantic world, Buck-Morss identifies, in the idea of a "sense" of taste, an "uncivilized and uncivilizable trace, a core of resistance to cultural domestication" that distinguishes it from later conceptions of the aesthetic (6). This aspect of taste—the "uncivilizable trace" that resists acculturation—is what the letter writer above identifies in Toussaint's unrestrained appetite. It is also, more accurately, what is on view in Jefferson's desire for culinary pleasure that keeps James Hemings in bondage, and in Madison's show of wealth that precludes Paul Jennings's release. Indeed, this "uncivilizable trace" is what best explains the paradox at the heart of republican taste: that the body and its "uncivilized" desires are as central to the production of republican taste as are any of its "domesticated" or cultivated manifestations. And yet, the bodies that possess the knowledge and perform the labor to produce this cultivated taste are not the same as those who claim to benefit from its moral force. In this way, the most transformative aspects of the sense of taste are, in those who claim to demonstrate good taste of the highest degree, shorn from their conditions of possibility. In ways that have not yet been fully acknowledged, these conditions of possibility instead remain in and are retained by the bodies of the enslaved men and women, such as Hemings and Jennings, who produce the taste on which the "free" republic depends.

As Buck-Morss's formulation also allows us to see, this same aspect of the sense of taste—its embodied and "uncivilizable trace"—ensures that a "core of resistance" remains. This is the aspect of taste that is consistently on display in James Hemings's culinary knowledge, and in Paul Jennings's tableside expertise. Their conscripted efforts in the conception, preparation, and presentation of meals help to constitute an expanded archive, one that documents a fuller range of the cultivation and expression of taste. This archive consists of a set of embodied cultural practices that, following Diana Taylor, resist the tendency of print archives to "separate[e] the source of 'knowledge' from the knower" (19). From this archive of eating—what Taylor would term a "repertoire"—we can glimpse how the sense of taste in the early republic was shaped as much by figures such as Hemings and Jennings as by the founders' abstracted ideals.

In this account of James Hemings and Paul Jennings, the men who prepared the food of presidents and served it at the highest seats of national power, I have attempted to identify places in the archive where we might reconnect knowledge with "the knower." I have also attempted to draw attention to the embodied cultural practices—the work of farming, cooking, and serving—that exist outside of our existing archive and that are merely gestured toward in the print record of the nation's founding. These embodied cultural practices also enable us, as scholars, to move beyond our concern with social and political contradiction in order to forge a new sense of the ways in which republican identity—the version enacted in the young United States and the version that would soon be made manifest in Haiti—is constituted by the interplay both between texts and bodies, and between subjective experience and acculturated response. Attending to the repertoire of republican taste, in which eating and aesthetics are inextricably intertwined, allows us to make better sense of our national cultural record by revealing the multiple meanings, or senses, of taste.

2

Appetite

Eating, Embodiment, and the Tasteful Subject

If the origins of the discourse of taste are most commonly traced to the British cultural critics of the early eighteenth century, the origins of the discourse of eating—if it could be described as such—are often attributed to a single man: the French epicure Alexandre Balthazar Grimod de la Reynière (1758–1837).[1] Grimod, as he is more commonly called, was known in his own time and today for his exuberant appetite, strong opinions, and sardonic wit. Yet he appeared uncharacteristically reserved when he reported to readers in his 1804 *Almanach des Gourmands,* the second annual volume of an eight-year run, about a potential new stop on his "itinéraire nutritif" (99).[2] The nutritive itinerary, subtitled "A Gourmand's Walk through Various Parisian Neighborhoods," provided an informal if opinionated account of where to acquire the most succulent roast duck, the freshest of oysters, and, at a restaurant on the corner of rue Mandar and rue Montorgueil, a wine-infused pâté of quail "fit for the table of the Gods" (99, 113).

But at the residence at 33 rue de Clichy, open to the public on Sunday afternoons, aspiring epicures could experience, according to the guide, an event "curious" as much as culinary: a demonstration of a "magnificent machine" that could electrocute a live turkey, resulting in a "truly admirable degree of tenderness" (Grimod, 224, 223). The machine's inventor, one Monsieur Beyer, was, according to Grimod, a scientist of some repute. Beyer based his design on the electrical experiments of Benjamin Franklin, who himself had noted in a 1750 letter to a friend—also a member of the Royal Society—that "birds killed in this manner eat *uncommonly* tender" (*Papers,* 4:111). Franklin had died just over a decade before the publication of Grimod's *Almanach,* but he had abandoned this particular avenue of experiment long before. Its apotheosis had been a "Party of Pleasure" on the banks of the Schuylkill in the summer of 1749, at which guests were served a dinner of turkey killed "by the Electrical Shock; and roasted by the electrical Jack, before a Fire kindled by the Electrified Bottle" (*Papers,* 3:352).[3] But by adapting the invention for everyday use, Beyer as much as Franklin, or so Grimod averred, was entitled to the "highest recognition by gourmands, and, more generally, those who take pleasure in eating perfectly cooked poultry and game, without being required to wait" (223, 224).

The nod to Beyer notwithstanding, Grimod's willingness to credit the "celebrated doctor Franklin" as the source of this innovation is unsurprising (223). Beginning in 1752, when Franklin's accounts of his experiments with electricity were first translated into French, he enjoyed distinguished status in that country.[4] Twenty-five years later, when he arrived in Paris in order to take up an appointment as the first U.S. ambassador to France—he was Thomas Jefferson's predecessor in that role—he "rode on his own coattails," as Stacy Schiff describes: "He was the world-renowned tamer of lightning, the man who had disarmed the heavens, who had vanquished superstition with reason" (3). Once established in Paris, in December 1776, Franklin would soon add an additional commendation to that list: the man who indulged his appetite. According to the "Accounts of Extravagance" that were published in U.S. newspapers during his time abroad, Franklin dined out six nights a week (*Papers*, 42:101).[5] This feat of appetitic indulgence earned him the admiration of the French and, just three years later, a incapacitating case of gout, which he famously documented in his satirical "Dialogue between Franklin and the Gout" (1780). In this regard, Franklin shared much with Grimod, who similarly "ate and drank too freely," and otherwise "too much indulged" his appetite (*Memoirs,* 3:327, 326). Indeed, both men exhibited a willingness to indulge their appetites and pleasures, often to the point of excess. Furthermore, both understood their excessive indulgence in philosophical terms: as evidence of the limits of the sense of taste as a moral or political guide, premised as it was upon the ability to subject one's appetite to reason.

As far back as Plato and Aristotle, the capacity for rational thought has been considered a key feature that separates human beings from all other living things.[6] And for just as long, that capacity has been doubted, challenged, and subjected to critique.[7] In many ways, the discourse of taste can be said to have been brought about not, as has been suggested thus far, as a direct extension of the basic Enlightenment belief in the human capacity for reason, but rather as a direct response to the doubts about reason that met Enlightenment humanism's rise. Only upon repeated insistence from key antagonists, most notably Thomas Hobbes, that appetite, and not reason, might be the dominant force that determined decisions of politics and morals, were the group of men that would come to be known as the taste philosophers prompted to theorize how such decisions came to be made.[8] Even today, appetite remains a major foil to the sense of taste, underscoring the importance of continued attention to what Sharon P. Holland, Marcia Ochoa, and Kyla Wazana Tompkins describe as the area of scholarly inquiry at the "intersection of race, food, humanity, and animality" (396–97). They place the appetite for food, as well as for sex and other bodily pleasures, in the domain of "the visceral," and propose that a renewed emphasis on the visceral aspects of human experience can help to "transform food studies, food systems, and food security narratives, which tend to privilege a kind of right, proper cultivation, into stories capable of making room for what might happen when civility goes awry" (398).

This chapter takes up the call to create stories that make room "for what might happen when civility goes awry" at precisely the moment when civility, itself, constituted a principal societal goal.[9] Through an examination of the works of three writers (and eaters) from around the time of the nation's founding, each of whom lived in or traveled to Europe at the time of the efflorescence of the discourse of taste, I serve up one possible set of stories for a transformed field of food studies. Each of these stories engages with the irrepressible force of appetite—for specific foods, for sensory pleasure, and for corporeal freedom—through which I identify the beginnings of critique of the dominant discourse of taste. Following Holland, Ochoa, and Tompkins, this critique resides in examples of the visceral aspects of appetite, in which animal instinct, sensory pleasure, and gustatory desire are each employed in order to challenge the purported stability of the sense of taste. Along with this critique comes a questioning of what I term the *tasteful subject*: the white male republican citizen viewed as uniquely capable of cultivating good taste. In formulating this concept and in identifying the questions it prompts, I draw from broader critiques of the Enlightenment subject, such as Alexander Weheliye's challenge to the exclusionary nature of what he terms the "world of Man" (10). Later chapters more closely align with Weheliye's aim of exploring the "cultural and political formations outside the world of Man that might offer alternative versions of humanity," in particular chapters 3 and 4, which explore alternatives to the theory of taste and its surrounding discourse (10). In pursuit of that eventual goal, this chapter focuses on challenges to the theory and discourse of taste that are issued from within the Enlightenment project. Similar to the "minoritarian enlightenment traditions" that Monique Allewaert identifies in her work on the American tropics, those which participate in the "disordering of the colonial projects that they also sustained," the figures whose writing (and eating) that I explore in this chapter similarly seek to "disorder" the dominant discourse that they nevertheless still—in different ways, and for different reasons—also simultaneously seek to maintain (22).

These figures include Franklin and Grimod, as well as one additional writer and interlocutor in the discourse of taste, the African American poet Phillis Wheatley. While Wheatley's status as an enslaved black woman would seem to strongly demarcate her life experience from the two (free) white men—as indeed it did, to no uncertain degree—her poetry directly engaged with the same theories of taste that Franklin and Grimod addressed in their work. As I will show, Wheatley's poetic investigations were thematically related, and at times directly connected, to the discussions in which Franklin and Grimod were also engaged. These discussions concerned the limits of taste, the force of appetite, and the freedom required to explore each. As I will argue, Franklin, Grimod, and Wheatley each understood eating as an entry point into a critique of the tasteful subject, as well as of the cultivated sense of taste that served as that subject's moral and political guide. And as we will see, each of these figures employed their actual bodies as well as the literary works their bodies produced in order to challenge the discourse of taste as it was then conceived.[10]

I begin with the body and body of work of Franklin. For it is in his lifelong obsession with eating, and writing about same, that he offers a rich set of examples through which to explore the personal, political, and philosophical ramifications of exerting (or, more accurately, *attempting* to exert) rational control over the appetites of the body. These examples expose an axis that positions enlightened restraint against excessive appetite. This excess is a form of appetite that Franklin associates with animals—with people who eat animals, with animals that eat, and with people who eat *like* animals. In Grimod, we find evidence of another attempt to position enlightenment against excess, in his case against an overly cultivated sense of taste that curtails the true pleasures of the palate. Through an analysis of his performative dinners as well as his published works, I show how Grimod stages a full-bodied critique of the tasteful subject. But it is Wheatley who offers this chapter's most complex critique of the boundedness of that idea. Through her direct engagement with contemporaneous aesthetic philosophy, Wheatley is able to put the lie to the enduring claims that the tasteful subject, its race and gender implied, could ever serve as the exemplar of either good taste or good citizenship. By countering the exclusionary definition of the tasteful subject with examples of her own tastefulness, as well as with arguments for how enslaved subjects might become refined according to the precise criteria laid out by the discourse of taste, she begins the required work of destabilizing that discourse from within.

I consider these figures separately and together because while each represents a unique position with respect to the discourse of taste, they share certain attributes and opinions. Grimod and Franklin were united by privilege; their shared social and economic status enabled them to mount critiques of the dominant discourse of taste without the fear of reprisal or personal cost. By the same token, Grimod and Wheatley shared select experiences of social difference; Grimod, who employed prosthetic hands, had no choice but to acknowledge his physical disability, just as Wheatley had no choice but to acknowledge the color of her skin.[11] While their shared life experiences end there, as Wheatley remained enslaved until the final years of her life and died in part due to starvation, they retain a connection for how they both strategically deployed their bodies, as they knew them to be perceived by their readers, in relation to their bodies of work.[12] A third comparison, between Wheatley and Franklin, helps to underscore this chapter's final argumentative claim: Franklin, because of his elevated status, could do or say (or eat) anything he so desired; Wheatley emphatically could not. Indeed, Wheatley, more intimately than either Franklin or Grimod, experienced the exclusions that inhered in the idea of the tasteful subject, as well as the limitations of the sense of taste itself. None of these figures articulate a complete alternative to the theory of taste, as do the figures discussed in later chapters of this book. But their critiques of the dominant discourse, framed in their own language, and mounted from within, begin the work of dismantling that exclusionary worldview.

Eating Animals and Animals That Eat

Franklin's "inordinate breakfast [of] four dishes of tea, with cream, and one or two buttered toasts, with slices of hung beef"—the meal that prompted rebuke from his personified gout—did not simply represent a strategic attempt to ingratiate himself with the French (*Memoirs*, 3:326). Rather, it reflected the culmination of nearly a lifetime of his having indulged in the pleasures of the palate. Franklin's *Autobiography* documents numerous examples of his struggles to hold his appetite at bay. In one of the most famous scenes, documenting the end of his vegetarian diet, Franklin is forced to reconsider his abstemiousness in light (and smell) of fish "hot out of the Frying Pan" (87). "I had formerly been a great Lover of Fish," he recalls, and therefore "balanc'd some time between Principle and Inclination: till I recollected, that when the Fish were opened, I saw smaller Fish taken out of their Stomachs: Then thought I, if you eat one another, I don't see why we mayn't eat you" (87–88). This episode has long been identified as among the most compelling examples of Franklin's awareness, as Betsy Erkkila explains, of the "instability of 'Reason' as the ground of the enlightened self and the new secular order he seeks to embody" (722). As an additional confirmation of its significance, Franklin includes this "return to eating Flesh" in the two-page outline of the work, although he makes no mention of the experiment with vegetarianism that preceded it (*Autobiography*, 268). But in the context of the discourse of taste, this anecdote performs additional philosophical work. For one, it indicates Franklin's awareness of the irrepressible force of appetite, as his "Dialogue with the Gout" will later confirm.[13] For another, it reveals Franklin's understanding of eating, as food writer Michael Pollan observes, as an act that "puts us in touch with all that we share with the other animals, and all that sets us apart" (10). By employing the fish's eating habits as a model for his own, Franklin acknowledges more than the malleability of reason as the grounds for the "enlightened self." He also accedes to the fundamental fluidity between the human animal and other living things.

The distinction between human and animal was central to the Enlightenment definition of the human subject, as scholars have long observed.[14] And while many episodes in the *Autobiography* touch on the distinction (or lack thereof) between humans and animals, Franklin dramatizes this philosophical concern most clearly in his depiction of Samuel Keimer, the owner of the Philadelphia print shop where he found his first formal employment.[15] This professional opportunity set Franklin on his future life course. And yet he consistently relegates Keimer to a role as his foil, characterizing him as inferior in every way. Franklin claims, for instance, that Keimer "kn[ew] nothing of Presswork," but Franklin, even on his first day of work, was able to "put his Press . . . into Order" (*Autobiography*, 78). He describes Keimer as a "Knave in his Composition," while positioning himself as an exemplar of expository style (79). Keimer, Franklin relates, was "very ignorant of the World," in contrast to Franklin's vaunted knowledge of international affairs (79). The comparisons continue, culminating in Franklin's account of his mastery over Keimer's mind. Franklin recalls how he "us'd to work [Keimer] so with [his] Socratic Method" to the point where Keimer "would hardly answer the most common Question, without asking first, *What do you intend to infer from that?*" (88). This intellectual contest results in a plea of nolo contendere for Keimer, whose abilities are no match for Franklin's enlightened mind.

Adding the proverbial insult to injury, Franklin conveys to his readers Keimer's other egregious fault: he "was usually a great Glutton" (*Autobiography*, 88). Contra Franklin, who learned early in life to exhibit "perfect Inattention" to the "Victuals on the Table, whether it was well or ill dressed, in or out of season, [or] of good or bad flavour," Keimer illustrates the negative impact of acquiescing to his "Tastes and Appetites" (55). While relating an anecdote in which the two decide to establish a "new sect," with doctrines ranging from not shaving their beards (Keimer's contribution) to not eating animals (obviously Franklin's), Franklin emphasizes Keimer's difficulty in adhering to the latter (88). He gleefully recalls:

> We had our Victuals dress'd and brought to us regularly by a
> Woman in the Neighbourhood, who had from me a List of
> 40 Dishes to be prepar'd for us at different times, in all which there
> was neither Fish Flesh nor Fowl. . . . I went on pleasantly, but poor
> Keimer suffer'd grievously, tir'd of the Project, long'd for the Flesh
> Pots of Egypt, and order'd a roast Pig. He invited me and two
> Women Friends to dine with him, but it being brought too soon
> upon table, he could not resist the Temptation, and ate it all up
> before we came. (88–89)

In contrast to Franklin's professed indifference to the "Victuals on the Table" and, perhaps more meaningfully, in contrast to his response to the temptation of fried Block Island cod—in which he attempts to find "balance" between his appetite and his inclination, and constructs a rational explanation for why he might indulge—Keimer is here described as wholly consumed by his appetites. He cannot even wait for Franklin to arrive before devouring the meal in its entirety. Keimer's desirousness is underscored by Franklin's mention of the "Women Friends" he invites to dine with them. With this additional detail, Franklin insinuates that Keimer is capable of none of the restraint that might distinguish his appetites from those of the other animals—appetites for food or even sexual pleasure. Extending Franklin's exploration, in the fish episode, of the tenuous boundary between animal appetite and human reason, Keimer's behavior, here, implicates him as nothing more (or less) than an animal that eats.[16]

Franklin continues to complicate the distinction (or lack thereof) between eating animals and animals that eat as he attempts to establish his professional independence from Keimer. In recounting his subsequent time in Keimer's print shop, Franklin takes every opportunity to portray Keimer as the embodiment of appetite, thereby reinforcing his own image as a paragon of restraint. When the men see the governor outside of the print shop, Franklin waits patiently upstairs. Keimer, on the other hand, "r[uns] down immediately" into the street (*Autobiography*, 80). And when Franklin's more measured response results in an invitation to accompany the governor to a tavern down the street, Keimer "star[es] like a Pig poison'd" (80). Here, Keimer does more than merely eat *like* an animal; he behaves as if he were the very animal he had recently consumed. As an embodiment of unrestrained appetite, Keimer comes to represent, for Franklin, the negative impact—professional as well as philosophical—of the slippage between human and animal that only reason has the power to hold at bay.

Franklin's meeting with the governor, as it would turn out, set in motion a series of events that allowed him to travel to England, the first of his many extended stays in that country. That particular sojourn, between 1724 and 1726, coincided with an extended public debate over the question of appetite's role in civil society.[17] One year before Franklin's arrival, in 1723, Bernard Mandeville had published an expanded version of his Hobbesian *Fable of the Bees* (1714). A response to the intellectual incursion of the early taste philosophers, who, as previously discussed, sought to attribute virtuous behavior to an innate moral sense, Mandeville's revised *Fable* reinforced the position that the impulse toward benevolence eschewed any internal basis. Based on the ideas expressed in Hobbes's *Leviathan* (1651), Mandeville argued that public virtue was simply a by-product of the satisfaction of instinctual desires.

Mandeville's primary interlocutor in this debate was Francis Hutcheson, whose 1725 *Inquiry into the Origins of Our Ideas of Beauty and Virtue* was (and still is) viewed as a foundational text of Scottish Enlightenment thought.[18] As for Franklin, it has been posited that his direct exposure to this particular intellectual struggle imparted "memorable exposure to the contemporary exchange between moral philosophy and practical psychology" (Douglas Anderson, 7). However, scholars have yet to draw out the significance of the Mandeville-Hutcheson debate for Franklin in terms of the conflict between appetite and reason, and the impact of that conflict on his ideas about the cultivation of virtue and taste. This is in large part due to the difficulty of subjecting Franklin's large and often contradictory body of work to any sustained analysis. It nevertheless bears mention that Franklin's only explicitly philosophical work, "A Dissertation on Liberty and Necessity, Pleasure and Pain," composed (and printed) while in London, so closely adhered to the Mandevillian view that it earned him an invitation to meet Mandeville himself. Although Franklin later repudiated that work as juvenilia, burning all but one copy, the "Dissertation" nonetheless points to an explicit awareness, later dramatized in the relationship between Franklin and Keimer, of the consequences—personal, public, and therefore political—of indulging in animal appetite rather than exercising enlightened restraint.[19]

But the tension between these presumed poles of appetite and restraint is precisely why eating served as such a compelling site of philosophical investigation for Franklin and his contemporaries, and continues to do so for scholars today.[20] After all, it is not only in the exercise of enlightened restraint but also in the ability to experience the pleasures of appetite that what distinguishes humans from other animals—and also what binds them together—comes most clearly into view.[21] Letters from Franklin's various travels abroad document the delight he took in receiving shipments of American foodstuffs otherwise unavailable in Europe. He repeatedly requested that his wife, Deborah, send him crates of Boston cranberries and Newtown Pippins (a variety of roasting apple, which was also a favorite of Jefferson's) (*Papers*, 8:90, 7:367). In addition, he once professed of Indian corn that "its green leaves roasted are a delicacy beyond expression" (43:74). During a mid-career trip to London in 1757,

Franklin had the opportunity to dine with David Hume himself, who, not only incidentally, "aimed to make his residence not only the intellectual but the gastronomic center of Edinburgh" (Nolan, 173). The historian J. Bennett Nolan reports that Hume "was very proud . . . of the culinary proficiency of his Peggy [Irvine, his cook], protesting that her sheep's head soup was the best in the world" (173). According to Nolan, Hume himself "loved to go into the kitchen and concoct a *soupe à la reine* after the recipe given him in France by Madame de Boufflers," and, apparently, he excelled: "Henry McKenzie, 'the man of feeling,' praised a *bouilli* which David cooked for him, and Boswell marveled at three kinds of ice cream" (173).

Ironically, it would be ice cream and its principal ingredient, sugar, that would ultimately force Franklin to interrogate the larger political and economic systems that enabled his gustatory pleasure.[22] In 1772, he published an editorial in the *London Chronicle* prompted by the ruling on the Somerset Case, the landmark court decision that held that slavery was not authorized by any extant English law. In the editorial, he asks, "Can sweetening our tea, etcetera, with sugar, be a circumstance of such absolute necessity? Can the petty pleasure thence arising to the taste, compensate for so much misery produced among our fellow creatures, and such a constant butchery of the human species by this pestilential detestable traffic in the bodies and souls of men?" (*Papers*, 19:187). In the decades that followed, which coincided with the final years of his life, Franklin would determine that the answer to this set of questions was a resounding "no." Because of its link to the "pestilential detestable traffic" of slave trade, sugar came to be viewed by Franklin, as by many others as the time, as "thoroughly dyed scarlet in grain" (*Papers*, 41:384).[23] It was a clear instance of how the sense of taste should be exercised in order to adhere to the morally correct position. The pleasure was "petty" in this case because it lacked the depth—ethical as much as gustatory—that a cultivated sense of taste could confer.

But even as specific foodstuffs became excised from the realm of tasteful eating—the result of another (purportedly) distinctly human quality, compassion—Franklin continued to acknowledge instances in which the force of appetite could not be curtailed. In a letter to his sister, Jane Mecom, in the final years of his life, Franklin describes his own public service in terms of an act of eating. He writes: "When I inform'd your good Friend Dr. Cooper that I was order'd to France being then 70 years old, and observ'd that the Publick having as it were eaten my

Flesh, seem'd now resolv'd to pick my Bones; [Dr. Cooper] replied that he approv'd their taste for that *the nearer the Bone the sweeter the Meat*" (*Papers*, 45:248). Franklin's humorous characterization of the sacrifice of public service—a core tenet of the moral sense philosophy to which Franklin would at least attempt to adhere—is here embodied to the utmost degree. Franklin describes the public's consumption of his body as not merely an assertion of appetite, but of a cannibalistic one: the public eats him to the bone. Not even animals (except, evidently, Franklin's iconic fish) participate in that practice. And yet, at least according to his sister's "Friend," the public demonstrates their good "taste" in doing so. On the surface, Franklin receives a witty compliment. But at a deeper level, this letter affirms how eating, the act that separates humans from animals, instead places the human on a continuum with animal instinct. The public cannot resist satisfying its appetite for Franklin's public service, just as Keimer cannot resist the taste of roast pig. In this way, this letter serves as an equal-but-opposite companion to Franklin's story of himself and the cod. In that case, human rationality is premised on animal rationality: if fish eat each other, then humans should be able to eat the fish. Here, however, we are shown how the act of eating, far more than a marker of civility, taste, or reason, instead connects us, as eating animals, to animals that eat. As Grimod will further imply, and as Wheatley will eventually confirm, these appetites—animalistic and, at times, approaching cannibalistic—are those which, contra the best aspirations of the taste philosophers, truly govern the world.

From Animal Appetite to Enlightened Pleasure

It was a similar view of the irrepressible force of appetite, as well as its pleasures, that Grimod sought to put on display when he hosted an infamous dinner—equal parts meal and performance—on an evening in early February 1783. The dinner was staged by the acting coach of Marie-Antoinette and was funded by Grimod's family wealth, evidently without his family's consent. It began by requiring the two dozen invited guests to wend their way through a series of dark antechambers before meeting with a "strange, terrifying monk" (qtd. in Spang, 88).[24] Upon uttering the password "Monsieur Grimod de la Reynière, defender of the people," the guests were then formally welcomed—in the form of incense perfumed upon them by staff dressed as choirboys—before entering into a dining chamber. There they were served a multicourse meal on a table with a coffin as its centerpiece, leading to the dinner being described in subsequent newspaper coverage as Grimod's "funeral dinner."[25] Eager to allow for the meal to be observed, if not tasted, by as many people as possible, Grimod opened a gallery overlooking the dining chamber to upward of three hundred additional viewers, who, as a result of limited seating capacity, were required to attend the meal in shifts.

In her analysis of the dinner's staging—one of the few scholarly accounts that can be found—Rebecca Spang proposes that "Grimod created a moment that indicted both the *grand couvert* and the exclusionary logic inherent in the Enlightenment's more universalist aspirations" (90).[26] Spang's analysis, which appears in the context of an argument about the rise of French restaurant culture, identifies two seemingly contradictory strands of Grimod's critique: the first of the *grand couvert,* the French royal tradition, popularized by Louis XIV, of allowing the public to observe the king and queen's evening meal; and the second of the secret rituals associated with freemasonry and other putatively democratic social groups. Grimod's dinner, which coincided with the final years of France's ancien régime (and, it should be noted, with Franklin's tenure as ambassador to that country, although there is no evidence that the two ever met), "commented simultaneously on the ceremonies of the absolutist court and on the new institutions that claimed to abolish ceremony and establish brotherhood," Spang explains (90). This same double critique would come to characterize Grimod's later writing, as will soon be discussed. But there remains an unexamined valence to Grimod's performance of pleasure, which has to do with Grimod himself: more specifically, how he employed his own cultivated appetite in order to challenge certain exclusions inherent in the discourse of taste.

In the context of an argument about Grimod's performance of appetite, certain additional details about his body and his experience with disability become germane. As a result of a genetic condition known today as Cenani-Lenz Syndrome, Grimod was born with his fingers fused together, and he required prostheses—dual assemblages of leather, parchment, and papier-mâché—in order to both eat and write.[27] He engaged in both acts with gusto; the former as evidenced by the dinner just described, and the latter as evidenced by his numerous publications, which included the eight-volume *Almanach des gourmands* (1803–12), as well as a manual for dinner party hosts (1808) and a variety of essays for popular journals of culture and taste. This literary output serves as the basis for most contemporary scholarship on Grimod, although that work remains scant, as his opinionated musings are often overlooked in favor of Jean Anthelme Brillat-Savarin's more developed culinary philosophy. But in his writing as well as his eating, Grimod offers a crucial critique—not evident in Brillat-Savarin's work—of both the narrowness of tasteful experience as it was then conceived, and the narrowness of the tasteful subject deemed capable of experiencing it.

In order to recognize the full extent of this critique, we must consider more of Grimod's biography. Born in 1758, Grimod was shunned by his aristocratic family almost immediately. In order to disabuse the public of any suggestion that his condition might be hereditary, his parents dropped the honorific "de" from his surname and baptismal papers, and listed his godparents as "the widow of a tailor and an illiterate carpenter" (Gigante, *Gusto*, 2). Ironically, this oppressive act would be what would protect him during the Reign of Terror, and what would ensure his social acceptance amid the upwelling of anti-aristocratic sentiment that followed. But his parents also pursued more fantastical means of ensuring that the family line would not come into question, concocting a tale of how he had been injured as a result of a childhood accident, in which an absentminded caregiver had dropped him into a pigpen, where he was attacked by the hungry hogs.[28] This story would not be dignified by its retelling were it not for the fact that, at his funeral dinner, Grimod seized on the pig as an emblem of sorts, which he used to contest the fictional as well as physical terms of his difference. According to one account, Grimod dressed up a pig in the clothes of his father and seated the animal at the head of the table (Downie, 191).[29] According to a second, the meal's first course consisted solely of pork (Spang, 88). According to a third, Grimod simply declared to his guests that he had descended from "pig farmers and grocers on his father's side" (Gigante, *Gusto*, 2). In any case, Grimod's use of the pig can be viewed as an attempt to reclaim the history that had been imposed upon him, and redirect its critical force.

The pig also represents part of Grimod's sustained attempt, further pursued in his writing, to reclaim and repurpose the pleasures of appetite. Here, a contrast between Grimod's performative embrace of the pig and Franklin's rejection of same—in the form of his characterization of Keimer's gluttony as akin to a "Pig poison'd"—becomes revealing. Whereas Franklin consistently seeks to distance himself from animal appetite, even as he admits to often falling under its sway, Grimod attempts a deliberate *detournement*. For Grimod, appetite need not be excised from the sense of taste, as Franklin (and the moral sense philosophers) would have it. Rather, après Grimod, appetite itself should be cultivated, celebrated, and indulged. In this way, Grimod's project is closely aligned with the work of Holland, Ochoa, and Tompkins, as discussed earlier in this chapter, who seek to embrace "what might happen when incivility goes awry." And here, an additional point of confluence might be observed: Holland and colleagues place their work at the intersection of food studies and queer theory, and Grimod's queering of his origin story—as well as of the discourse of taste—would seem to directly support these scholars' claims. At his funeral dinner as in his published work, Grimod insists on the value of a sense of taste that originates in the body and remains connected to its pleasures. He emphatically rejects the belief that embodied pleasure, and any "incivility" it might encourage, must be removed in order for the sense of taste to be refined.

As a person whose body marked him for exclusion from the most elite Parisian circles—because of his extraordinary appetite as much as his "extraordinary body"—Grimod himself helps underscore a central point of contrast with Franklin.[30] After all, Franklin, in spite of his own extraordinary appetite, remained secure in the innermost sanctums of social capital and political power. While firmly ensconced within similar circles, and while Franklin was in France the very same ones, Grimod remained never fully embraced. Not only was his writing consistently derided as "the product of a deranged mind," but as a result of the funeral dinner, followed by several other stunts in short succession, Grimod himself was shunned by his family for a second time (Spang, 159). Through a *lettre de cachet*—a letter signed by the king used to authorize a person's imprisonment on the grounds of maintaining public order—he was forcibly sent to live in a monastery, the Abbaye Domèvre-sur-Vezouse. He lived in the abbaye for two years, where, according to Gigante, he further refined his palate and also learned to cook with the monks, who were known for "mak[ing] the most of their grounds, flowing with fresh fish and produce" (*Gusto*, 2). He then moved to Lyon, the culinary capital of southern France, where he established himself as a commercial food trader. When he returned to Paris in 1794, at the height of the Reign of Terror, he was able to employ his professional credentials, combined with the baptismal papers that attested to his ignoble origins, in order to regain control of his family's residence. (His father had died earlier that year.) It was at the Hôtel de la Reynière that Grimod rode out the revolution, and when Napoleon seized power in November 1799 he began to write.

In the *Almanach des gourmands*, which appeared several years later, Grimod was able to convey his knowledge of the aristocratic eating practices that he acquired in his youth, and that he further refined at the monastery, to a larger reading public. And this public was indeed large; the first volume of the *Almanach* went through four editions, totaling twenty thousand copies and securing Grimod's reputation as "unquestionably, the single most famous eater in First-Empire France" (Spang, 152). In the preface to that volume, Grimod seemingly excoriates the uneducated class of nouveaux riches for turning "toward purely animal pleasures" (29). Their "hearts have suddenly transformed into gullets; their emotions are no longer more than sensations; and their desires only appetites," he writes (29). With the chain of oppositions that he establishes between "heart" and "gullet," "emotion" and "sensation," and "desire" and "appetite," Grimod's project would seem to closely align with the central aims and language of the discourse of taste. However, in the same way that Grimod levied his indictment of tasteful behavior at both sides in his infamous funeral dinner, here, in the *Almanach,* he also issues a double critique: on the one hand, of the "animal" appetites that those uninitiated in the art of eating might exhibit, and, on the other, of those whose tastes are so refined that they fail to experience the pleasures of the palate to their full effect.

In the *Almanach,* Grimod thus seeks to model a new form of enlightened appetite. This form of appetite draws its conceptual language from the dominant discourse of taste, even as it is deliberately distanced from that same discourse. He articulates its key features most clearly in the essay "On Gourmands and Gourmandise," which appears in the *Almanach's* third volume (1806). In that essay, he writes:

> The Gourmand is more than just a creature whom Nature has graced with an excellent stomach and vast appetite; all vigorous men of sound constitution enjoy the same privilege; rather, he also possesses an enlightened sense of taste, the first principle of which lies in an exceptionally delicate palate developed through extensive experience. All his senses must work in constant concert with

that of taste, for he must contemplate his food before it even nears his lips. Suffice to say that his gaze must be penetrating, his ear alert, his sense of touch keen, and his tongue able. Thus the Gourmand, whom the Academy depicts as a course creature, is characterized instead by extreme delicacy; only his health need be robust. (Qtd. in Gigante, *Gusto*, 12)

Unlike contemporaneous writings that seek to characterize the sense of taste, Grimod both begins and ends with the body. He specifies that "an excellent stomach" and a "vast appetite" are just as important as an "enlightened sense of taste." But this sense of taste is not one that is employed in the interest of aesthetic or moral judgment, or of political decision making. Rather, it is focused on the body and its pleasures alone.[31] All of the senses "must work in constant concert with that of taste," he explains, specifying what each sense can contribute to the pleasures of the palate. Ending his account with the same themes he emphasizes at the outset, he confirms that the "health" of the body is the most important attribute for the gourmand to maintain.

Grimod's emphasis on embodied pleasure over and above the pleasures that derive from behaving with virtue or benevolence, or from appreciating a work of art, is illustrated most visibly in the series of frontispieces that begin each volume of the *Almanach*. The engraving that accompanies the first volume, titled "The Library of the Nineteenth-Century Gourmand," depicts "a study decorated in the most modern taste." (Each frontispiece is accompanied by several paragraphs of textual description.) In the foreground is "a table laden with refined fare, enough for fifteen people," yet the table is set for only two. There is also a serving table and two sideboards, each laden with food. Hanging from the ceiling in the place of a chandelier is a "monstrous Bayonne ham." The perspective of the image, coupled with the relative sparseness of the side walls, draws the viewer's gaze toward the bookcase that spans the full length of the back wall: the library named in the engraving's title. But there are no books on the shelves. Instead, the shelves are laden with "all manner of foodstuffs, among which one can see a suckling pig, various sorts of patés, enormous saveloys, and other such delicacies, along with a good number of bottles of wine and liquor, jars of fruit either crystalized or preserved, etc." (qtd. in Gigante, *Gusto*, 283). Here, then, is a literal depiction of Grimod's central aim: to replace the more rarefied arts, namely,

Figure 5. This frontispiece, titled "The Library of the Nineteenth-Century Gourmand," which depicts a library in which the books have been replaced by food, introduces the first volume of Grimod de la Reynière's Almanach des gourmands (1805). Courtesy of HathiTrust.

literature, with eating alone. The books that to the taste philosophers signaled the highest degree of aesthetic discernment are exchanged for the foods that to Grimod signal the highest degree of embodied pleasure.[32]

Another frontispiece, which announces the third volume of the *Almanach,* depicts a scene more anchored in reality. Titled "A Jury of Gourmand Tasters in Session," the engraving depicts eight men in jackets and wigs seated around a dining table. These men are "professors in the art of Gourmandise," we are told, and together they constitute the "Tasting Jury." The Tasting Jury was the brainchild of Grimod, in which a group of men—no fewer than five but no more than twelve—gathered each Tuesday, not unlike the Judges' Table on the reality television series *Top Chef,* to debate the relative merits of the foodstuffs under consideration for potential inclusion in future editions of the *Almanach*.[33] In the scene depicted in the frontispiece, the men "are tasting the Paté that was seen in volume two's print; on their faces one can observe the depth of reflection that is the hallmark of a Gourmand carrying out his duties," Grimod explains (qtd. in Gigante, *Gusto,* 294). By his use of the phrase "depth of reflection," Grimod emphasizes how the opinions of the Tasting Jury are informed by the discourse of taste—think of Jefferson's various invocations of the concept, as discussed in chapter 1. Grimod further emphasizes how the judges "deliberate without distinction and with complete independence" (294). While each member casts his own vote, the final verdicts are pronounced collectively, Grimod explains. In these ways, the Tasting Jury seems to lay "a claim to objectivity and universality, asking to be taken as the aesthetic standard of a group of ideal critics: the fantasy of Enlightenment taste theory come true," as Gigante has observed (xxiv).

Yet Grimod remains insistent that his project is one of cultivating appetite and not one of cultivating taste. As he admits in an essay on the Tasting Jury, published in the fifth volume of the *Almanach,* he was prompted to assemble the jury primarily because of the physical limitations of his appetite. "We," Grimod explains, speaking of himself in the plural, "felt that our abilities and our methods were insufficient to evaluate so many objects, and that in spite of our zeal, our love for art, and our vast appetite, we could not proceed alone; the best stomach has its limits" (554). It is thus additional men with stomachs that he requires as much as men who possess a cultivated sense of taste. In assembling his additional jury members, Grimod continues to emphasize the need for men who possess robust physical capabilities such as "jaws which had been exercised for many years" (554). He seeks participants who are each distinguished by his "palate, by his tact, his delicacy, and his sensitivity" (554).[34] Insisting that "the Almanac and the Tasting Jury have become inseparable, [that] one promulgates the decisions of the other; [that] they lend each other mutual aid, and are, in a sense, a community of God," Grimod refuses to allow any untethering of the sense of taste from the bodies that experience its pleasures (555).

Grimod's emphasis on embodied pleasure, and on the appetites that produce it, is confirmed by his decision to explicitly excise politics from his table. Citing an essay in the eighth and final volume of the *Almanach,* Spang explains Grimod's rationale: "When confronted with an elaborate

Séance d'un Jury de Gourmands dégustateurs.

Figure 6. "A Jury of Gourmand Tasters in Session," the frontispiece to the third volume of the Almanach des gourmands (1807), documents the process by which foodstuffs were considered for inclusion in the book. Courtesy of HathiTrust.

pheasant pâté or a truffled roast turkey, the true connoisseur often could not control his own eating—how could he attempt, Grimod asked, to govern others?" (158). Here, Grimod openly admits the futility of attempting to subject appetite to reason in ways that Franklin, for one, was unwilling to fully acknowledge. In Grimod's emphatic rejection of politics at the table resides his most valuable critique as it applies to the notion of republican taste. One's taste cannot be trusted to weigh in on decisions disconnected from the body because the body, in the end, is the sense of taste's most trusted guide. This is an opinion that Franklin likely shared, but could not allow to overshadow his public persona, dedicated as he was to continuing to cultivate—if not always to exhibit—tasteful behavior. But Grimod, who through a combination of choice and circumstance remained primarily accountable to himself, could mount his critique of the discourse of taste with clarity, conviction, and gusto.

Enslavement and Refinement as Figure and Fact

Grimod does not mention the issue of slavery even once in the more than one thousand pages that constitute the *Almanach*'s eight volumes. This fact is not unsurprising, given the political censorship to which the *Almanach* was subjected, as well as the fact that France had abolished the practice nearly a decade earlier—right around the time that James Hemings began his culinary apprenticeship in Paris.[35] But a fact that has proven more surprising, at least to some, was that Franklin similarly avoided addressing the issue of slavery head-on. While he occasionally opined on the negative impact of slavery in his writing, he took until three weeks before his death, in 1790, to adopt an explicitly antislavery stance.[36] Here, it is equally important to acknowledge Franklin himself enslaved several people over the course of his life and "never systematically divested of them" (Waldstreicher, "Benjamin Franklin," para. 8). He took two of these enslaved men, Peter and King, with him to London when he traveled there for the third time, in 1764, in order to serve as a representative of Pennsylvania before King George III.[37] And in the summer of 1773, as he was nearing the end of this particular stay, Franklin took time to visit Phillis Wheatley, "the black Poetess," as he described her in a letter to his nephew-in-law, and "offer'd her any Services I could do her" (*Papers*, 20:291).

There exists no additional information about the conversation that transpired, save for Franklin's mention, later in the letter, that Nathaniel Wheatley, Phillis Wheatley's enslaver, "was not pleased with the Visit" and that perhaps for that reason Franklin "heard nothing since of her." Wheatley, however, was sufficiently affected by the encounter that she planned to dedicate her second volume of poetry, unfortunately never published, to Franklin himself.[38] But this trace of a connection between Wheatley and Franklin has nevertheless continued to resonate for scholars, most notably Henry Louis Gates Jr., who included this account in the Jefferson Lecture he delivered to the National Endowment for the Humanities in 2002, in large part because it remains powerfully incomplete.[39] For Wheatley and Franklin held much in common: they were both separated

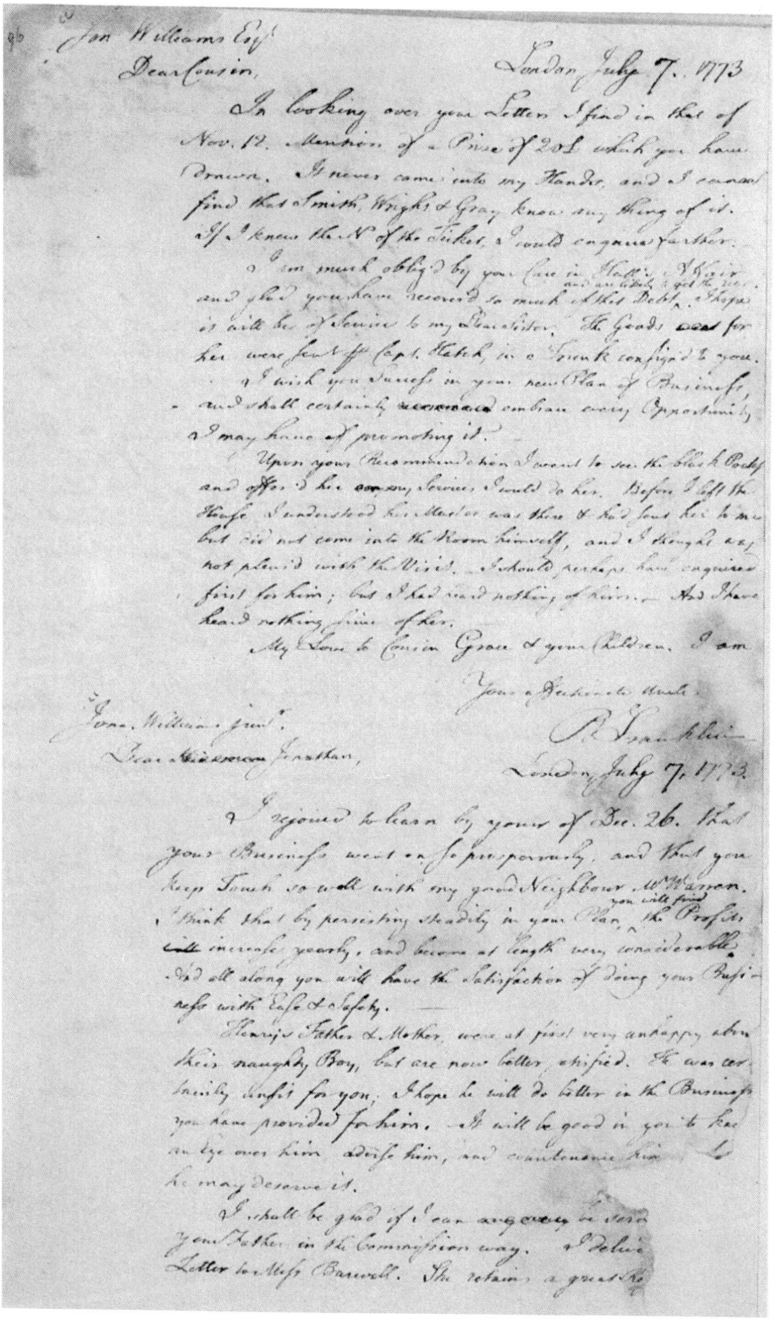

Figure 7. The letter at top, written from Benjamin Franklin to his nephew-in-law, Jonathan Williams Sr., on July 7, 1773, provides the only extant documentation of Franklin's meeting with Phillis Wheatley. Courtesy of the Library of Congress, Manuscript Division, Benjamin Franklin Papers.

from their parents at a young age; they were both primarily self-taught; and they both read prolifically, including key texts associated with the discourse of taste. Had Wheatley's enslaved status not precluded her from engaging with Franklin on an equal plane, this encounter in London would perhaps have been the first of many meetings of minds. But it was not, and for this reason, the silence that Franklin registers, and that he commits to the archive in his remark to his nephew that he had "heard nothing since," expands with significance. More specifically, it punctuates the moral and political limits of the tasteful subject, swayed as he was—as Franklin and Grimod both suggest—by the forces of appetite.

A simple comparison between Wheatley, an enslaved black woman, and Franklin, a free white man, attests to the basic truth of this claim.[40] But a reading of Wheatley that foregrounds her racialized subject position over her body of work is "too simple and ignores an obvious fact," as Tara Bynum asserts. "Eighteenth-century African-American authors rarely discuss what it means to be part of a cohesive racialized community," she writes, and Wheatley, in particular, "does not write about race as a collective and embodied experience" (para. 9). What Wheatley does write about, however, is aesthetic theory; more specifically, she writes about the embodied aspects of sensory experience that prompt her own imaginative pleasure as well as others' far less cerebral desires. Indeed, it is in her poetry that her strongest engagement with and critique of the discourse of taste resides.

Wheatley's engagement with contemporaneous aesthetic theory is illustrated most clearly in the poem "On Imagination," which was published in her *Poems on Various Subjects, Religious and Moral* (1773), the volume that her trip to London helped to secure. An extended apostrophe to the imagination, the poem begins with a direct address to its eponymous subject: "THY various works, imperial queen, we see, / How bright their forms! how deck'd with pomp by thee! / Thy wond'rous acts in beauteous order stand, / And all attest how potent is thine hand" (ll. 1–4). Here, Wheatley personifies the imagination as an "imperial queen," whom she credits as the source of a range of "wond'rous acts" of creation. In his reading of these lines, Edward Cahill emphasizes how Wheatley seems to figure several key concepts associated with eighteenth-century aesthetic theory: "The 'various' range of its 'works' and the brightness of their 'forms' describe the infinite diversity of sensible impressions and elaborate trains of association that await the perceiver. Likewise, the alignment of 'wond'rous acts' and 'beauteous order' suggests a reconciliation of the contending forces of sublimity and beauty, a world of antagonistic images and perceptions brought under despotic control by the imagination's queenly power" (58–59).

As Cahill also suggests, there is also a complex set of power dynamics embedded within the poem. At first, Wheatley appears to defer to the queen of the imagination. But in her demands, as voiced in the next quatrain, that the personified imagination "befriend" her own "attempts" at creative expression and further "triumph in my song," Wheatley asserts her own position of dominance over the imagination (ll. 6, 8). This dominance is additionally complicated by the third quatrain, which reads: "Now here, now there, the roving *Fancy* flies, / Till some lov'd object strikes her wand'ring eyes, / Whose silken fetters all the senses bind, / And soft captivity involves the mind" (ll. 9–12). Here, Wheatley's use of the term "fancy" serves as an assertion of her ability to engage in philosophical debate as well as imaginative creation. As explained by Joseph Addison in his essay "Pleasures of the Imagination," which was published in the *Spectator* in 1712 and was canonical even then, the term "fancy" is employed "promiscuously," carrying a broader and less formal range of connotations than the term "imagination" (qtd. in Gigante, *Great Age*, 79).[41] In her poem, Wheatley thus draws upon this connotation of promiscuity in order to underscore the far-ranging nature of the imagination's "roving" as well as its "wand'ring eyes."

In this philosophical context, Wheatley's subsequent evocation of the "silken fetters" of fancy, those that "all the senses bind," and of the "soft captivity" that "involves the mind" acquires an additional layer of meaning. Then, as now, one could not read these phrases without considering Wheatley's own "captivity." But Wheatley does not explicitly reference her own enslavement in this poem. Brad Pasanek suggests that she might have borrowed the phrase "silken fetters" from how Mark Akenside, the British poet and physician, "influentially" described "the pleasures of aesthetic reverie" in the 1774 edition of his two-book poem, *The Pleasures of Imagination* (131). (As the title suggests, Akenside's poem was directly inspired by Addison's essay.) In his analysis of these lines, Cahill focuses on a more direct allusion to Addison: his 1713 play, *Cato: A Tragedy*—"the most quoted Whig literary work in America at the time"—in which the phrase "soft captivity" first appears (59). By choosing to engage with common cultural reference points rather than invoke her own experience,

Wheatley additionally underscores her ability to participate in the "bracketing of selfhood demanded by republican virtue," Cahill asserts (60). With this claim, Cahill points to how Wheatley exhibits republican taste of the highest degree. She is able to set aside her own desire for physical freedom—the satisfaction of which, one might assume, would take precedence over all others—as she considers how she might satisfy the broader desire, on the part of the public, for further investigation into the workings of the imagination.

In this way, "On Imagination" points to how Wheatley seemingly seeks to contribute to the development of the discourse of taste rather than invite its undoing. And in this regard, she diverges from both Franklin and Grimod in meaningful ways. Consider how Franklin's intervention into the discourse of taste, if it could be described as such, centers on appetite and its role in destabilizing the rational order imposed by the sense of taste, even as he continues to uphold the cultivation of good taste as a goal. Grimod's intervention into that discourse also centers on appetite, but his goal is to elevate appetite from its base status such that the embodied aspects of pleasure remain. Wheatley's contribution, in contrast to both, seems in this case primarily constructive. If it performs a critique, it is through the figure of Wheatley herself as she models her ability to adhere to the highest standards of taste—and to participate in lofty philosophical conversations about same—with the subtext of her race, her gender, and her enslaved status deliberately, even tastefully, unnamed.

In point of fact, Wheatley does not employ the word "taste" in her work, choosing instead to focus on the related concepts of imagination and reason, as she does not only in "On Imagination" but in many of her other works. She was assuredly familiar with the discourse of taste, however, and not only from her engagement with Addison and perhaps Akenside, as described above. The first advertisement for the volume that would become *Poems on Various Subjects,* which appeared in the *Boston Censor* in 1772, and which, Julian Mason believes, Wheatley herself helped to craft, positioned her "Genius" as exceptional in view of her "uncultivated" African origins (*Wheatley,* 165).[42] This axis of cultivated genius against uncultivated barbarism (Wheatley is described in the advertisement as being until recently a "Barbarian") was another key concept in the discourse of taste. It underscores how issues of cultivation, and in particular, their racialized dimensions, were almost certainly never far from Wheatley's mind.

Wheatley engages with ideas about cultivation and race most directly in her famous (and infamous) poem "On Being Brought from Africa to America." Also included in *Poems on Various Subjects,* the poem consists in its entirety of four rhyming couplets, and centers on Wheatley's seemingly positive assessment the impact of her capture and conscripted transport to New England. Nevertheless, the poem also contains several more subtle critiques—of the perversions of Christianity, of racial prejudice, and of the slave trade, among others. In issuing these critiques, "On Being Brought" exemplifies what Rafia Zafar has described as the "veritable tightrope walk" that Wheatley was required to perform as an enslaved black woman offering an opinion at all (*Mask,* 25). Placed in the context of Wheatley's deep engagement with aesthetic theory, as well as of her awareness of the cultivated taste that defined the republican citizenship that she was denied, the poem acquires an additional critical valence that has not yet been fully explored; namely, how Wheatley asserts the ability of black people, considered as a group, to participate in the project of cultivating good taste.

The poem reads as follows:

'Twas mercy brought me from my *Pagan* land,
Taught my benighted soul to understand
That there's a God, that there's a *Saviour* too:
Once I redemption neither sought nor knew.
Some view our sable race with scornful eye,
"Their colour is a diabolic die."
Remember, *Christians, Negros,* black as *Cain,*
May be refin'd, and join th' angelic train.

It is in the final couplet, "Remember, *Christians, Negroes,* black as *Cain,* / May be refin'd, and join th' angelic train," that this assertion comes into focus (ll. 7–8). Indeed, these are the lines that are most often explicated—by Gates, Zafar, Vincent Carretta, and others—in the interest of illuminating the subversive elements of this ostensibly concessionist poem. By issuing her reprimand as one Christian to another, it is said, Wheatley mitigates the effect of a fundamentally radical act: an enslaved black woman admonishing her white reading audience for its racist beliefs. Wheatley's use of apposition introduces additional semantic instability, and potential subversion, in that she may also intend to imply that the (white) "*Christians*" are morally "black as *Cain*," and therefore in most need of refinement; this is an interpretation that is often put forth in the Wheatley scholarship.

But it is around the word "refin'd" itself that the significance of the poem for an argument about taste and its cultivation begins to coalesce. After all, the idea of refinement, and the term itself, was central to the discourse of taste at the time. Lord Shaftesbury, for example, describes how the "Justness of Thought and Style, Refinement in Manners, good Breeding, and Politeness of every kind, can come only from the Trial and Experience of what is best" (10). Later theorists, including many of the moral sense philosophers, would take up the term in more detail, although it is unknown as to whether Wheatley was familiar with their works.[43] Regardless, Wheatley's use of the term acquires additional significance for the discourse of taste when considering its resonance with several other words that she employs in the poem. In the third couplet, for example, Wheatley comments that "some view" the "colour" of her "sable race" as "a diabolical die" (ll. 5–6). Here, it has been suggested, her invocation of "a diabolical die" references the indigo dye that constituted one of the primary items trafficked through the slave trade. It further suggests that we might read her use of the word "refin'd" as an allusion to refined sugar, another principal commodity associated with the slave trade. Wheatley's couplet thus recalls Franklin's characterization of sugar as being "thoroughly dyed scarlet in grain," the language he employs when explaining his decision to abstain from eating sugar. More broadly, Timothy Morton has theorized this connection as the "'blood sugar' topos," a phrase he uses to describe the "powerful and ambiguous metaphor" widely pervasive in British Romantic texts "in which sugar stands for the blood of the slaves" (88). Here, Wheatley would seem to similarly implicate the institution of slavery, and in particular, those who sustain the slave trade through their emphatically unrefined taste for sugar, among other commercial goods.

But one additional word choice, also associated with the slave trade, complicates this satisfying reading. With the line "Remember, *Christians*, *Negros*, black as *Cain*," Wheatley may also be punning aurally on sugar cane.[44] In this interpretation, it is either white "*Christians*" or unconverted

"*Negroes*" or both who, prior to moral or religious conversation, exist in an unrefined state akin to "black" cane syrup. The complications introduced by this intimation are twofold, and split apart the double meaning that inheres in the sense of taste. At the level of gustatory taste, there is the implication (and, for most, the reality) that unrefined cane syrup does not taste as good as refined sugar. But at the level of aesthetic taste, or refinement, to express good taste would be to express a preference for refined sugar, and, implicitly, to retain a dependence on the slave trade that enables its production. Lending additional complexity to this interpretive valence, Wheatley does not figure a taste for refined sugar as the end product of the process of refinement. Rather, it is the people themselves who become refined into white sugar, all the more delicious to consume.[45]

Considered in this way, Wheatley levies a critique at the discourse of taste in ways that do not diverge from but rather sharpen and extend those of Franklin and Grimod. With Franklin's emphasis on unrestrained appetite, which he illustrates through his characterization of Keimer as a person who both eats pig and looks like one; and with Grimod's emphasis on gustatory pleasure, which he dramatizes at his funeral dinner with an actual pig seated at his table, or perhaps simply a decadent course of all pork, Wheatley's figuration of people as sugar becomes illuminated as the most striking instantiation of how the pleasure of appetite—even when cultivated, and perhaps *especially* when cultivated— can very quickly transform into cannibalistic desire. She issues no direct indictment of the sense of taste. By all accounts, she attempted to express her own cultivated taste to the highest degree. But the excess of meaning imparted by "On Being Brought" opens up the discourse of taste to additional questioning. This questioning would be further pursued in the decades to come, as discussed in chapters 3 and 4, as the hypocrisies brought about by the persistence of slavery continued to mount.

Eating Bodies and Bodies of Work

In spite of her publisher's claim that he sought to submit the "striking" contents of Wheatley's *Poems on Various Subjects* to the "unabashed candor of the impartial public," as he wrote in an advertisement that appeared in a London newspaper the day before the book's release, Wheatley was strongly encouraged by her benefactor, Selina Hastings, countess of Huntingdon, to include a portrait of herself as the frontispiece to the book. Robert Calef, who authored the letter that registers this request in the archive, wrote: "I do imagine it can be Easily done, and think would contribute greatly to the Sale of the Book" (qtd. in Carretta, 93).[46] Whether this was also the rationale underlying the countess's initial request remains unknown. But in the context of the various advertisements for the volume that emphasize Wheatley's race, coupled with the authenticating documents that precede her poems in the book, scholars have come to understand the inclusion of the portrait to be motivated by curiosity at best, and suspicion at worst. The irony of the racism that imposed this burden of proof is that the frontispiece—which depicts Wheatley at her writing table, her quill pen poised on the page—is now recognized as the first portrait in the history of the United States to depict a woman, of any race, in the act of writing.[47]

It is generally assumed that there exists no analogous portrait of Grimod, a further testament to the divergent social and cultural demands made on the two writers. But upon inspecting the frontispiece to the third volume of the *Almanach*, the one that depicts the Tasting Jury in session, a small detail suggests that this might not be the case. The detail involves the jury member who is depicted with his back toward the viewer, his face rendered only partially visible as he turns toward the jury's scribe. He is identified in the description of the frontispiece as the "Secretary of the Society" (qtd. in Gigante, *Gusto*, 284). Because we know Grimod to have appointed himself as the Tasting Jury's secretary for life, we can begin to wonder: Could this man be Grimod?

The detail that offers the most confirmation of this claim relates to one of the man's hands. It is accentuated by the lower half of the sleeve of the jacket that he wears, which is drawn in what seems to be deliberate shadow. (The half shadow cast over the rest of the engraving, which originates from the left of the frame, is less opaque than the dark etching employed to color the jacket sleeve.) The hand is drawn in this way, we might speculate, because it is a prosthesis. Perhaps the artist wishes us to know that it is Grimod's hand, and only Grimod's, that is responsible for translating the judgments of the Tasting Jury to the printed page. As pictured, the hand rests against the desk of the scribe, tracing the edge of the pages of notes. It serves as the link—visual, physical, and symbolic—between eating and the archive.

Much has been written on the symbolic valences of the prosthesis.[48] In keeping with this line of inquiry, it is tempting to interpret Grimod's

Figure 8. The frontispiece to Phillis Wheatley's Poems on Various Subjects, Religious and Moral (London, 1773), attributed to Scipio Moorhead, is believed to be the first portrait of an American woman of any race depicted in the act of writing. Courtesy of the Library of Congress, Rare Book and Special Collections Division.

prosthetic hands, as pictured in the frontispiece and as employed in his life, as an uncannily apt emblem of how Cary Wolfe understands the project of posthumanist critique of naming and explaining "the embodiment and the embeddedness of the human being in not just its biological but also its technological world, the prosthetic coevolution of the human animal with the technicity of tools and external archival mechanisms (such as language and culture)" (xv). In the image, we can clearly see how Grimod is presented as embodied and embedded in both biological and technical worlds, just as we can clearly see the "prosthetic coevolution" of the Tasting Jury and the "archival mechanisms" that record it. But against this strain of scholarship, as disability studies scholar Michael Davidson reminds us, "there are cases in which a prosthesis is *still* a prosthesis" (137). By this, Davidson suggests, and rightly so, that any analysis of a prosthesis should also entail attention to the lived experience of the person who employs it, as well as to the social, political, and technological conditions that determine its everyday use.

At Davidson's behest, we might return to what we know of how Grimod experienced his disability in his life, and how he employed that experience as the starting point for his critique of the dominant discourse of taste. His was one that sought to release the restrictions placed on sensory pleasure, over and above the restrictions placed on his participation in that discourse. Wheatley, similarly, did not address the question of her participation in that discourse directly. Rather, she took active steps to ensure that her ideas were heard. She sent copies of her poems to George Washington, who, in 1776, wrote to compliment her on her "elegant Lines" (qtd. in Carretta, 176). It is possible that even the king to whom she addressed "To the King's Most Excellent Majesty. 1768" was another of her readers.[49] Thomas Jefferson's dismissive opinion of her work, as documented in the *Notes on the State of Virginia* and as discussed in chapter 1, nevertheless confirms her role as an important interlocutor in that debate. But for Franklin, the limits of the discourse of taste remained, at most, an inconvenience. His status as a prototypal Enlightenment subject meant that he was rarely prompted to consider who else might have been excluded from consideration as a tasteful subject, or who might experience the most deleterious effects of those subjects' failures to regulate their own sense of taste. They remained errors of judgment that, like the "errata" of his life, could be corrected after the fact.

It seems fitting, then, that Franklin chose to figure his body as a book, in marked contrast to how Wheatley and Grimod, in different ways, could not avoid others choosing to interpret their bodies as such. In his famous fictitious epitaph, composed at the age of twenty-two—when he was not more than a year or two older than Wheatley was when she published *Poems on Various Subjects*—Franklin famously describes his own dead body "Like the Cover of an Old Book / Its Contents torn Out," buried in the ground as "Food for Worms" (*Papers*, 1:109). This collapse of the distinction between body and book has offered evidence to many scholars, including Michael Warner, of the "perfect reciprocity" that Franklin shared with the printed page (71). Not only in the pages that Franklin himself composed, but also in the archive that documents his life, there is ample evidence of his every inclination—a privilege not accorded to either Wheatley or Grimod.

But by centering the idea of eating in the archive we are prompted to consider what cannot ever be recorded: the embodied pleasures that Grimod sought to elevate to the status of taste, and the instinctual appetites that Franklin sought to acknowledge, if never fully address. That Franklin's body, in the end, becomes "Food for Worms" further underscores how even the textual record offers insufficient evidence of eating, as the record itself—the book of Franklin's body—is consumed. In this chapter, I have sought to demonstrate how the act of eating, and the "visceral" aspects of human experience, serve as a valuable point of entry into discussions of taste precisely because they resist being recorded in the archive—indeed resist being controlled in any way. For us as scholars in the present, tasked with identifying and unraveling the legacies of Enlightenment humanism in our own cultures, as for those who experienced the exclusions of that regime firsthand, the act of eating serves as an accessible and therefore powerful example of the flaws in that view. While none of the figures discussed in this chapter fully broke from the dominant discourse, their experiences of eating, and the pleasures that resulted, perform the important work of weakening the strictures of taste so that alternatives to that theory can emerge.

3

Satisfaction

Aesthetics, Speculation, and the Theory of Cookbooks

In the early 1850s, at the age of nineteen, Malinda Russell, a free black woman whose grandparents had been enslaved, set off from eastern Tennessee, where she was born and raised, to seek a new life in Liberia. Russell's decision to leave her home was by all accounts not undertaken lightly. In anticipation of her journey, she set aside substantial personal savings and obtained a certificate attesting to her character. The certificate, signed by several acquaintances—presumably white—attested to Russell's "fine disposition and business-doing habits" and affirmed her "moral deportment" before concluding: "We have little doubt, should she reach Liberia, in Africa, to which place she is now bound, that she will make a valuable citizen" (qtd. in Russell, 3). However, Russell never even reached the East Coast. In or around Lynchburg, Virginia, she was robbed by a member of her traveling party, which required that she find immediate employment. It was in Lynchburg, Russell would later explain, "where I commenced cooking" (3).

It was cooking that would secure Russell's livelihood, and eventually her historical legacy. Widowed after only four years of marriage and left the sole caretaker of a disabled son, Russell returned home to Tennessee, settling first in the foothills of the Great Smoky Mountains and then in more metropolitan Greenville, where she opened a well-regarded pastry shop.[1] Her recipes for "Puff Paste," "Butter Pastry," and various cakes and "jumbles" (cookies made with mace, clove, nutmeg, or "any spice you like") came to constitute the core of *A Domestic Cookbook: Containing a Careful Selection of Useful Receipts for the Kitchen,* which she self-published in 1866 (24). While there exist two earlier African American–authored kitchen manuals—Robert Roberts's *The House Servant's Directory* (1827) and Tunis Campbell's *Hotel Keepers, Head Waiters, and Housekeepers' Guide* (1848), both of which contain recipes alongside an abundance of other helpful information—Russell's *Domestic Cookbook* was the first to focus exclusively on cooking. As a result, it has earned recent distinction, and coverage in the *New York Times,* as the earliest African American–authored cookbook presently known.[2] That Russell was a woman is also significant, and points to how the cookbook, if not an exclusively female genre (although it would become increasingly so over the course of the nineteenth century), functions as a valuable record of the production of a range of alternatives to the dominant discourse of taste.[3]

Indeed, if the first chapter of this book sought to amplify the cultural contributions of figures such as James Hemings and Paul Jennings, those who, through their culinary repertoire, directly contributed to the development of a distinctly republican sense of taste, and the second chapter sought to expose the fissures in the theory of the sense of taste through the bodies and bodies of work of Benjamin Franklin, Alexandre Balthazar Grimod de la Reynière, and Phillis Wheatley, this chapter aims to document an alternative to that theory: what I describe as the *speculative aesthetics* of the early United States.[4] In doing so, I follow Fred Moten, Ivy Wilson, David Kazanjian, and others who, in drawing broadly from the concept of speculation, advocate for "reading apparently descriptive texts as theoretical texts that speculate upon their own conjectures" (Kazanjian, "Scenes of Speculation," 79).[5] In his analysis of the epistolary archive of colonial Liberia—not coincidentally, the site of Russell's intended (but never actualized) home—Kazanjian demonstrates how certain key words, such as "free," expand with theoretical significance when placed in the context of contemporaneous philosophical debates.[6] In doing so, such words can "sound a kind of interrogative backbeat to the descriptive discourse against which they are set and by which they are often engulfed," he explains ("Speculative Freedom," 871). This approach, when applied to the genre of the cookbook, which like the letter is a primarily descriptive form, rewards us with views that diverge from the dominant philosophical model of taste of the time.

By proposing a speculative approach to ideas about eating, my aim is twofold: first, following Kazanjian and others, I invite readers to consider how the genre of the cookbook might be more fully recognized for the philosophical work that it performs. To this end, Russell's *Domestic Cookbook* is particularly instructive, as it employs form as much as content in order to express its ideological agenda. But by positing *A Domestic Cookbook* as imbued with aesthetic significance in particular, my aim is also, importantly, to expand our vista of what aesthetic philosophy in the early United States[10] more fully entailed. For if it is true, as Edward Cahill and Edward Larkin have recently claimed, that in the early United States and in the decades before, the idea of the aesthetic was "defined not only by privilege but also by difference, not only by the status of the subject but also the nature of its experience," then it is incumbent upon us, as scholars of that era, to loosen the strictures of our own definition of what constituted aesthetic experience at that time, as well as of which subjects we tend to associate with its various forms (243). Doing so will enable us, in the present, to identify a wider range of aesthetic expression—indeed, of aesthetic philosophy—in the past.

I have previously discussed how the concept of aesthetic taste preceded the term "aesthetic" by many decades, and longer still if prehistories of taste are taken into account.[7] But another way to understand the delayed emergence of the term "aesthetic" is to posit the concept of aesthetic taste as inherently speculative; in other words, as a concept that is fully theorized and, as a reflection of that theory, necessarily imprecise. Consider that philosophers and cultural critics concerned themselves with the broad scope and range of significance of the idea of aesthetic taste from their very first explorations of the "mental sense" of beauty and its relationship to virtue.[8] In the early United States, as Cahill has documented, "ideas about pleasure, fancy, association, taste, genius, beauty, and sublimity permeated literary culture. Educated Americans read about, reflected upon, discussed and debated such ideas with remarkable frequency and intensity (2). And yet, a full century after the term "aesthetic" was introduced into English, those who sought to pin down its meaning—as did Elizabeth Palmer Peabody in her *Aesthetic Papers,* published in 1849, for example—continued to make recourse to "the real presence of an idea," which the "user" of the term still "cannot himself fully grasp or account for" (1).[9] Thus while most scholars of early American aesthetics, including Cahill, flag the term "aesthetic" as a "necessarily anachronistic" but nonetheless "useful placeholder" for a set of concepts that would later cohere, I propose that the idea of the aesthetic in that era should be understood as a coherent concept, one defined by its speculative core (3).[10] An understanding of aesthetic taste as inherently speculative serves to acknowledge any formulation of the concept as conjectural, and therefore as a precise encapsulation of the indeterminate space between sensory experience and acculturated response in which judgments of taste take place.

This chapter thus seeks to distill the speculative theories of aesthetics that were developed in parallel with, and often in direct opposition to, the dominant theory of republican taste. Here, I look to *A Domestic Cookbook* for evidence of how the preparation and presentation of food constitutes an additional form of aesthetic expression, one that contests the exclusionary nature of the tasteful subject more directly than the writing about eating discussed in chapter 2. Employing a speculative approach to Russell's text, I amplify the philosophical significance of her writing and, in particular, her emphasis on satisfaction, positing it as a provisional aesthetic theory that acknowledges the force of appetite as much as the influence of taste and that insists upon the equivalence of financial success and aesthetic pleasure. I show how Russell's philosophy of satisfaction challenges the nature of both subjective judgment and civic virtue, offering a means of expressing national belonging that depends upon economic rather than political agency. Tracing the intertwined taste traditions that Russell documents in her volume, I connect her oppositional aesthetics to three key culinary antecedents: Amelia Simmons's *American Cookery* (1796), the text often described as the first American cookbook; Mary Randolph's *The Virginia House-Wife* (1824), the text often considered the first southern cookbook, and which Russell cites as the "plan" for her text; and the lived experience of Fannie Steward, the "colored cook, of Virginia" whom Russell credits with her culinary training and about whom little else is known (5).[11] Placed among these antecedents, the aesthetic work of *A Domestic Cookbook* emerges as an extension of, and a challenge to, the dominant philosophical model of taste at the time. Replacing the cultivation of civic virtue with the satisfaction of financial need, Russell's cookbook presents a method of expressing personal agency, and therefore national belonging, that does not depend on formal mechanisms of political expression. Her suggestions about how a person might value herself, independent of legal definitions of citizenship, illustrate how acts of cooking and eating—in both their material and aesthetic manifestations—open up new political and philosophical as well as culinary terrain.

The Philosophy of Satisfaction

By her own account, Malinda Russell possessed a culinary acumen of the highest degree. On the title page of *A Domestic Cookbook,* her byline reads "Mrs. Malinda Russell, an Experienced Cook," and the evidence that she offers in the introduction underscores the depth of her experience and skill: "I have made cooking my employment for the last twenty years, in the first families of Tennessee, (my native place,) Virginia, North Carolina, and Kentucky. I know my Receipts to be good, as they have always given satisfaction" (5). As indicated by this statement, cooking consistently enabled Russell to find employment, even as she was required to reestablish herself in new locales; and cooking consistently accorded her with a sense of self-worth, even as she encountered significant adversity—physical and psychological as much as financial. For the robbery that Russell experienced en route to Liberia was, unfortunately, only the first in a series of hardships she would encounter over the course of her adult life. After securing a degree of financial stability, not to mention professional fulfillment, as proprietor of her own pastry shop, Russell was robbed again. In the "Short History of the Author" that begins her cookbook, she explains: "I kept a pastry shop for about six years, and, by hard labor and economy, saved a considerable sum of money for the support of myself and my son, which was taken from me on the 16th of January, 1864, by a guerilla party, who threatened my life if I revealed who they were" (4). To avoid future harm, Russell "follow[ed] a flag of truce" out of the South, eventually making her way to the town of Paw Paw, Michigan (4). While she remained steadfast in her desire to return to Greenville to "recover [her] property," she "resolved to make" Paw Paw her temporary "home" (4). There, in what she called "the Garden of the West," her spirit of determination and her capacity for resilience—and, most explicitly, her sense of the "satisfaction" elicited by her food—enabled her to remake her life once again.

Whether or not Russell ever recovered her pastry shop remains unknown; the town of Paw Paw burned to the ground several months after the publication of *A Domestic Cookbook,* eliminating the possibility of tracing Russell through any local records there, as Jan Longone, the curator responsible for acquiring Russell's cookbook for the University of Michigan Libraries, unfortunately discovered.[12] But the strength of Russell's

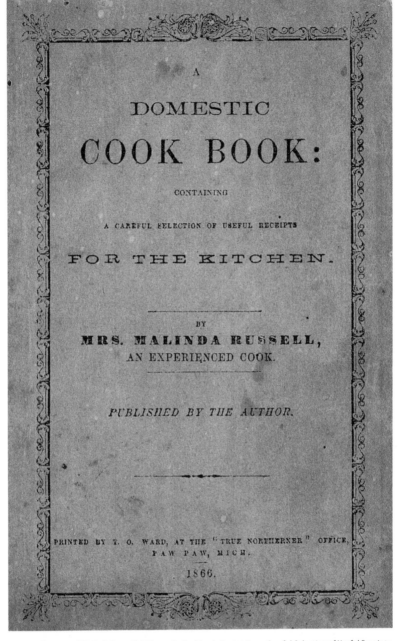

A

DOMESTIC
COOK BOOK:

CONTAINING

A CAREFUL SELECTION OF USEFUL RECEIPTS

FOR THE KITCHEN.

BY

MRS. MALINDA RUSSELL,

AN EXPERIENCED COOK.

PUBLISHED BY THE AUTHOR.

PRINTED BY T. O. WARD, AT THE "TRUE NORTHERNER" OFFICE, PAW PAW, MICH.

1866.

Figure 9. The cover of Malinda Russell's A Domestic Cookbook: Containing a Careful Selection of Useful Receipts for the Kitchen *(1866). Russell's cookbook is the first African American–authored cookbook presently known. Courtesy of HathiTrust/University of Michigan Library (Special Collections Research Center, Janice Bluestein Longone Culinary Archive).*

desire to return to Greenville—and of her conviction that cooking would provide her with the means to do so—is clearly documented in the lines that close the "Short History": "This is one reason why I publish my Cook Book, hoping to receive enough from the sale of it to enable me to return home. I know my book will sell well where I have cooked, and am sure those using my receipts will be well satisfied" (4).

The phrase Russell employs as the marker of her recipes' quality and worth, "well satisfied," echoes her previous account of the "satisfaction" exhibited by the families who experienced her capable cookery. The term is never used again in the cookbook, as the recipes that follow contain only short descriptions of how to prepare each dish, as was typical for the genre at the time. But I believe its meaning lingers. Of a sort with the philosophically charged terms that Kazanjian points to as evidence of speculative theory—those that we can set apart from the descriptive discourse that surrounds them in order to draw deeper significance from the text as a whole—"satisfaction" here signals the multiple lenses, philosophical as much as culinary or autobiographical, through which Russell's cookbook can be read.

In this way, Russell's theory of satisfaction offers a counterpoint to the discourse of taste that has been the focus of the preceding chapters, as it was for the dominant culture of the time. "All of the major Enlightenment philosophers of taste," as Denise Gigante explains, referring to the Scottish moral sense philosophers such as Hutcheson and Hume, were concerned with "sublimating the tasteful essence of selfhood from its own matters and motions, appetites and aversions, passions and physical sensibilities" (*Taste*, 3). That concern carried over the Atlantic into the thoughts, if rarely the actions, of figures such as Washington, Jefferson, Madison, and Franklin, as I have argued thus far. Russell, by contrast, as a professional cook, was required to enlist her culinary acumen in the service of the senses directly. Employed as a cook for the "first families" of several southern states—families much like, if not directly related to, the Washingtons, Jeffersons, and Madisons—Russell concerned herself with deposing her own good taste back into others' gustatory pleasure (5). Indeed, Russell was required to speculate herself about the "matters and motions, appetites and aversions, passions and physical sensibilities" of the families for whom she cooked, as her ability to satisfy those desires, as much as her ability to satisfy their senses of taste, would determine whether they would be pleased with her food and therefore retain her services. Russell's emphasis on satisfaction thus reflects a necessary embrace of the physical gratification that results from eating, placing the pleasures of appetite and taste on an equal plane. Furthermore, Russell, like all those whose livelihoods were dependent upon the tastes of others, was required to sublimate her own desires in order to satisfy those she served. Another version of the "bracketing of republican selfhood" that Cahill describes with respect to Phillis Wheatley, as discussed in chapter 2, the satisfaction that Russell successfully elicits in others reflects the high degree of her own tasteful restraint, as much as it does her ability to produce pleasure in the palates and the minds of others.

Russell's emphasis on the consistently pleasurable effects of her cooking helps to further announce the significance of satisfaction as an alternative to the philosophical concept of taste. Taste remains rooted in the individual, cultivated from within, even as it is eventually expressed to a like-minded public.[13] Put another way: taste retains its internal locus even as the influences that shape its cultivation derive from broader cultural influences and find expression in larger social groups.[14] Satisfaction, by contrast, does not need to originate in the individual; it can be elicited in others, as the example of Russell's cooking makes clear. This externalizable, transmissible quality of satisfaction made it indispensable to professional cooks such as Russell, who were required to enlist their personal taste in the interests of those they served. Russell's assertion that her recipes "have always *given* satisfaction" (emphasis added) additionally underscores the transmissible quality.

Teresa Brennan has theorized the transmission of affect as "a process that is social in origin but biological and physical in effect" (3). This process, originating in the social but experienced by and within the body, can also describe the transmission of taste. Also like the transmission of affect, the transmission of taste is sometimes bidirectional. In other words, the effects of satisfaction at times reflect back upon the original source. Robert Roberts surmises as much in his *House Servant's Directory* (1827). Written with professional household workers in mind, Roberts's text is explicit about its intention to "lay before the public those general rules and directions for servants to go by as shall give satisfaction to their employers, and gain a good reputation for themselves" (x). More clearly than Russell, Roberts explains how the ability to "give satisfaction" can result in personal "gain." In this way, Roberts contests the dominant model of the sense of taste, as explored in previous chapters, in which "good reputation" extends from shared participation in (and shared judgments about) experiences of eating, among other aestheticized acts. For domestic workers such as Roberts and cooks such as Russell, however, good reputation is established indirectly, a result of the degree of satisfaction that they are able to transmit to those who consume their tasteful food. This good reputation holds even as they cannot share it directly while seated around a common table.[15]

This indirect relation between the preparation of tasteful food and the experience of others' satisfaction is, ultimately, what enables the oppositional qualities of Russell's aesthetic theory to begin to cohere. We have previously seen how, in the early United States, the cultivation of personal taste was widely understood as corresponding to the cultivation of civic virtue, a quality that in turn prepared citizens to participate appropriately in their new democracy. By contrast, the experience of satisfaction carries no such assumption of political agency.[16] For Russell in particular, this dissociation from formal mechanisms of enfranchisement is important. With the Fourteenth Amendment still two years from passage at the time that she authored her cookbook, Russell harbored no illusions about the partial nature of her rights as a citizen. The story of the loss of her pastry shop bears this out. Her primary reason for being "compelled" to abandon her shop is her decision to express her "Union principles" (5). In other words, rather than empower her or align with a larger coalition, her exercising one of the foundational rights of the republic—the right to political speech—results in the forced separation from her job and her community. Her rejection of the promise of republican taste in favor of a homegrown philosophy of satisfaction thus reflects an acute awareness of the legal limits placed on her political subjectivity, and the beginnings of an attempt to achieve agency, both personal and political, through other means.

Like many other black Americans denied basic legal rights, Russell identifies economic success as a more reliable method of asserting both her politics and her taste. This view is suggested in the vision of Russell becoming a "valuable citizen" of Liberia, as documented in one of the letters she quotes at the beginning of her cookbook; and it is confirmed throughout the volume's prefatory pages, in which Russell makes clear how she pursues the satisfaction of her own financial needs in equal measure to the satisfaction of others' pleasures and tastes. In her account of her departure from her pastry shop, for example, she emphasizes the "considerable sum of money" that it enables her to earn, which in turn allows her to "support myself and son." The pain that she experiences as a result of being forced to abandon her shop is thus financial as much as physical. For if Russell's life was defined by its culinary achievements, it was also defined by her financial distress. At every juncture—from the robbery en route to Liberia that set her culinary career in motion to the economic burden of supporting herself and her son that led her to open her pastry shop to the loss of wages (a result of her "advanced" age) that prompted the publication of her cookbook—Russell's culinary aspirations were consistently accompanied by (if not directly motivated by) instances of intense financial need. Taking these economic obligations into account, Russell's emphasis on satisfaction acquires an additional conceptual valence, one that derives from the word's frequent usage in the context of satisfying debts.

As a helpful point of contrast, one might consider the "little satisfaction" exhibited by the character of Hepzibah Pyncheon in Nathaniel Hawthorne's *The House of the Seven Gables* upon the opening of her own little shop (52). Published in 1851, right around the time that Russell opened her pastry shop, Hawthorne's novel documents the financial and political decline of one of the "first families" of New England, the northern equivalent of those for whom Russell cooked. In fact, Hawthorne invokes the "ghosts of departed cook-maids" when attempting to convey the extent of the Pyncheon family's fall from power (99). Unlike Russell, however, Hepzibah exhibits little business acumen; she gives her first customer his purchase—significantly, a cookie shaped like Jim Crow—away for free.[17] Even when her young cousin, Phoebe, joins her in the shop and enables it to achieve a modicum of success, Hepzibah takes little pleasure in her renewed ability to pay her family's debts. By comparison, Russell's embrace of a philosophy of satisfaction enables her to take pleasure in the act of satisfying her personal financial obligations as much as satisfying of others' tastes.

At the same time, Russell understands her pursuit of her own financial satisfaction as an undertaking that, like the cultivation of personal taste, impacts a community beyond herself. Immediately following her pronouncement about her satisfying cookery, she takes another step to acknowledge the extended benefits of her decision to capitalize on her culinary expertise. She explains: "I have been advised to have my Receipts published, as they are valuable, and every family has use for them" (5). Positioned as the central clause in the sentence, the "value" of her recipes functions as a conceptual as well as semantic hinge; it indicates the recipes' economic utility for herself and their culinary utility for others. When she adds, in the final line of the same paragraph, "I have put out this book with the intention of benefiting the public as well as myself," she clarifies her belief in how personal profit and public "benefit" can coincide (5). As an alternative to the republican model in which the cultivation of personal taste leads to the cultivation of civic virtue, Russell proposes a paradigm in which her own economic satisfaction contributes to the culinary satisfaction of others, which in turn contributes to the public good.

With this connection between personal satisfaction and the public good well established, Russell's sense of satisfaction begins to resonate with the theories of liberal capitalism that were then beginning to find expression in national policy.[18] Not only in the "hard labor and economy" that she exhibits in her pastry shop, but also in the letters she quotes early in the cookbook, which affirm her "fine disposition and business-doing habits," as well as in the advertisement for her washhouse that she also cites, which touts her "proficiency in her business," Russell takes pains to not only demonstrate but also document her entrepreneurial expertise. Consistent with the entrepreneurial ethos established by Franklin in his *Autobiography,* and taken up in many of the slave narratives that, as Rafia Zafar has demonstrated, would have been well-known reference points for nineteenth-century readers of *A Domestic Cookbook,* Russell positions her entrepreneurialism as evidence of her place in the nation.[19] By replacing political with economic agency, Russell seems to offer a corrective to the concept of republican taste, which does not account for how nonvoting subjects can contribute to the public good. In a speculative reading, then, Russell's oppositional aesthetics emerge through her insistence that her expressions of economic agency are equivalent to others' expressions of personal taste. Her life philosophy is revealed as one that admits the role of pleasure as a productive contribution to both personal profit and public good. It expands the definition of civic virtue to include the pursuit of financial gain, and insists that economic agency as much as political agency impacts the good of the nation.[20]

Orphaned Subjects and Scriptive Texts

Seventy years before Malinda Russell entered the office of the *True Northerner* newspaper, in Paw Paw, in order to inquire about the possibility of printing *A Domestic Cookbook,* another aspiring cookbook author, a white woman by the name of Amelia Simmons, approached the offices of Hudson & Goodwin, in Hartford, Connecticut, with her own proposition: there had yet to be a cookbook that was "adapted to this country, and to all grades of life" (1).[21] Orphaned at a young age, and having been "reduced to the necessity" of finding employment as a cook, Simmons had amassed the requisite amount of culinary knowledge and life experience to be able to author such a book (3). Was it not true that the "rising generation of *Females* in America" were owed a culinary education as much as each "Lady of fashion and fortune"? (3). And should that education not include recipes that made use of "every article brought into market" (6)? None of the British texts that were then in circulation, such as Eliza Smith's *Compleat Houswife* (1727), Hannah Glasse's *Art of Cookery Made Plain and Easy* (1747), and Susannah Carter's *Frugal Housewife; Or, Complete Woman Cook* (1772), included recipes for "Tasty Indian Pudding," "Pompkin" pie, or turkey with "cramberry-sauce [sic]," for example (31, 34, 13). By bringing together indigenous American ingredients with British cooking techniques, Simmons authored what culinary historian Mark McWilliams would later describe, in his book on the subject, as a "culinary declaration of independence" for the United States (308).[22]

As hyperbolic as it may seem, McWilliams's assertion is not far from the truth. Simmons's cookbook was as important for American culinary history as its title is long to behold: *American Cookery, or the Art of Dressing Viands, Fish, Poultry, and Vegetables, and the Best Modes of Making Pastes, Puffs, Pies, Tarts, Puddings, Custards, and Preserves, and All Kinds of Cakes, from the Imperial Plum to Plain Cake: Adapted to This Country, and All Grades of Life.* Published in 1796, *American Cookery,* as it is known, was met with a "call . . . so great, and [a] sale so rapid" that the author found herself "not only encouraged, but under a necessity of publishing a second edition" (5). That edition, published later that year in Albany, New York, was followed by a third, in 1804, and many more through the first decades of the nineteenth century.[23] With this strong response, Simmons almost certainly secured her own status as a member of the "rising generation" of women to whom she addressed her own valuable recipes. But as the contrast to Russell makes clear, Simmons's success, both social and financial, owes as much to her whiteness as it does to her culinary expertise. Unlike Russell, herself an orphan whose status as a black woman amplified her experience of social and economic precarity, Simmons experienced her orphanhood as aligning her more closely with, not distancing her more fully from, the project of cultivating republican taste.

On the title page of her cookbook, Simmons describes herself as an "American orphan," in what is at once a (presumed) reflection of her actual circumstances and a deliberate deployment of the trope, common at the time, to describe the severed relation between colony and king (2).[24] In her analysis of the cookbook, Glynis Ridley reads this self-bestowed epithet as evidence of Simmons's belief in the view, pervasive at the time, of a distinctly American capacity for "social mobility and [an] inclusiveness that sees all treated equally" (116). Simmons underscores her own adherence to an ideology of self-improvement with the clarity of her stated desire to help others who "by the loss of their parents, or other unfortunate circumstances, are reduced to the necessity of going into families in the line of domestics, or taking refuge with their friends or relations, and doing those things which are really essential to the perfecting them as good wives, and useful members of society" (3). Unsurprisingly for the late eighteenth century, Simmons does not acknowledge how black women such as Russell, whose own "unfortunate circumstances" would otherwise seem to place her among Simmons's intended readers, faced many more obstacles to becoming "good wives, and useful members of society" than simply the lack of practical knowledge about how to cook. Another kind of "American orphan," Russell's diminished sense of national belonging was owed to the racism and sexism that denied her full participation in the U.S. government, and the resultant social and economic circumstances that required her to move away from her family, along with the death of her mother "when [she] was quite young" (3). Russell's rejection of the fantasy of direct political agency becomes, from this vantage point, an equal-but-opposite response to the same national culture (and commensurate legal policy) that embraced Simmons as an emblem of the newly independent state.

Russell's aesthetic philosophy thus emerges not only from within her text, but also in response to texts such as Simmons's that, like the ideas expressed by Jefferson and Madison (and Washington to some degree), unreflectively bind the cultivation of taste to the cultivation of virtuous citizenship. For Simmons, as for the founders, the connection between good taste and good citizenship is simply assumed; it does not include a consideration of the human costs of producing good taste, nor of who is

AMERICAN COOKE

OR THE ART OF DRESSING

VIANDS, FISH, POULTRY and VEGETABLES,

AND THE BEST MODES OF MAKING

PASTES, PUFFS, PIES, TARTS, PUDDINGS, CUSTARDS AND PRESERVES,

AND ALL KINDS OF

CAKES,

FROM THE IMPERIAL PLUMB TO PLAIN CAKE.

ADAPTED TO THIS COUNTRY,

AND ALL GRADES OF LIFE.

By Amelia Simmons,

AN AMERICAN ORPHAN.

PUBLISHED ACCORDING TO ACT OF CONGRESS.

HARTFORD:

PRINTED BY HUDSON & GOODWIN,

FOR THE AUTHOR.

1796.

Figure 10. The title page of Amelia Simmons's American Cookery (1796). Simmons's cookbook is commonly credited as the first "American" cookbook. Courtesy of the Library of Congress, Rare Book and Special Collections Division.

prevented from exhibiting either good taste or good citizenship. Along these lines, it is significant that Simmons follows her advice to her orphan readers about how to become "useful members of society" with a statement about the crucial need to cultivate a strong sense of personal taste: "The orphan, tho' left to the care of virtuous guardians, will find it essentially necessary to have an opinion and determination of her own," she intones (3). Here, Simmons sounds the refrain of the discourse of taste, underscoring the positive impact of exercising good taste—an "opinion and determination of [one's] own"—on both family and nation. In this context, the orphan becomes a symbol of the independence of thought required to sustain the nation's growth. She assumes that her orphan readers each possess an equal ability to participate in U.S. democracy, one that, as Erica Armstrong Dunbar has explained, did not accurately account for the "class barriers" that prevented "most women, black or white," from participating in it (24). And Simmons certainly does not account for figures such as Russell, whose ability to express her personal taste was severely curtailed by her social standing, legal status, and financial needs. "The domestic sphere was simply different for black women," Dunbar further explains: "free African American women found their status as free people challenged every day as millions of black men and women remained enslaved" (24–25).

In spite of her lack of acknowledgment of issues of race or of slavery, Simmons's insistence on the importance of taste nevertheless helps to illuminate how her text, and Russell's, both perform aesthetic work.[25] Culinary scholars often observe how the cookbook is set apart from other literary genres by the fact that recipes it contains are intended not only to be read but also enacted. A cookbook's recipes "demand a certain set of actions, performed in a certain sequence, to produce a certain product," points out culinary historian Jessamyn Neuhaus (95). As any cook well knows, however, recipes also involve a degree of improvisation. This fact is also often noted by culinary scholars, but it is most helpfully theorized by cultural historian Robin Bernstein. She looks to domestic artifacts such as dolls, handkerchiefs, and pincushions in order to develop a notion of what she calls the "scriptive thing" (12).[26] Such artifacts, Bernstein explains, function "like playscripts, broadly structuring a performance while allowing for agency and unleashing original, live variations that may not be individually predictable" (12). The recipe is not a physical object like those Bernstein treats. However, we might similarly consider how the recipe "scripts" the behavior of its reader-turned-cook, establishing a broad framework within which the reader can improvise her own "variation," or otherwise assert her own culinary expertise. Like the playscript Bernstein uses as her model, the recipe facilitates the "agency" of its reader/cook within any number of larger constraints, social and political as much as formal. The result has additional implications in terms of both taste and significance that, to borrow another phrase from Bernstein, both "include and exceed" the original dish (12).

As an example of how the recipe functions as a "scriptive" text, consider a typical recipe from *American Cookery,* such as "To make the best Bacon," the first to appear in the book: "To each ham put one ounce of saltpeter, one pint bay salt, one pint molasses, shake together 6 or 8 weeks, or when a large quantity is together, bast [*sic*] them with the liquor every day; when taken out to dry, smoke three weeks with cobs or malt fumes. To every ham may be added a cheek, if you stow away a barrel and not alter the composition, some add a shoulder. For transportation or exportation, double the period of smoking [*sic*]" (5–6). This recipe, like so many others, is simultaneously evocative and nondescript. It conjures a strong enough sense of the completed dish such that the reader/cook will be compelled to follow it, and yet its plain instructions reflect the requirement that the reader/cook will be able to follow them with ease. With regard to the latter, "To make the best Bacon" exemplifies the demands on the reader/cook that characterize the recipe as a genre. But its details are also worthy of note. Here, the instructions to first cure the meat, then dry and smoke it include the additional space for improvisation that the notion of the "scriptive thing" helps to unfold—here, the choice of smoking with either "cobs or malt fumes" and the option of adding an additional pork cheek or shoulder to increase the yield, as well as the indication that the bacon may (or may not) be intended for travel or export. Suggesting multiple outcomes while not requiring any particular one, the recipe facilitates a form of culinary agency that is fundamentally bounded, yet remains open to individual acts of interpretation and expression.

Considered in the context of aesthetic theory, these dual notions of agency—the one constrained by the author, intended to be followed with precision and care, and the other improvisatory, open to individual interpretation and expression—can be understood as corresponding to the contrasting forces that make judgments of taste so complex. Indeed, the central philosophical "problem" of taste, as Carolyn Korsmeyer describes it, resides in the necessary reconciliation of certain universal standards with a person's internal sensory response (46). While it is impossible to know with any certainty whether, or to what degree, Simmons was aware of any of the more formal articulations of this problem in circulation at the time, her cookbook is at least engaged with one version of the issue. As she advocates for each of her orphan readers to cultivate "an opinion and determination of her own," she makes sure to clarify that the reader must still adhere to certain standards: "By having an opinion and determination," Simmons explains, "I would not be understood to mean an obstinate perseverance in trifles, which borders on obstinacy—by no means, but only an adherence to those rules and maxims which have stood the test of ages" (4). The recipes that follow, then, reinforce this model of exercising individual "opinion and determination," but only within social and cultural constraints.

This model, of cultivating personal taste within predetermined social standards, is one that Russell also acknowledges, and then reconfigures through her writing. After all, her cookbook begins not with a treatise on taste, but with a detailed account of her own life story. Her recipes, similarly, are framed so as to foreground her own unique contributions to others' tables. As a primary example of how she foregrounds her unique expertise, consider "To Make Lard Pastry," the recipe that describes how to make the pastry dough for which she was renowned: "Two quarts flour, one and a half lb lard; divide the lard into four parts; rub one part into the flour with a knife, mix with cold water to a consistent dough, roll the dough into sheets, spreading the remainder of the lard over them, folding the sheets and rolling again; salt-spoon of salt. Nice and flaky" (22). In terms of style, "To Make Lard Pastry" retains the sparseness that characterizes the recipe as a genre in the nineteenth century. Russell relates the necessary ingredients with minimal elaboration, a reflection most likely of their familiarity to both herself and her readers. But in her account of how to assemble the dough, she provides a notable amount of detail. Russell relates no fewer than seven steps required to achieve her "nice and flaky" pastry. (Simmons, by contrast, includes only four steps in the recipe for lard pastry that she includes in her book.)[27] By following these instructions with a qualitative assessment—unusual both for *A Domestic Cookbook* and for the genre as a whole—Russell conveys her belief that readers who successfully adhere to her instructions will be well satisfied by the result.

At the same time, the closing phrase reinforces Russell's own experience and skill. After all, the pastry will only be "nice and flaky" if the reader follows the recipe correctly—a daunting task that, as David S. Shields observes in his study of late eighteenth- and early nineteenth-century pastry cooks, requires nothing short of "mastery" (*Provisions*, 112).[28] "To Make Lard Pastry" thus mirrors the more explicit assertions of expertise that Russell includes in her introduction, affirming the uniquely satisfying qualities of Russell's own cooking. In contrast to Simmons, who frames her cookbook as an exercise in cultivating taste, Russell understands that her place in the nation is bound to the pleasure that she herself can produce in those who consume her food. Her status as a black woman, even two generations removed from the nation's original sin, carries none of the benefits of citizenship automatically accorded to Simmons or to her white orphan readers. Russell's orphanhood, instead, informs a philosophy in which the satisfaction of the nation is only possible by satisfying each and every one of its citizens, each and every time that Russell offers up a dish.

Recipes, Regulation, and Resistance

Despite the historical trajectory that links Amelia Simmons, the self-appointed "American orphan," with Malinda Russell, the orphan that America made, Russell does not acknowledge Simmons's influence, at least not explicitly. In *A Domestic Cookbook*, Russell cites two other sources for her culinary expertise. As she writes: "I learned my trade of FANNY STEWARD, a colored cook, of Virginia, and have since learned many new things in the art of Cooking. I cook after the plan of the 'VIRGINIA HOUSEWIFE'" (n.p.). While presented as statements of fact, the coupling of these particular references—to Steward, the "colored cook, of Virginia" about whom little else is known, and to *The Virginia House-Wife; or, Methodical Cook* (1824) by Mary Randolph, a member of one of the "first families of Virginia" to which Russell traces her lineage—reflects an awareness, on the part of Russell, of the multiple sources that contribute to culinary knowledge (Russell, 3).[29] It also reinforces her seeming attempt, throughout *A Domestic Cookbook*, to reconfigure the relation between personal taste and civic virtue. For if her acknowledgment of Steward as the source of her culinary knowledge affirms the primary role of experiential knowledge in the production of gustatory pleasure, her reference to the "plan" of the *Virginia House-Wife* points to a related understanding of how cookbooks structure that knowledge in order to produce particular political subjects as well as educated cooks.

Randolph's cookbook is notable for how it records her own attempt to employ techniques of regulation and management in order to distill the tasteful aspects of cooking from the labor and knowledge required to produce it. In the introduction she declares, "The prosperity and happiness of a family depend greatly on the order and regularity established in it," and in the recipes that follow she indicates the processes by which this "order and regularity" can be achieved: a high degree of precision with respect to what and how much of each ingredient to include, an equally high degree of detail about the process by which to prepare the dish, and a heightened attention to strategies for saving both money and time (xii). Like the recipes of both Simmons and Russell, Randolph's read not only as instructions for implementing a particular set of dishes, but also for implementing a particular political subjectivity: one with implications for the individuals whom Randolph herself employed in her kitchen, and for the women readers who would, following Randolph, become arbiters of national taste.

Randolph characterizes her system in terms of what she calls "method" (ix). In the opening lines of the preface, she explains how she developed this approach in response to her own lack of experience in the kitchen. Characterizing herself as a "Tyro" (from the Latin *tiro*, meaning "young soldier" or "new recruit"), she recalls: "The difficulties I encountered when I first entered on the duties of a House-keeping life, from the want of books sufficiently clear and concise to impart knowledge to a Tyro, compelled me to study the subject, and by actual experiment to reduce every thing in the culinary line, to proper weights and measures" (ix). Randolph contrasts her cookbook with the texts that she herself encountered as a young housewife, almost certainly including Simmons's, which lacked "sufficiently clear and concise" instructions for novice cooks such as herself. She emphasizes the "proper weights and measures" that characterize her recipes—the result, she claims, of "actual experiment"—as the feature that most distinguishes her cookbook from others. The food that results is both "economical" and delicious for "when the ingredients employed were given in just proportions, the article made was always equally good" (ix).

Randolph views her "methodical" approach to cooking as one that can be easily adapted to apply to housekeeping in general. The title page of *The Virginia House-Wife* features the motto "Method is the soul of management," and in the preface Randolph makes clear that her approach extends from the management of the cooking process to the management of the entire home. She counsels that "a regular system must be introduced into each department [of the house], which may be modified until matured, and should then pass into an inviolable law" (ix). More explicitly than either Simmons or Russell, Randolph employs the language of governance—here, the mention of "inviolable law"—in order to advocate for the political impact of her methodical cookery. She asserts that the "government of the family bears a Lilliputian relation to the government of a nation," in a line that indicates the depth of her political as well as literary engagement (ix). The daughter of a participant in the Virginia Convention of 1776, and a relation by marriage to Thomas Jefferson, who complimented her "valuable little volume" upon its publication, Randolph was intimately familiar with what the government of both family and nation entailed (Jefferson, "Letter"). Amplifying the language of regulation with references to the actual legislative process, Randolph's cookbook advances a vision of household management that connects it to national politics in terms of both process and effect.

Of course, personal as well as national politics were already abundant in Randolph's kitchen, long before she began writing her cookbook. First as the mistress of Presqu'ile Plantation, where she resided during the first years of her married life between 1780 and 1798, and then as the owner of a well-regarded boardinghouse, which she opened upon her return to the city of Richmond in 1798, Randolph relied upon an enslaved staff of at least nine persons in order to prepare the "fine food" for which she was known (qtd. in Kierner, 210).[30] The presence of these individuals—formally documented in the 1810 census but qualitatively registered in every meal that Randolph served—suggests that, even as she promoted her "actual" kitchen experience, Randolph herself likely never prepared the recipes printed in her book. Culinary historians have long noted this fact, if obliquely. Karen Hess, for one, acknowledges that Randolph "was a fine practitioner who knew her way about the kitchen but the actual cooking and toil fell to black women" (The Virginia House-Wife, xl). Marcie Cohen Ferris states the case more strongly: "Slavery built the table of Mary Randolph" (88). The scriptive power of Randolph's recipes, then, is revealed for how it shifts the source of good taste from the process of cooking to the regulation thereof.[31] Not dissimilar from the attempt by James Madison (who when presented with a copy of The Virginia House-Wife tellingly professed to be unable to "decide on [its] merit" on account of his own lack of "practice on the table")

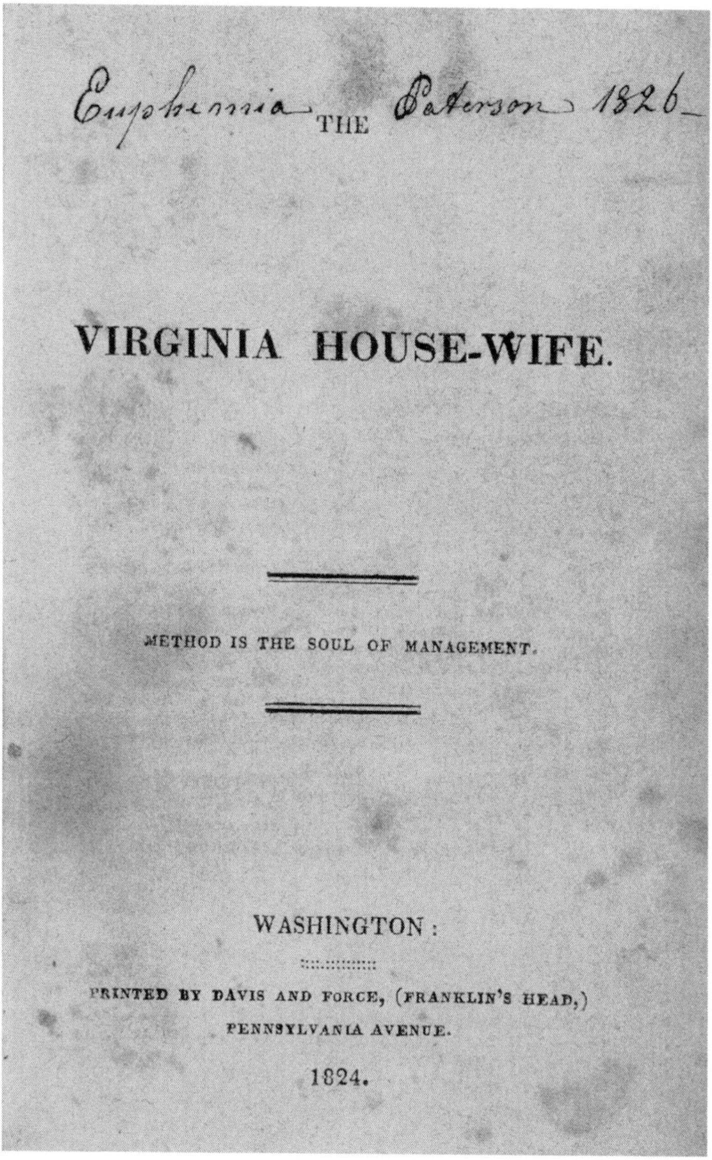

Euphemia THE *Paterson* 1826

VIRGINIA HOUSE-WIFE.

METHOD IS THE SOUL OF MANAGEMENT.

WASHINGTON :

PRINTED BY DAVIS AND FORCE, (FRANKLIN'S HEAD,)
PENNSYLVANIA AVENUE.

1824.

Figure 11. The title page of Mary Randolph's The Virginia House-Wife *(1824). Malinda Russell cites Randolph's cookbook as one of two sources of her own culinary knowledge; the other is "Fanny Steward, a colored cook of Virginia." Courtesy of the Library of Congress, Rare Book and Special Collections Division.*

to separate the "art" of cultivation from the physical labor of farming, Randolph's efforts to separate the managerial aspects of food preparation from the physical labor of cooking enable her—and her white readers—to take credit for any impact food and eating might have on the "prosperity and happiness" of both family and nation (xii).[32]

Unlike Madison's approach, however, which was premised on a distancing of the process of cultivation from the labor required to produce it, Randolph's emphasis on management enables the mistress of the house, otherwise far removed from the actual work of cooking, to reinsert herself into the cooking process. In her advice to "Virginia ladies," for instance, when Randolph declares, "Let all the articles intended for the dinner, pass in review before her: have the butter, sugar, flour, meal, lard, given out in proper quantities; the catsup, spice, wine, whatever may be wanted for each dish, measured to the cook," she describes a method for asserting practical as much as symbolic control over the cooking process (xi–xii). While presented under the guise of ensuring consistency in the kitchen, the act of meting out the individual ingredients for each dish plainly illustrates the interrelation of measurement, management, and control. And this claim to improving consistency was indeed a guise: the enslaved women working in the kitchen knew far more about consistent cooking than any plantation mistress. The passive voice employed in Randolph's phrasing underscores this point. These enslaved cooks should be credited for making food taste good *in spite of* any attempt on behalf of a mistress to control the process, as Psyche Williams-Forson's discussion of the power dynamics involved in white-authored cookbooks helps to suggest.[33] Indeed, the formal systems of measurement and accounting by which food was distributed to enslaved plantation laborers functioned to "regulate the dense cultural import of cooking and eating for the enslaved," as Christopher Farrish has observed (194). Randolph's method of household management performs a similarly regulatory function, one that serves to regulate power as much as process and that asserts social as much as culinary control.

The recipes of *The Virginia House-Wife* are revealing for how they procedurally enforce this method of culinary and social control. An undercurrent of each recipe included in the book, this enforcement is nowhere more evident than in the recipes that make use of ingredients and techniques introduced to the Americas through the transatlantic slave trade. As a primary example, consider Randolph's recipe for "Ochra

Soup," which is often celebrated in discussions of southern food for how it "introduces" the West African ingredient to American palates:

> Get two double handsful of young ochra, wash and slice thin, add two onions chopped fine, put into a gallon of water at a very early hour in an earthen pipkin, or very nice iron pot: it must be kept steadily simmering, but not boiling: put in pepper and salt. At 12 o'clock, put in a handful of Lima beans, at half past one o'clock, add three young cimlins cleaned and cut in small pieces, a fowl, or knuckle of veal, a bit of bacon or pork that has been boiled, and six tomatas, with the skin taken off when nearly done; thicken with a spoonful of butter, mixed with one of flour. Have rice boiled to eat with it. (34–35)

In keeping with Randolph's stated aims, this recipe is characterized by the (relative) precision of its required ingredients ("two double handsful of young ochra," "three young cimlins," "one [spoonful] of flour"), the detail of its methods of preparation ("wash and slice thin," "steadily simmering, but not boiling"), the specificity of its cooking times ("at 12 o'clock," "at half past one o'clock," "when nearly done"), and even its inclusion of recommended cookware ("an earthen pipkin, or a very nice iron pot"). Ostensibly included as information for the inexperienced cook, these detailed instructions also enable the mistress of the house to easily implement Randolph's method of (micro)management. Considered in terms of how it formalizes the embodied and experiential knowledge of the kitchen, Randolph's recipe is also significant for how it enacts a forcible transfer of culinary knowledge from enslaved cook to household mistress.[34]

Less immediately evident, although equally operational, is how the precision of Randolph's recipes facilitates the shift in cultural and political, and therefore aesthetic, value that she points toward in her introductory account. More specifically, her efforts to distill the managerial aspects of food preparation into recipe form allow her to invest the management of the cooking process with the aesthetic significance that other cookbook authors, including both Simmons and Russell, would associate with cooking itself. Randolph hints at this conceptual shift throughout *The Virginia House-Wife*, but it is most clearly articulated in a section that appears midway through the volume, titled, "Important Observations on Roasting,

Boiling, Frying, &c." There, Randolph proclaims: "Profusion is not elegance—a dinner justly calculated for the company, and consisting for the great part of small articles, correctly prepared, and neatly served up, will make a much more pleasing appearance to the sight, and give a far greater gratification to the appetite, than a table loaded with food, and from the multiplicity of dishes, unavoidably neglected in the preparation, and served up cold" (27). In this statement, Randolph offers a vision of an elegant dinner that elicits both a "pleasing appearance to the sight" and "gratification to the appetite," the signal attributes of the discourse of taste. But she is quick to distinguish a "table loaded with food" from her own ideal: "a dinner justly calculated for the company." The former may reflect the ability to cook a "multiplicity of dishes," but only the latter can convey the ability to manage the home. Organization and execution, the aspects of cooking over which the mistress maintains control, are, for Randolph, the most valid manifestations of virtue and taste.

Russell's citation of the "plan" of *The Virginia House-Wife* thus emerges as an acknowledgment of the role of method in shaping the tastes of both family and nation. But her pairing of Randolph's "plan" with Steward's "trade" points to an acknowledgment of a more potent source of culinary knowledge: the "art of Cooking" itself (5). Russell's decision to preface her cookbook with neither a treatise on taste, following Simmons, nor a polemic on management, following Randolph, but with a detailed personal history does more than serve as an "authenticating document" for her own expertise, as Zafar has claimed (18). It also works to secure the contributions of cooks such as Steward, who labored in the kitchen without written recognition, to the development of a distinct regional cuisine.[35] Indeed, Russell's method, while modeled after Randolph's "plan," extends beyond managerial virtue to include both the experiential knowledge gained through kitchen work and the entrepreneurial skill cultivated through daily life. She employs her cookbook as a platform for her personal philosophy of satisfaction, strategically reinforced through the lineage established by her reference to Randolph's text, and by her acknowledgment of Steward's expertise. Even more so than Russell's, the details of Steward's life story are difficult to recover.[36] But we can hold open a space of recognition by acknowledging the experience and improvisation required to transform a recipe—recorded either on the page or in the mind—into a pleasurable, satisfying dish.

Satisfaction in the Wake of Slavery

Mary Randolph and her husband David Meade Randolph, then federal marshal for the state of Virginia, were safely ensconced in their Richmond mansion, Moldavia, on Saturday, August 30, 1800, when the city experienced the "most terrible thunder Storm, accompanied with an enormous rain" that some "ever witnessed" (qtd. in Egerton, 69).[37] Unbeknownst to Richmond's white inhabitants, including the Randolph family, the storm upended what might otherwise have become the largest slave revolt in U.S. history. Gabriel's Rebellion, as the event came to be known, was envisioned by the eponymous twenty-four-year-old, a literate blacksmith who was born into slavery on a Henrico County tobacco plantation, as nothing short of revolution. Inspired by recent events in France and Haiti, Gabriel spent the summer of 1800 recruiting hundreds of men to his cause. He planned for an army of ten thousand, organized in three columns, that would march on Richmond with "cutlasses, knives, pikes, and muskets" (qtd. in Egerton, 50). James Monroe, then governor of Virginia, would be taken hostage as the rebels seized the munitions held in the magazine at Capitol Square.

The rain slowed down the plan, however, giving several would-be participants time to reconsider. One of these participants was an enslaved man named Pharoah, who mentioned his doubts to another man, Tom, enslaved in the same household, who in turn suggested that they tell their enslaver, Mosby Sheppard.[38] From that moment, a response as rapid and as destructive as the lightning that accompanied the storm resulted in thirty-seven of the rebels being captured and sentenced to death. Forced to speak in the hours before they were hanged, the rebels' testimony provides contemporary scholars with the primary (if at times conflicting) record of the rebellion's never-realized goals. One of the captured rebels, an enslaved man named Ben Woolfolk, who offered one of the most extensive accounts of the intended events, testified that "none were to be spared of the Whites, except quakers Methodists and French people" ("Testimony"). This line captured the imagination (and fears) of the white population of Richmond, and in the years that followed, it transformed into local legend. In her 1883 novelization of the events, *Judith: A Chronicle of Old Virginia*, for instance, Marion Harland (herself a cookbook author) reports that Gabriel planned to establish himself "King of Virginia," killing all who resisted (22).[39] In her 1923 pseudo-historical account, *Richmond, Its People, and Its Story*, Mary Newton Stanard provides even more (embellished) detail: "All the people of Richmond were to be massacred save those who begged for quarter or agreed to join the movement. All blacks who refused to join were to be killed" as well (84). Interestingly, Stanard identifies one additional life to be spared: none other than Mary Randolph, whom Gabriel would make "his queen because she knew so much about cooking" (84).

This "odd item," as historian Jonathan Daniels describes it in his popular biography of the Randolph family, is almost certainly apocryphal (186).[40] But Randolph's retroactive insertion into the events of August 1800 underscores the verifiable fact that food and eating played a key role in the rebellion. Many of the captured men referenced a series of barbecues that allowed them to "concert the plan of Insurrection" ("Testimony").[41] The organizing function of these barbecues seems consistent with scholarship on the sociality of the communal meals prepared and consumed by the enslaved during their time away from their labors.[42] These meals usually took place on Sunday evenings, the one time each week when the enslaved laborers were permitted to rest, and sometimes worship and gather with others. That the meals mentioned in the testimony were barbecues, coupled with the stormy weather, additionally recalls the legend of Bois Caïman: the organizing meeting and ceremony that is often cited as the start of the Haitian Revolution. That event, similarly characterized by a mixture of fiction and fact, also took place "while the storm raged and lightning shot across the sky" and was called under the "pretext of a meal."[43] The multiple shared elements between these two events begin to suggest how satisfaction can shift from a protocapitalist to a revolutionary register.

The revolutionary potential of a theory of satisfaction is further reinforced by the insertion of "Queen Molly," as she was known to her friends, into the account of the ascension of "King Gabriel," as he would be known to history. In doing so, Stanard and her peers might have sought to insert an element of control, in the form of Randolph herself, into the narrative of a plot that threatened to overturn their own social and political order.[44] Randolph's tightly regulated kitchen would work symbolically, perhaps, to mitigate the psychological threat of what endured, in their minds, as an expression of unregulation of the highest degree. Here, then, in the retelling of the events, if not in the original "plan of Insurrection," we see the desire for revolution—indeed for revenge—conceptually contained by Randolph's peerless "method of management."

But an additional bit of evidence that emerged at the trial, provided by another captured rebel named Ben, suggests a second reason for the retroactive insertion of Mary Randolph into the story of Gabriel's Rebellion. Unlike Ben Woolfolk, "Prosser's Ben," as this man was described, offered an account that did not sentence the white inhabitants of Richmond to certain death. He reported, rather, "That if the White people agreed to their freedom they would then hoist a White flag, and [Gabriel] would dine and drink with the merchants of the City" ("Testimony"). Douglas Egerton, the author of the most comprehensive account of the events, reads this report as evidence that Gabriel "understood that simple liberation was not sufficient," and that "he wanted the fully acknowledged position of equality with the master class—political, social, and economic—that was the antithesis of human bondage" (51).[45] Certainly, the notion that Gabriel, the leader of a newly emancipated class of black citizens, would "dine and drink" with his white compatriots suggests a strong understanding of the "political, social, and economic" symbolism of a shared meal. But placed in the context of Mary Randolph, the ideology of household management to which she adhered, and the enslaved household staff upon whom she relied to enforce it, the dinner acquires additional significance. Forcing Randolph, the captive wife, to prepare a meal for the leader of the revolution and the "merchants of the City" turns the (literal) table on any philosophy that linked civic virtue to the exercise of enlightened restraint. After all, Gabriel did not represent moderation in the slightest; he planned for violent revolution. A far cry from Jefferson's tasteful "little dinner," which linked the cultivation and expression of taste to the cultivation and expression of civic virtue, Gabriel's seemingly conciliatory dinner becomes, instead, an enactment of the total surrender of the tasteful master class. According to this account, Gabriel sought the satisfaction of seeing himself liberated from bondage, as well as his oppressors forced to confront, across the dining table, the new world order that his rebellion had, at long last, brought about.

Gabriel's sense of satisfaction—the pleasure of knowing that an oppressive system had been toppled, and that a form of higher justice had been served—contrasts sharply with the satisfaction sought by Malinda Russell—the pleasure of achieving economic success within that same oppressive system, and that would result in the modest goal of "return[ing] home" (3). But their shared emphasis on satisfaction, over and above personal taste, points to how the precarity that characterized all black lives in the early republic, both those enslaved and those free, shaped a range of personal philosophies and aesthetic expressions, from armed insurrection to "Almond Sponge Cake" (Russell, 9). Acknowledging how "slavery's continual unfolding" has prompted a wide range of material and aesthetic response, Christina Sharpe has recently called for a "new analytic," one that can better account for the experience that connects enslaved men like Gabriel, across time and circumstances, to free black women like Russell; and one that can also connect both Gabriel and Russell, across history and geography, to those "seeking a resolution to blackness's ongoing and irreversible abjection" in the present (18, 14). In formulating this analytic, Sharpe contests the goal of resolution itself, instead calling upon scholars to "imagine otherwise from what we know *now* in the wake of slavery" today (18).

To support this project, we might begin to imagine otherwise from our position in the present, further speculating about what we know about the archive of the early United States. In reimagining what we know about the subjects whose lives are documented in or, alternately, erased from the archive, we might also reimagine what we know about the theories that governed their lives. In this chapter, I have sought to model a method for imagining aesthetic theory otherwise. This is a method that accepts the interrelation of aesthetics and politics as a matter of course, but does not limit itself to formal definitions of either aesthetic theory or political expression. In addition to the standard sites in which such theories are developed and ideas are expressed, it looks to cooking and recipes for evidence of theories that are enacted at the table, and at times even served, in order to achieve their fullest form. This method rejects the notion that philosophy is defined by a single genre or style, in favor of a more capacious understanding of what constitutes aesthetic thought. And it insists that the actors involved in the production and presentation of food understood their own labor, in its own time, as performing aesthetic work. This method enhances our existing understanding of aesthetics by introducing additional theories developed from alternate conceptual models, and within alternate material conditions. These are theories identified in the present that can be used to speculate about how they might have been used to contest the dominant ideologies of their time.

4

Imagination

Food, Fiction, and the Limits of Taste

In the second chapter of *Incidents in the Life of a Slave Girl* (1861), Harriet Jacobs introduces the malevolent physician, Dr. Flint, who will serve as the primary source of misery for Linda Brent, the eponymous "slave girl."[1] By marrying the sister of Brent's mistress, Flint is able to take legal possession of Brent and remove her from the (relative) comfort of her grandmother's house. In a series of episodes that gather emotional impact as they accrue—a narrative technique often noted by scholars who seek to emphasize the literary dimensions of Jacobs's otherwise autobiographical account—Jacobs documents the multiple forms of violence that Dr. Flint inflicts on the enslaved members of his household and plantation staff.[2] One of the earliest of these episodes centers on the household kitchen. Jacobs describes how the cook and her children, in spite of preparing every meal for the Flint family, "could get nothing to eat except what [Mrs. Flint] chose to give them" (12). As a result, they often went hungry. By contrast, Dr. and Mrs. Flint were not only well provisioned; we are told that Dr. Flint "was an epicure" (12). Evidently, in spite of his inhumane treatment of the very people who prepared his food, this most vile of enslavers possessed a cultivated sense of taste.

Unlike the qualities associated with good taste outlined by figures such as Jefferson and Madison, and explored—and challenged—by figures including Franklin, Grimod, Wheatley, and Russell, Jacobs associates an entirely different set of qualities with her exemplary epicure. Following her initial assessment of Dr. Flint's sense of taste, Jacobs elaborates the rationale for her incriminating indictment: "The cook never sent a dinner to [Flint's] table without fear and trembling; for if there happened to be a dish not to his liking, he would either order her to be whipped, or compel her to eat every mouthful of it in his presence" (12). Jacobs, speaking as Brent, goes on to recall the most extreme example of this particular form of abuse, one prompted by the family's pet dog, who had long been a "nuisance in the house": "The cook was ordered to make some Indian mush for [the dog]. He refused to eat, and when his head was held over it, the froth flowed from his mouth into the basin. He died a few minutes after. When Dr. Flint came in, he said the mush had not been well cooked, and that was the reason the animal would not eat it. He sent for the cook, and compelled her to eat it. He thought that the woman's stomach was stronger than the dog's; but her sufferings afterwards proved that he was mistaken" (12). Here is evidence that is literally revolting: the cook is forced to consume the mixture of Indian mush and canine froth that is, as evinced by the woman's subsequent "sufferings," not only psychologically distressing but physically toxic.[3] The epicure, in this context, is revealed as a person defined not, *pace* Grimod, by his cultivated appetite, and certainly not, *pace* Jefferson, by any claim to virtue, but instead as the complete reverse: as an individual who, because of his status as a man of taste, feels the need to violently enforce the distinction between himself and those he perceives as beneath him, those who, either through the preparation of food, or through other expressions of their own personal preferences, might challenge the basis of his culinary (or corporeal) authority.

Jacobs's characterization of Flint as a man of taste is evident throughout the book, as she similarly indicts his sensibility and his morals. In so doing, Jacobs suggests that the end result of a cultivated sense of taste, as expressed in one's choices in what to eat and how to behave, is an erasure of humanity. As we have seen in various ways throughout this book, the persistence of slavery severely compromises all of the claims, not infrequent in the late colonial era and the early United States, that link the cultivation of good taste to the expression of virtuous citizenship. As an increasing number of formerly enslaved people, such as Jacobs, began to tell their stories—and did so in a narrative style intended to activate the sympathies of their readers—the act of eating emerged as an even more robust example of the failings of a philosophy that linked good taste to good citizenship.[4] In this chapter, I will examine how abolitionist writers, Jacobs among them, employed narrative techniques to challenge an ideology of taste that was by then all-pervasive. In their ability to imagine new registers for the sense of taste, these abolitionist writers both contribute to and critique the dominant sense of taste of the antebellum United States. I further contend that these contributions and critiques, manifested in the imaginative worlds evoked by abolitionist fiction and slave narratives, rejected the premise that personal taste, if left unexamined, could ever propel U.S. citizens toward abolishing slavery at a national level. I unpack the assumptions embedded in a philosophy that insisted upon the close relation between imagination and taste. In doing so, I show how the authors of slave narratives, as well as of abolitionist fiction, employ literary techniques in order to interrogate the circumstances—both personal and political—that contribute to the fundamental disjunction between imagination and taste.

I will explore this disjunction through a series of close readings from key abolitionist texts, each of which prominently features food and eating. This exploration, like all those in this book, is informed by the discourse of taste. Here, I also consider more recent insights into the complex role of the imagination in the literature of the antebellum United States. For example, Christopher Castiglia, in *Interior States,* posits that the fictional works of that era, in contrast to the nation's actual political institutions, serve as the basis for "socially possible" but not yet realized political configurations (12). Such works, which are "centered in their understandings and deployments of imagination," express an understanding of fiction as invested with the capacity to call into being future possible worlds, he later explains ("Revolution," 404). This compelling argument must nevertheless be set against the important body of work that challenges the presumption that possible futures can be imagined at all. In the years since Saidiya Hartman called attention to the ethical considerations of engaging with a contemporaneous archive—the archive of slavery—that by definition conscribes its subjects to social death, scholars of that archive, as well as the contemporary writers who seek to engage with it, have sought to develop new interpretive strategies independent of assumptions about either knowledge or futurity. I have previously discussed Hartman's technique of "critical fabulation," as well as additional approaches such as the one demonstrated by Marisa Fuentes, which stretches archival fragments "along the bias grain."[5] To these scholarly approaches, we might add Madhu Dubey's theorization of how, in the realm of fiction, authors of neo-slave narratives seek to "situate themselves against history, suggesting that we can best comprehend the truth of slavery by abandoning historical modes of knowing" altogether (780).

Connecting these current methodologies to the strategies employed by two nineteenth-century writers—Jacobs, who, as a result of the constraints of the slave narrative as a genre perhaps best exemplifies the deliberate deployment of fictional techniques; and the editor of her narrative, Lydia Maria Child, who, as a white woman, could more explicitly engage in imaginative fiction—I show how each understood her writing as expressing an attitude toward the future and its transformative possibilities (or lack thereof). I further argue that, in their contrasting approaches, Jacobs and Child each elaborate a theory of the imagination and its relation to taste: Jacobs of how, as a result of the fundamentally incommunicable aspects of the experience of enslavement, the imagination is fundamentally severed from both sympathy and taste; and Child of how the imagination can at times shape personal taste, thereby prompting sympathy across divergent contexts and circumstances.

As should now be clear, I read the works of these women alongside each other not to gain insight into the power structures that governed their relationship, as the majority of scholarship on the subject seeks to do; nor do I seek to further refine the politics of the slave narrative as a genre, as another dominant strain of literary scholarship might be described.[6] Rather, I take Jacobs and Child's shared attention to—and awareness of—the significance of cooking and eating as the grounds for a comparative analysis of their views, both suspicious and hopeful, about the transformative capabilities of taste. More specifically, I undertake an analysis of Child's deliberately staged scenes of eating in her first novel, *Hobomok, a Tale of Early Times* (1824), in order to establish her lifelong view of the close relation between the experience of eating and the sense of taste, and of the significance of both for the archive of the early United States. I then turn to a later, less considered work, the short story "Willie Wharton" (1863), in order to demonstrate her strategic deployment of the imagination in order to encourage individual citizens to reassess their personal standards of taste. Returning to Jacobs's *Incidents,* and, in particular, to her contrasting portrayals of her own and her grandmother's worldviews, I illustrate Jacobs's refusal to accept imaginative sympathy as sufficient grounds for shared understanding between those who have endured enslavement and those who have always lived in freedom. For Jacobs, the notion that a narrative of slavery could ever prompt sympathetic response is a falsehood. I argue that Jacobs, instead, understands and deploys the techniques of fiction within the context of a narrative of her life in order to underscore the fundamental disconnection between sympathy, imagination, and taste. Considering their works together, we begin to arrive at a more expansive conception of the uses of fiction both as a technique to imagine futures that do not depend on presuppositions of possibility and as a tool to excavate pasts that do not depend on an archive that is static or fixed. The sense of taste, as both a metaphor for subjective judgment and as a model of encountering the world, here offers an undertraveled entry point into both imagined pleasures and unrecorded pasts.

The Fiction of Early American Taste

Lydia Maria Child was already deeply attuned to the impact of eating when she published her cookbook *The Frugal Housewife* in 1829 to immediate and widespread acclaim.[7] The daughter of a baker whose "Medford crackers" could be purchased throughout New England and were, for a time, even exported to England, Child identified herself, throughout her life, with the class of farmers and mechanics who proudly "work with their *hands*" (qtd. in Karcher, 127). She saw little distinction between the work of her writing and the labor of her cooking; both pursuits expressed aspects of the sense of taste, inspired by figures including Benjamin Franklin, that she sought to instill in her readers.[8] Her family's Thanksgiving tradition further reflects this tasteful citizenship: "All the humble friends of the Francis household—[the teacher] 'Ma'am Betty,' the washerwoman, the wood-sawyer, and the journeymen . . . some twenty or thirty in all—were summoned to a preliminary entertainment," in which they "partook of an immense chicken pie, pumpkin pies (made in milk-pans), and heaps of donuts" and "went away loaded with [her father's] crackers and bread" (Higginson, 41). The scene struck Thomas Wentworth Higginson, himself an arbiter of national taste, as "such plain application" of Child's magnanimous beliefs that he included this anecdote, alongside his account of her literary and political accomplishments, in his profile of the author that appeared in *Eminent Women of the Age* (41).

Child was one the many "eminent women" of the age who helped to usher in a new era of literary production in the United States. After decades of relying on England, among other nations, for the majority of its reading material; and after decades of experimentation on the part of U.S. authors with respect to genre, subject matter, style, and tone, U.S. citizens could, by the 1820s, begin to point to novels and short stories, poems and essays, that reflected a variety of national cultural concerns.[9] Child's own oeuvre was exceptionally vast and wide-ranging, and reflected her experimentation with many of these same genres, subjects, and styles. In addition to *The Frugal Housewife* and *Hobomok*, Child published a widely circulated children's magazine, *The Juvenile Miscellany* (1826–36), a radical (for its time) antislavery text, *An Appeal in Favor of That Class of Americans Called Africans* (1833), and a weekly newspaper column, "Letters from New York" (1842–43), among an abundance of other works. But exceptionally important for the argument of this book is that it is Child, perhaps more than any other person involved in establishing this new American literary culture, who engages with the sense of taste across its gustatory and aesthetic registers. Not only through her cookbook, but also through her novels and short stories, which often featured scenes of food and eating, Child illustrates her adherence to a view of taste as both gustatory and aesthetic, and imbued with cultural, moral, and political significance.

In the opening scene of *Hobomok*, for example, the principal narrator, an Englishman from the Isle of Wight, descends from the ship that had served as his home for the past several months, hoping to find a "second Canaan" (7). Instead, he found the "six miserable hovels" that together "constituted the whole settlement of Naumkeak," the Puritan colony that he would soon make his home (7). Shortly thereafter, the narrator is invited to a breakfast with his colonial compatriots. The meal "consisted only of roasted pumpkin, a plentiful supply of clams, and coarse cakes made of pounded maize," the narrator recalls. "But unpalatable as it proved, even to me, it was cheerfully partaken by the noble inmates of that miserable hut" (9). Here, Child explicitly contrasts the narrator's refined British palate, which prevents him from deriving pleasure from the "plentiful" breakfast, with the delight experienced by the "noble inmates" of Naumkeak. Child, with her characteristic ability to infuse ideology into engaging narrative description, clearly stages this scene in order to emphasize how adapting to the environment of New England is fundamentally premised upon a change in personal taste. Through this example of eating, Child also affirms her adherence to the discourse of taste, as described in the Introduction, as formulated by the Scottish philosophers and then filtered through their nineteenth-century inheritors in Europe and in the United States, as both a specific register of sensory experience and a metaphorical model for one's encounter with the world.

In addition, by specifying the particular components of the meal—pumpkin, clams, and maize—Child deliberately inscribes the regional ingredients of the Northeastern seaboard into a national cultural memory. That emerging memory was almost certainly at odds with historical reality: English colonists did not uniformly embrace indigenous foodstuffs at that time, nor were they readily able to cultivate them.[10] Historical accounts, which Child most likely read, emphasize the widespread aversion to indigenous foods and methods of preparation.[11] Culinary historian Trudy Eden references an account by John Smith, recorded in 1608, of the Jamestown settlers refusing to eat "this savage trash" (3). Even with twenty years and six hundred miles separating the establishment of Jamestown from the Naumkeak settlement—Child's novel begins in 1629—Anglo-American eating habits were far from stable. (One might also cite Mary Rowlandson's 1682 account of her reluctant culinary conversion, which also included a similar description of the "filthy trash" consumed by her Nargansett, Wampanoag, and Nashaway/Nipmuc captors [147].) By imagining a meal of native foodstuffs as the first scene of her novel, Child supplements factual accounts of the nation's origin story to include references to the specific foods that, she believed, best reflected the simplicity and abundance of early colonial life. Whether those foodstuffs were actually valued by the early colonists for those reasons was less important, from her perspective, than their ideological valences in her own time. In other words, Child sought to apply the virtuous tenets that, in the 1820s, were increasingly accepted as constitutive of a distinctly republican sense of taste, backward two centuries to one of the nation's most pivotal origin stories.[12]

In *Hobomok,* as in her later writings, Child employs imagined epicurean tableaux in order to assert not only that the sense of taste is central to the cultivation of a unitary national cultural identity, but that it can—and in fact should—be purposefully refined. For instance, in the second significant scene of eating that appears in the book, the meal that welcomes Lady Arabella Johnson, a symbol of old world aristocracy, to the Naumkeak settlement, Mary Conant, the novel's protagonist, leads Arabella to a "pine table" covered with a "damask" cloth (97). Once seated at the table, Mary professes, "I have honored you more than we ever did any guests in America" (97). In their subsequent conversation, Mary discloses her concern that the meal may prove as unpalatable to Arabella as that first breakfast did to the narrator. And if Child's nineteenth-century readers fail to immediately interpret the cultural significance of the meal, Arabella's response makes its meaning explicit: "I have come into the wilderness too," she states, "and I must learn to eat hominy and milk, and forget the substantial plum puddings of England" (97). Both in her words and through her actions, Arabella affirms her commitment to bravely adapting her sense of taste to the realities of daily life in New England.

The version of taste that Arabella seeks to acquire, built upon the plain flavors of "hominy and milk" and the simple living symbolized by the "pine table," hinges on the notion of virtue implicit in republican taste. This notion was developed in the late colonial era and into the early republic through the likes of Jefferson and Madison, as we have learned, even as Child sets the novel over a century before that time. In doing so, Child here invests the preference for simple New England ingredients with additional national cultural import (and thus perhaps anticipates how she would frame her cookbook, published a short five years later, as a treatise on the virtues, both moral and political, of economical eating). Lady Arabella, when subsequently entreated to "taste" some venison, a luxurious dish prepared especially for her, declines the offer (97). "No, thank you," she responds, "I am going to try some of Mary's pumpkin and milk" (98). This example of the rejection of British luxury in favor of American simplicity is among the many instances that, as Mark McWilliams has argued, establish Child as a crucial voice in constructing the "myth" of the origins of what he understands as "republican simplicity," one that coalesced in the literary works of the early nineteenth century (365). Considered in a philosophical as well a cultural context, Arabella's decision to acquire a taste for "pumpkin and milk" also underscores Child's belief in the deliberateness with which her version of republican taste must be acquired.

Child further reinforces her belief in the intention required for the proper acquisition of taste, as well as its New England features, through a range of forms of culture not limited to food. For instance, Mary recognizes in her first lover, Charles Brown, a man with whom she can exult in the natural beauty of the New England landscape. When Brown is then banished from Naumkeak as a result of his Episcopalian faith, Mary despairs at her Puritan brethren who cannot contemplate the "latent treasures of the mind or the rich sympathies of taste" that she and Brown could uniquely perceive (91). For Child, then, it is not simply personal taste but sympathy with others that creates the grounds for common understanding. After Brown's banishment, Mary turns to the Indian, Hobomok, "whose language was brief, figurative, and poetic," and with whom she might once again share the "sympathies of taste," the same phrase previously employed to describe her connection with Brown (121). By restaging the relation with Brown, built on a shared aesthetic sensibility and sympathetic communion, Child does more than assert the equal status of Anglo-American and indigenous peoples—the focal point for most of the book's readers, now as then. She also begins to assert that taste and sympathy go hand in hand, and that the latter can, like the former, be cultivated. Child thus extends the Scottish Enlightenment argument about the relationship between personal taste and civic virtue, updating it to account for the power of sympathy that would occupy increasing intellectual attention as the nineteenth century unfolded.

In this regard, the novel's final scene is quite revealing: when Brown returns to Naumkeak in search of Mary, after it is revealed that he has not perished at sea as previously believed, Hobomok informs Brown of his own marriage to Mary. His language is characteristically poetic: "The handsome English bird hath for three years lain in my bosom; and her milk hath nourished the son of Hobomok" (139). Thus the "son of Hobomok," an embodiment of the literal consummation of Anglo- and Native American cultures, is "nourished" by Mary's "milk" to develop appropriately (white) American taste. The fact that the child is later sent away to boarding school in Cambridge, and then sent to England to continue his studies, where his Indian identity is all but lost, underscores how Child's version of national taste was strongly biased against indigenous influences. But Hobomok's final vision of his son, a scene of "Mary feeding her Indian boy from his little wooden bowl," which he observes from a hidden vantage point before he disappears into the wilderness—another damaging trope—offers an unequivocal message about Child's view of the value of taste: that the act of eating, enhanced by sympathetic bonds, would play a pivotal role in the development, cultivation, and consolidation of a national culture (141).

Sympathetic Taste and National Wholeness

William Lloyd Garrison, the fiery abolitionist, had yet to meet Child in person when, in an 1829 editorial column, he declared her to be the "first woman in the republic" (85). Citing her ability to "impart useful hints to the government as well as to the family circle," Garrison urged Child to pursue a broader audience for her writing, which by that point included, in addition to *Hobomok* and a follow-up novel, dozens of stories directed at children, most with an emphasis on social and political change (85). Just over a decade later, in 1841, Garrison would give Child the opportunity to do just that when he offered her the editorship of the *National Anti-Slavery Standard,* the official newspaper of the American Anti-Slavery Society. Child consented, and in May of that year began to implement her editorial strategy: a deliberate attempt to include a "large proportion of literary and miscellaneous matter" so that she might bring additional U.S. citizens, primarily women and children, to "look candidly at antislavery principles, by drawing them in with the garland of imagination and taste" (191). In these lines, Child reasserts her belief in the capacity of personal taste, as activated by a sympathetic imagination, to guide her readers toward justice. The "garland" that unites those two concepts further reflects Child's own technique—visible in the *Standard* as in her other work—of employing artful yet precise presentation in order to ensure (to the best of her abilities) that her readers would absorb her intended lesson.

Child's tenure as editor of the *Standard* proved short-lived, however. In an example characteristic of the gender-inflected criticism that she sustained throughout her time at the paper's helm and that pushed her to resign her editorship after less than two years, Maria Weston Chapman, one of the more radical voices of the American Anti-Slavery Society, accused Child of "substituting 'flapdoodle' for the 'roast Beef' the *Standard* needed" (qtd. in Karcher, 268). After stepping down, Child continued to maintain an active political agenda. From that point on, however, she viewed her chief vocation as a writer of fiction. "Formed as my character now is," she explained in an 1844 letter to Francis Shaw, "I cannot do otherwise than make literature the honest agent of my conscience and my heart" (qtd. in Karcher, 301). This realization marked the start of a distinct second half of her long and prolific life, where she focused almost exclusively on literature, and on fiction in particular. For it was through fiction that Child identified her most powerful method of instilling the "sympathies of taste" in others. In this work, Child remained bound to the antislavery cause while recommitting herself to the cause of Indian rights that had defined her earliest literary interventions, such as *Hobomok.* In the case of both displaced Native peoples and enslaved African Americans, Child identified the sense of taste as the mechanism that would prompt the collective action that, she continued to believe, would bring about necessary social and political change.

In "Willie Wharton," a short story that appeared in the *Atlantic Monthly* in 1863, Child consolidates the national sense of taste that she began to formulate in *Hobomok*. This was one that, while inclusive in its conception of citizenship and premised on admirable political ideals, remained limited by her narrow sense of what American culture should properly entail. For the most part, the plot of "Willie Wharton" follows a traditional trajectory of captivity and restoration: the eponymous protagonist, lost in the woods as a child, is carried away by Indians; twenty years later, he returns to his family—with his Indian wife, A-lee-lah. Child's story becomes an important exploration of the cultivation of taste as she depicts the Wharton family's embrace of A-lee-lah and their thoughtful (if, from a twenty-first-century vantage point, fundamentally misguided) attempts at cultural conversion. Child confirms her own colonialist biases at the same time that she mounts a critique of those less progressive than herself, as she demonstrates both how readily A-lee-lah adapts her instinctual affinities in order to conform to white standards of taste and how stubbornly certain other characters, bound by their cultural and racial prejudices, resist accepting A-lee-lah's full membership in their society.

As opposed to the New England setting of *Hobomok,* Child locates this story about the cultural and philosophical dimensions of the development of a national sense of taste in "one of our Western States" (*Hobomok,* 253). She also chooses a contemporary time frame. Indicating an awareness of the rapidity of U.S. colonial expansion, the narrator of "Willie Wharton" notes how the "landscape had greatly changed" during the two decades that Willie had been away from his family (271). But Child also presents Willie's absence from his family in terms of his absence from the table. During his time away, the narrator reports that Willie's "chair retained its place at the table" even as "out of the family he was nearly forgotten" (271). Underscoring a point that her dedicated readers would already have intuited, Child insists that the dining table serves as the foundation, both material and metaphoric, from which national taste extends.

Child further emphasizes the extended significance of the table, and of the particular foods it holds, as she stages Willie's return to his family on Thanksgiving Day. Recalling Child's own family tradition, the narrator relates how "wild turkeys were prepared for roasting, and the kitchen was redolent of pies and plum-pudding" and how the entire extended family, "Father, Emma, Uncle George, Aunt Mary, Bessie and her young

Squire, Charles's wife, baby, and all," were there to welcome Willie to his familial—and implied cultural—home (*Hobomok*, 275). Although it would not be until six months after the publication of this story that Thanksgiving Day would be declared a national holiday, Child's readers would have nevertheless understood the cultural implications of this festive scene. By the 1860s, foods native to New England such as wild turkey and pumpkin pie had become bound to a national origin story, in large part owing to Child's literary pursuits. Child's readers would therefore have easily interpreted the bounty of the Wharton Thanksgiving table as symbolizing the nation, as well as the family, as a cultural whole.[13]

Child further accentuates the consolidating function of food and eating as she describes how the Wharton family "guide[s]" the newly arrived couple "into increasing conformity with civilized habits" (*Hobomok*, 285). As in the scene of Mary Conant feeding the "son of Hobomok" described above, Child again emphasizes the experience of eating, as much as the particular foods consumed, as important to the process of individual acculturation. Significantly, at the dinner Willie's brother Charles takes "every precaution to have his brother appear as little as possible like a savage," including supervising the preparation of the food to be served: "Without mentioning that [Willie] would like raw meat better than all their dainties, [his brother] went to the kitchen to superintend the cooking of some Indian succotash, and buffalo-steak *very slightly broiled*" (*Hobomok*, 277). This subtle shift toward the Anglo-American style of preparing meat instead of indulging the (presumed) Indian preference for serving meat raw, establishes the Wharton family's approach—consistent with Child's own view—of gradually exposing Willie and A-lee-lah to more culturally sanctioned principles of manners and taste.

In her analysis of another short story of Child's, a tale involving a white girl, Mary French, and her black friend, Susan Easton, who are kidnapped and sold into slavery, Brigitte Fielder underscores how Child crafts each character so as to represent a specific attitude toward antiblack racism.[14] Here, Child's deliberate depiction of a range of responses to Willie and A-lee-lah's relationship appears to be deployed with a similar intent: encouraging readers to evaluate, for themselves, the appropriateness of each character's response. The members of Willie's immediate family, for example, act on their conviction that both Willie and his Indian wife are capable of internalizing appropriately "American" standards of taste. As they gently acclimate Willie and A-lee-lah to the family's cultural preferences, Willie demonstrates immediate acuity. The narrator describes how Willie regains his use of the English language "with a rapidity that might have seemed miraculous, were it not a well-known fact that one's native tongue forgotten is always easily restored" (*Hobomok*, 277). The Whartons devote additional attention to A-lee-lah, who, it is implied, has much more to learn, but they employ the same method as with Willie. Just as "everything was done to attract William to [the American] mode of life, but still no remark was made when he gave a preference to Indian customs," so, too, with regard to A-lee-lah, the family "agree[s] not to manifest any distaste for Indian fashions" (280, 282). Under this regime, A-lee-lah becomes "almost as skillful at her needle as she [once] was weaving baskets and wampum" (287). In addition, "her taste for music improved" and "her taste in dress changed also" (287). In this way, Child conveys to her readers her own belief in the natural affinities of indigenous peoples for white American culture, affinities that, according to the overall message of "Willie Wharton," need only to be cultivated and refined. To be clear: Child does nothing to overturn the insidious view of indigenous cultures as easily displaced; this is the same sentiment she expresses by plotting Hobomok's silent disappearance into the wilderness in *Hobomok*. With that said, Child nonetheless frames A-lee-lah's ability to be "guided" into "conformity" with the conventions of white society as a positive trait.[15]

In a manner that again recalls *Hobomok*, and in what would become a recurrent theme of her fiction, Child concludes "Willie Wharton" with a short account of the child of Willie and A-lee-lah. However, Child's description of the girl, Jenny, offers a subtle evolution from her portrayal of the son of Hobomok and Mary Conant. The son of Hobomok, whose "Indian appellation" is "silently omitted" only "by degrees," is sent away to England; colonial America cannot yet embrace him or the mixture of cultures that he represents (*Hobomok*, 150). Jenny, on the other hand, whose name does not disclose her multiracial background, flourishes in the United States of the 1860s. The narrator relates that she is "universally admitted to be the prettiest and brightest child in the village" (287). Mr. Wharton reports that "her busy little mind makes him think of his Willie, at her age," and her Uncle Charles "says he has no fault to find with her, for she has her mother's beautiful eyes and wears her hair 'like folks'" (287). Taken together, these comments suggest that

Jenny's cultivated intellect derives from Willie, as part of her white inheritance. And with the mention that she "has her mother's beautiful eyes," she appears to transform her Indian beauty so as to adhere to white standards of taste.

With the cultural (and gender) hierarchy encoded in this description of Jenny, it is difficult not to view the overall message of "Willie Wharton" in terms of the "imperial process of civilizing" that Amy Kaplan identifies in her influential essay on one of Child's contemporaries, and occasional contributor to the *Juvenile Miscellany,* Sarah Josepha Hale (184).[16] It is nevertheless worth considering that in contrast to Hale's exclusionary conception of the "American" home—which, according to Kaplan, "makes race central to woman's sphere not only by excluding nonwhites from domestic nationalism but also by seeing the capacity for domesticity as an innate, defining characteristic of the Anglo-Saxon race"—Child's story of Willie and A-lee-lah Wharton suggests a more inclusive conception of the nation (198). Still, it remains difficult to overlook Child's inclination to subsume indigenous cultural influences within an already dominant Anglo-American national identity. What I will suggest is not that we disregard these significant contradictions.[17] Rather, following Fielder, I believe that we can understand Child most effectively when we closely examine the responses of individual characters to evaluate the more specific views that each represents. Child's divergent characterizations of the Whartons' extended family, friends, and neighbors, and their varied difficulties in accepting A-lee-lah, thus become a localized critique of the negative effects of prejudice—if not white cultural supremacy—on that era's sense of taste. By incorporating these negative responses into her narrative, Child reinforces her own position on the value of the sense of taste. Because the sense of taste is instilled and assessed from within, it is less susceptible to the damaging social pressures that can interfere with personal judgments made by other means.

In fact, "Willie Wharton" offers a direct indictment of standards of taste that are adopted without regard to inner principle. Shortly after Willie's return, for example, his cousin Bessie remarks to her father: "I feel as if I ought to invite William and his wife to dine with us, but if any of my husband's family should come in, I should feel *so* mortified to have them see a woman with a blanket over her shoulders sitting at my table!" (*Hobomok,* 283). "Besides," she adds, "they like raw meat, and that is dreadful!" (283). From this account, it is clear that although Bessie "feel[s]" that she should welcome Willie and his wife with an invitation to a family dinner, she cannot reconcile her instinctual kindness with her concern for others' judgments of A-lee-lah and, perhaps more significantly, their judgments of her.

In keeping with Child's view, it is ultimately Bessie's behavior, and not A-lee-lah's, that is cast as being worthy of further scrutiny. Bessie's father, offering a "philosophical way of viewing the subject," suggests that the issue is, both literally and figuratively, a matter of taste (*Hobomok*, 283). "Certainly it is not pleasant," he states, "but I once dined in Boston, at a house of high civilization, where the odor of venison and of Stilton cheese produced much more internal disturbance than I have ever experienced from any of their Indian messes" (283). This example of a meal at a "house of high civilization" that nonetheless smelled worse and "produced much more internal disturbance" than "any of their Indian messes" exposes the difference between a thoughtless adherence to social standards and the cultivation of taste from within. The father's "philosophical way of viewing the subject" reveals to his daughter, and to Child's readers, the deeper significance that is present, even if not always acknowledged, in many matters of taste. It reveals, moreover, how Child understood her readers' ability to inhabit her characters' subject positions—in other words, to activate their sympathetic imagination—as the process that would lead to the cultivation of their own, socially aware sense of taste.

In the most generous of interpretations, it could be said that the hegemony of white culture is challenged by the events described in "Willie Wharton" (*Hobomok*, 260). After all, Willie and A-lee-lah are first identified as "representatives of races widely separated by moral and intellectual culture" (260). Upon their return, however, the "more enlightened portion of the community" responds in a positive manner to the couple, while others who are "not distinguished either for moral or intellectual culture"—the same phrase first used to distinguish Anglo-American from Indian—"sneer" at the Wharton family's decision to embrace them (285). Child contrasts these undistinguished citizens with Willie's parents, who "had been so long in the habit of regulating their actions by their own principles"; not surprisingly, his parents make the more tolerant choice in welcoming A-lee-lah into their home and family (284). By adopting the language of self-regulation—the same language employed by Jefferson, Madison, and Franklin in their discussions of the transformation of appetite into taste, as discussed in previous chapters—Child suggests that personal taste can and should guide each U.S. citizen in his or her interactions with others, and ideally in his or her political action as well.

The Limits of Fiction, the Limits of Taste

It would be nearly seven years between the winter of 1853/54, when Harriet Jacobs began to set aside her "evenings to write," and the fall of 1860, when she at last secured a publisher for her book (qtd. in Jacobs, xviii). After turning down her first publishing opportunity, which would have required that her narrative be introduced by Harriet Beecher Stowe, whom Jacobs had cause to distrust, she accepted the suggestion of another publisher, Thayer and Eldridge, that she enlist Lydia Maria Child to write the preface. Jacobs had yet to meet Child in person and "past experience made [her] tremble at the thought of approaching another Sattellite [sic] of so great magnitude," as Jacobs wrote to her friend and confidant Amy Post (qtd. in Jacobs, 247). But upon meeting Child, Jacobs discovered her to be a "whole souled Woman—we soon found the way to each others heart" (qtd. in Jacobs, 247). Child took a month to edit Jacobs's manuscript, with her work primarily consisting of condensing and rearranging certain sections of the original document.[18] And after a several-month delay, largely owing to financial difficulties on behalf of the press, *Incidents in the Life of a Slave Girl* was published in an edition of three thousand copies in the final weeks of December 1861.

Unlike Child and her explicit embrace of fiction—which, in addition to Indian rights, she employed to shed light on the injustices of slavery as well as on the prejudice faced by formerly enslaved people—Jacobs, a person who herself was formerly enslaved and who sought to narrate her own life story, was required to reject fiction as a matter of course. The "Preface by the Author" begins with a direct address that makes this constraint clear: "Reader, be assured this narrative is no fiction" (1). Because of the "incredible" life events described in the volume, and because of the immensity of the "wrongs inflicted by Slavery," Jacobs could not afford to have her narrative interpreted as anything less than the truth (1).[19] But the truth, Jacobs goes on to explain, is not equivalent to complete knowledge, nor is it enough to lead to true understanding. Anticipating the remarks made by Toni Morrison, in "The Site of Memory," about the distinctions among fiction, fact, and truth, Jacobs similarly understands how the "crucial distinction . . . is not the difference between fact and fiction, but the distinction between fact and truth" (93). Here, I seek to focus this broad conceptual inquiry by centering on Jacobs's understanding of the sense of taste. I am interested in how Jacobs, in starkly different ways from Child, frames the uses and limits of taste in relation both to the hopeful imaginativeness of fiction and to the sympathetic imaginativeness of fact.

Although many circumstances separated the lives of Jacobs and Child, they shared an awareness of the function of food and eating as a catalyst for more philosophical thinking about the outward expression and social and political impact of the sense of taste. Like Child's father, Convers Francis, Jacobs's grandmother, whose name we now know to be Molly Horniblow, was a baker who was "much praised for her cooking" (6). Grandmother Horniblow's "nice crackers," like Francis's northern version of same, "became so famous in the neighborhood that many people were desirous of obtaining them," as Jacobs writes in the first pages of *Incidents* (6). It need hardly be observed that the life circumstances of Francis and Horniblow, like those of their literary progeny, sharply differed. Whereas Francis, a white man from New England, could pursue any entrepreneurial opportunity as he so pleased, Horniblow, who would only gain her freedom at the age of fifty, was required to "ask permission of her mistress to bake crackers at night, after all the household work was done" (6). One need only consider the contrast between the festive atmosphere of Thanksgiving Eve in the Francis household, as documented by Thomas Higginson, in which Francis freely dispensed his crackers to his departing guests; and the fatigue that likely greeted Molly Horniblow each night as, instead of retiring to bed at the end of a full day of enforced labor, was required to draw from untold personal reserves in order to pursue her "midnight bakings" (6). More sharply than even Malinda Russell, whose own baking business facilitated a form of economic agency, as discussed in chapter 3, Molly Horniblow recognized this rare ability to monetize her confectionery skill as the once-in-a-lifetime opportunity that would lead to her own, and her family's, liberation (6).[20]

At the same time, Jacobs's grandmother's baking business, like Child's father's and also like Russell's, offered her a certain similarity of exposure to the extended implications of the pleasures of the palate for herself and for others. In *Incidents*—and here I return to the fictional names employed in the narrative—Brent explains how her grandmother's business allowed her to "receive[] portions of the crackers, cakes, and preserves, she made to sell," providing Brent with essential sustenance when her slave rations proved insufficient (6). As she subsequently explains, "Little attention was paid to the slaves' meals in Dr. Flint's house" (10). But, she continues: "I gave myself no trouble on that score, for on my various errands I passed my grandmother's house, where there was always something to spare for me. I was frequently threatened with punishment if I stopped there; and my grandmother, to avoid detaining me, often stood at the gate with something for my breakfast or dinner. I was indebted to *her* for all my comforts, spiritual or temporal" (10–11). As the narrator indicates, it is her grandmother's baking, enhanced by the mobility accorded by her status as a freewoman, that enables her to support Brent during her time in bondage. From that single action—standing by the gate with food ready to go—in which is encoded a depth of foresight and compassion along with the liberty to enact both, Brent derives "comforts" far more significant than the comfort of food alone.

As *Incidents* unfolds, Brent elaborates on the "comforts" that extend from her grandmother's baking business. She explains how after she and her brother "ceased to be children," they became "indebted to [their grandmother] for many more important services" than baking alone (6). Those "services" ranged from the emotional support that Aunt Martha, as Brent refers to her grandmother, offered upon the failed pursuit of Brent's first lover; the constant vigilance that she provided during the time when Brent's brother and children were jailed; and her largest and most significant "service," the emotional endurance required to protect Brent while she hid, for seven years, in the garret above her Aunt Martha's home. While Brent experiences the effects of these services at far remove from her grandmother's baking, they remain linked to that original activity. For Aunt Martha is only able to secure her own freedom as a result of the relationships she had forged through her baking business; because she "had for a long time supplied many families with crackers and preserves," Brent narrates, "every body who knew her respected her intelligence and good character" (21). Thus when Dr. Flint reneges on his promise to free Aunt Martha, the families who had for so long purchased her food schemed instead to purchase her freedom. The material affordances and concomitant mental reserves that Aunt Martha is able to accumulate as a free woman, those that equip her to endure the anguish of her granddaughter trapped in her "loophole of retreat," derive directly from the benefits of her baking.

These benefits, both financial and emotional, affect the long-term prospects represented by Brent and her grandmother. In a poignant passage, Jacobs employs the "charms of the old oven" synecdochically for Aunt Martha's (relatively) charmed life (17). She contrasts Aunt Martha's "hopefulness" with Brent and her brother's justified pessimism: "We longed for a home like hers. There we always found sweet balsam for our troubles. She was so loving, so sympathizing! She always met us with a smile, and listened with patience to all our sorrows. She spoke so hopefully, that unconsciously the clouds gave place to sunshine. There was a grand big oven there, too, that baked bread and nice things for the town, and we knew there was always a choice bit in store for us" (17). Here, Brent reveals how her grandmother's optimistic view of the future relates to her access to her "grand big oven." For in addition to, or perhaps because of, Aunt Martha's financial security, her emotional reserves, and, of course, her physical freedom, she is able to maintain her "loving" and "sympathizing" qualities and speak "hopefully" about the future. Her ability to look ahead to a place and time when her family will be free, even after enduring fifty years of enslavement herself, reflects a view that is not shared by her granddaughter. Brent explains that, for herself and her brother, "even the charms of the old oven failed to reconcile us to our hard lot" (17). The difference in circumstances between Brent and her grandmother, Jacobs suggests, affects their divergent abilities to envision (or a failure to envision) future possible worlds.

In contrast to Jacobs's own view, Child identified Aunt Martha's hopeful outlook as the more valuable of the two. Not only did she suggest that Jacobs conclude *Incidents* with an account of the death of her "good old grandmother," advice that Jacobs evidently took to heart, but she also identified, in the transformative power of hopefulness, a lesson that might be extracted and applied to the education of others (201). In the immediate aftermath of emancipation, Child compiled *The Freedmen's Book* (1865), an anthology of biographies and vignettes about prominent black cultural figures that was intended to educate newly free black citizens about their own possible futures. In it, she included Jacobs's account of Aunt Martha to "illustrate the power of character over circumstances" (218). For Child, the hopefulness of the "good grandmother," as Child titled the excerpt, aligned beautifully with her personal views. Not surprisingly, in the excerpt, all mention of Brent's struggle was excluded.

For Jacobs, however, hopefulness about the future remained ill-advised, and, as she demonstrates throughout *Incidents,* at times impossible even to contemplate. Brent consistently finds her hopes vanquished and her desires suppressed. When Dr. Flint denies her "love-dream" to marry her childhood friend, a freeborn carpenter who lived in the neighborhood, Brent reflects that her "lamp of hope had gone out" (38, 42). That "lamp of hope" remains extinguished through the end of *Incidents,* which concludes with Brent's melancholy observation that the "dream of my life is not yet realized" (201). Reminiscent of her childhood "long[ing]" for a home like her grandmother's, a longing that is connected to her grandmother's oven, Brent informs the reader that she does "not sit with my children in a home of my own" (201). Ceding the final lines to Brent's "tender memories" of her "good old grandmother," which she describes as "light, fleecy clouds floating over a dark and troubled sea," Jacobs concludes *Incidents* by underscoring the distinction between Aunt Martha's ethereal hope and Brent's more pragmatic, albeit world-weary view (201).

Throughout *Incidents,* Jacobs deftly translates her own hesitancy about hope for the future into a series of lessons about both the psychological traumas of slavery, and the practical limits of literature. Scholars have long sought to unpack the implications of the slave narrative as a genre, at times explicitly referring to Jacobs's text as an exemplar of how the impossibility of describing—and therefore imagining—the horrors of slavery becomes a defining feature of the form.[21] One of the most frequently examined passages in the book, unsurprisingly, is Jacobs's indictment of her white readers' ability to ever truly imagine themselves as enslaved, an indictment that follows Brent's revelation of her decision to begin a relationship with another enslaver, Mr. Sands: "Pity me, and pardon me, O virtuous reader! You never knew what it is to be a slave; to be entirely unprotected by law or custom; to have the laws reduce you to the condition of a chattel, entirely subject to the will of another. You never exhausted your ingenuity in avoiding the snares, and eluding the power of a hated tyrant; you never shuddered at the sound of his footsteps, and trembled within hearing of his voice" (55). Here, Brent seeks to defend her actions that, if judged by white moral standards, would be deemed sinful and beyond repair. In reminding readers that they "never knew" and could never know "what it is like to be a slave," Jacobs underscores the fundamental impossibility of white readers imagining the conditions of enslavement.

What is less immediately evident is how this failure of imagination is linked to a failure of taste. The theory of the imagination that is promoted by Child—of a sympathetic impulse that is directed and sustained by personal taste—is, Jacobs seems to suggest, incompatible with her condition of enslavement. At the most basic level, one does not have the freedom to exercise personal taste when "entirely subject to the will of another." The anticipatory terror that Brent describes—"shudder[ing] at the sound of his footsteps" that signal the approach of her abuser, "trembl[ing]" at the sound of his voice—are indeed a form of imagination, but one that is categorically different from the sympathetic imagination that Child hopes to encourage in the readers of her own work and presumably Jacobs's as well. This imaginative terror is neither guided nor assessed by personal taste; it is elicited by the actions of a powerful other, and evaluated only in terms of survival.[22]

For Jacobs, the fundamental limitations of the sense of taste as both a method of governing personal behavior and as a means of eliciting sympathetic response are evident from among her earliest life experiences. She incorporates this view into *Incidents* as she describes, early in the narrative, how Brent is required to "spen[d] the day gathering flowers and weaving them into festoons" for an "evening party" at her mistress's house, rather than being granted permission to attend her father's funeral (10). This striking contrast between the indulgence of carefree pleasures over the most profound experience of compassion sets the stage for a lifetime of incompatibilities between white taste and black suffering. Returning to the episode that began this chapter concerning Dr. Flint's perverted sense of taste, it becomes more understandable as to why Jacobs ties the failure of taste to the failure of sympathy. Both in the case of Dr. Flint, who exhibits good taste in eating while simultaneously revealing the most repugnant moral views, and in the case of her readers, who assume that their personal taste offers sufficient grounds for understanding, Jacobs emphasizes the privileged assumptions that underlie each view.

Jacobs's aim, in recording her narrative, is to lead her readers to a sense of sympathetic obligation toward—but, crucially, not shared sympathy with—those who remain in bondage. As Franny Nudelman helpfully summarizes, "Sentimental narration assumes that emotional experience can be directly embodied, and thus perfectly communicated, in written language" (944). Because of her firsthand knowledge of how certain experiences cannot be communicated, especially across such divergent social roles, Jacobs justifiably rejects this assumption out of hand. From the first lines of the preface, she is explicit about her desire not "to excite sympathy for [her] own sufferings," but instead to "arouse the women of the North to realizing a sense of the condition of the two millions of women in the South, still in bondage, suffering what [she] suffered, and most of them far worse" (1). The "sense" of the condition of the women who remain enslaved is far different from the sense of sympathetic taste that, Child insists, will impel northern white women to action. This "sense" may elicit emotional response, which in turn may prompt action, but it cannot guarantee perfect understanding; nor does Jacob believe it should do so. A different form of imagination, disconnected from taste, is characteristic of Jacobs's experience of enslavement.

Imagination, (Im)Possibility, and the Archive of Slavery

Halfway through *The Underground Railroad,* Colson Whitehead's 2016 award-winning novel that reimagines the abolitionist network as an actual system of tunnels and track, the novel's protagonist, Cora, a fugitive from a Georgia plantation, arrives in North Carolina. Initially unsure as to what to expect, Cora quickly discovers that she has entered a "sort of hell," with mutilated corpses strung up on trees marking the path into town (153). Her personal hell reveals itself more slowly, however, as, upon her arrival at the home of the train station agent, Martin Wells, she is quickly secreted up to the attic, where she is hurried into a "cramped nook" that "came to a point three feet from the floor and ran fifteen feet in length" (154). In the nook, Cora cannot stand upright, and the "only source of light and air [is] a hole in the wall that faced the street" (154). She remains "imprisoned" in the attic for months until, betrayed by the Wells family housekeeper, she is recaptured by the malevolent slave catcher, Ridgeway, who had been pursuing her since her initial flight from Georgia (161). Martin and his wife are summarily hanged, presumably to join the line of corpses that had augured their demise those many months ago. Cora, meanwhile, back in the possession of Ridgeway, is carried west to Tennessee, where she will continue her quest for freedom.

Whitehead, a contemporary novelist, must imagine the events that set his plot in motion. But the conditions that Cora endures during her imprisonment in the "nook" have a strong basis in fact and recall the "garret" of identical dimensions and constraints in which Harriet Jacobs hid, above her grandmother's house (also in North Carolina) for the seven years that it took to enact her escape (114). Whitehead is explicit about his indebtedness to Jacobs, naming her along with Frederick Douglass in the book's acknowledgments section. But in reimagining Jacobs's narrative in a fictional context, Whitehead introduces his own view of the role of the imagination—and, interestingly, of the role of the sense of taste—with respect to the archive of slavery. It is not insignificant that each station stop on his underground railroad, while diverging in design and level of completeness, always contains a table (or a picnic basket) resplendent with food; nor is it inconsequential that the first exchange that Cora has with the wagon driver who will at last convey her away from the South is about Cora's hunger. Cora's hunger, for both food and for freedom, serves as a continual reminder of her humanity within a set of conditions that derives its ideological power, in large part, by insisting on the inhumanity of the enslaved.[23]

From his own vantage point in the twenty-first century, Whitehead is highly attuned to both the material and the ideological distortions effected by the institution of slavery. Through a combination of his use of an omniscient narrator, who reveals Cora's inner life to the reader, and his emphasis on the daily needs of his characters—including and especially eating—Whitehead takes the opportunity to himself reimagine, if not to redress, those distortions. For example, it is Cora's plot of land, which she employs to grow the yams and okra that, as culinary historians have shown, often supplemented the meager rations on plantations in the Deep South, that animates the opening of the novel. As we have learned throughout this book, however, few detailed accounts of such farming practices exist in the literature of that era. In order to evoke Cora's plot, Whitehead most likely synthesized information drawn from his own archival research with an array of narrative techniques, allowing the plot of land to accumulate symbolic significance first as a material manifestation of Cora's severed bond with her mother, then as an example of the powers of ownership to which she was otherwise unequivocally subject, and, finally, as a symbol of America itself, that "shadow of something that lived elsewhere," that "ghost in the darkness, like her" (180). In so doing, Whitehead offers evidence of the imaginative capacities of his enslaved characters, just as he contests the racialized nature of the nineteenth-century imagination itself.[24]

In *Sites of Slavery: Citizenship and Racial Democracy in the Post-Civil Rights Imagination,* Salamishah Tillet considers how, in neo-slave narratives like *The Underground Railroad,* historical flashpoints, such as Jefferson's relationship with Sally Hemings, as well as physical places, such as Gorée Island, in Senegal, through which Phillis Wheatley might have passed, are reconfigured "in order to accommodate the constitutive sites of American history that the national memory has forgotten or excised" (26).[25] Crucially for Tillet, "contemporary black writers and artists do not disaggregate slavery from the narrative of American democracy. Instead of representing slavery as the foil to American democracy, contemporary African Americans foreground slavery as the mnemonic property of the entire nation" (32). Although Tillet does not consider Whitehead's novel, which was published after her own book, his physical reimagining of the original underground railroad, as well as his elaboration of the symbolic significance of Cora's plot of land, would seem to strongly support Tillet's thesis about the desire of contemporary black authors to elaborate a "democratic aesthetic" that "privilege[s] the idea and ideal of democracy, yet all the while remaining skeptical of its materialization" (34). In *The Underground Railroad,* both Cora's land and the railroad itself are explicitly figured as emblems of the United States. In the novel's denouement, Elijah Lander—the charismatic leader of the utopian farm that shelters Cora upon her escape from Ridgeway and that would soon be set ablaze in a violent attack—names three fundamental "delusions" that shape the lives of formerly enslaved people: the existence of the farm; the belief that its inhabitants can ever psychologically "escape" slavery; and the United States itself, the delusion he calls the "grandest of all" (285). Lander's "delusion" that links the shadow of slavery to the nation as a whole is the same "mnemonic property" that characterizes Tillet's "democratic aesthetic": the belief that, in spite of conditions that impede its full materialization, there exist examples of democracy's promise. Lander's farm, Cora's land, and the Underground Railroad all serve as sites for imagining otherwise, even as they also serve as reminders of imagination's limits.

In this chapter, I have attempted to show how examples of food and eating, both real and fictional, enable the writers who record them to contemplate their extended significance for the cultivation of taste, for the experience of sympathy, and for the expression of the imagination. I have also attempted to call attention to the crucial distinction between imagination and possibility, concepts that, without the interventions of enslaved writers like Jacobs, we might unreflexively assume to be aligned.

These writers, because of their circumscribed social and political agency, were only authorized to present accountings of their own lives. But their work also hints at the separation of imagination from possibility, and deliberately so. For the authors of neo-slave narratives who have learned from this original work, and, ideally, for the scholars who also seek to understand it, this separation, in turn, becomes the site of fictional imaginings of imperfect futures. Both the imagined potential—and fundamental impossibility—of fully witnessing these futures is what an attention to eating in the nineteenth century allows us as scholars in the present to see.

5

Absence

Slavery and Silence in the Archive of Eating

On February 22, 1801, Thomas Jefferson sat down to compose a letter to a friend in Baltimore. The friend, William Evans, ran a bustling inn, recognizable to passersby by its sign depicting an "Indian Queen."[1] For those who stayed there, however, the inn was more memorable for its large "common Table," which could seat between seventy and eighty dinner guests, in addition to "many private tables handsomely served."[2] But when Jefferson wrote to Evans, he was concerned with tables closer to home. As Jefferson was also aware, Evans's inn served as a primary relay point for mail routes up and down the East Coast. Jefferson hoped that Evans's central position in that physical communication network would also allow him to convey a message in person, and so he posed a seemingly innocuous request: "You mentioned to me in conversation here that you sometimes saw my former servant James, & that he made his engagements such as to keep himself always free to come to me. Could I get the favor of you to send for him & tell him I shall be glad to receive him as soon as he can come to me?" (*Papers*, 33:38). Less than two weeks away from assuming the presidency—his inauguration would take place on March 4 of that year—Jefferson apologized for troubling Evans with his inquiry. As he writes: "The truth is that I am so much embarrassed in composing a good houshold [*sic*] for myself, as in providing a good administration for our country" (*Papers*, 33:39). As we saw in chapter 1, and as we have throughout this book, the process of "composing a good houshold" and of "providing a good administration for our country" were, for Jefferson, very much aligned.

After signing the letter, Jefferson put down his pen and moistened a sheet of copying paper, which he had imported from London expressly for this task. After placing the copying paper over the original document, the iron-gall ink still wet, he encased the two sheets in adhesive paper

(paper that had been waxed or oiled to prevent the ink from evaporating) and placed the entire stack in his customized copying press. He then rotated the brass crank affixed to the side of the device, which in turn advanced a roller; the pressure of the roller forced the ink through the porous copying paper, resulting in a facsimile of the original document that, once dry, could be turned over and read from the back.[3] Satisfied with the reproduction, Jefferson summoned his secretary to file the press copy and then sent the original off to Evans in the mail. For reasons more complex—and more tragic—than he could know at the time, Jefferson's difficulties in enlisting his "former servant James" as a member of his White House staff would soon be acutely felt. For the "James" he hoped to contact was none other than James Hemings, Jefferson's skillful chef. And not more than eight months later, as described in chapter 1, James Hemings would take his own life.

I hold that tragic act in abeyance as I consider Jefferson's own archival practice, for it reveals as much about how we have come to know about the "melancholy circumstances" of Hemings's final days as it does about the celebrated contributions of Jefferson's long and storied life (*Papers*, 35:542). Over the years, many scholars have commented on Jefferson's awareness of his own historical legacy, as well as of his desire to influence that legacy through his personal archive. This archive was directly constituted by the choices that Jefferson made about which conversations to record in writing, which of those records to then copy and file, and, therefore, which to preserve.[4] It has even been suggested that Jefferson, because of his role as a "founding father," his function in establishing the Library of Congress, and his own acute case of Derridean archive fever, functions as a "synecdoche for the American archive" as a whole (Elmer, 23).[5] The sheer size of the Jefferson archive—an estimated seventy thousand documents, a number that includes the eighteen thousand letters that Jefferson himself composed, copied, and filed, as well as every additional "known extant letter or Jefferson-related paper"—suggests that it can tell us much about the nation's early years, perhaps including the role of James Hemings in establishing its cultural foundation.[6] But the size of the Jefferson archive masks one of its additional defining features, one that makes it an even more meaningful approximation of the archive of the early United States as a whole: its silences.

Since the 1990s, the term "archival silence" has been increasingly employed by archivists, as well as by scholars across the humanities, to describe the gaps that are created by information that is absent from the archival record.[7] The "silence" of this term is intended to evoke the resonant space left by those gaps—the absence of records relating to figures like Hemings—whose voices we yearn to listen to and learn from but which can no longer be accessed in their full richness and depth. Michel-Rolph Trouillot describes how such silences can enter the archive at any of four crucial moments: "The moment of fact creation (the making of *sources*); the moment of fact assembly (the making of *archives*); the moment of fact retrieval (the making of *narratives*); and the moment of retrospective significance (the making of *history*) in the final instance" (26). Trouillot takes as his focus the historical narrative of the Haitian Revolution, but his observations about the forms of silence that enter into and shape that story also apply to the stories told through the Jefferson archive—and as I have argued throughout this book, through the entire archive of the early United States.

Thus far, I have focused on the gaps left by the food that is absent from this archive. But behind the food, as I have shown, are the people who prepared, served, and consumed it. Theirs are the voices that can best tell us about its flavors, as well as about its significance for the cultivation and expression of republican taste. And yet, because of each of the four sources of archival silence that Trouillot identifies—"the making of *sources*," "the making of *narrative*," "the making of *archives*," and "the making of *history*"—these voices cannot speak to us from the documents that might otherwise convey their thoughts and ideas. And these silences persist into the present, even as we live in what has been called the Information Age. In the era of Google, Siri, and Alexa, it is easy to assume that any information we might seek can be made accessible through quick command. But the ease—and error—of this assumption invest the Jefferson archive, and the faint traces of the life of James Hemings that it records, with additional significance. This takes the form of the technological veil that they cast over each of the four sources of archival silence that Trouillot describes.

As I intended my account of Jefferson's personal archiving process to suggest, Jefferson was himself also strongly committed to technology use. He was even what we might call today an "early adopter." He sought to acquire "one of those copying Machines" in 1783, almost as soon he learned of its existence, and in 1804 he would purchase one of the first polygraph devices, which represented the next generation of copying technology (*Papers*, 15:585).[8] In this context, it becomes additionally relevant to consider how I first encountered the letter to Evans quoted at the outset of this chapter: neither in its original pen and ink, nor in the press copy, but in the *Papers of Thomas Jefferson Digital Edition,* which I accessed through a web browser running on my laptop as I sat at home—then in Brooklyn—right on my living room couch.

As I write now, in Atlanta, in 2019, it is almost certain that every scholar who employs archival materials as part of their research has experienced a version of this archival future shock. Ed Folsom has made much of the "epic transformation" of the archive, by which he refers to the dramatic shift from print to digital archival form that has taken place over the past twenty or so years (1571). This shift is characterized not only by the increased availability of digitized content, but also by the proliferations of pathways that can be used to access that content, most notably by the affordance known colloquially as "search."[9] By entering a single keyword, or sometimes a set of keywords or a short phrase, into an empty text field, scholars can simply and effortlessly access the documents most relevant to their research. But search is only *seemingly* simple and effortless, and here again the letter to Evans is instructive. For I was able to locate this letter only because of a fortuitous confluence of technological affordances, design decisions, editorial oversight, and prior research, which, both separately and together, were in fact quite complex.

Recall the content of the letter to Evans, and note that Jefferson does not identify Hemings with any more specificity than as a man formerly in his employ. In fact, the name "Hemings" does not appear in the letter at all. The reason that Evans's letter appeared in the list of results for a search on "James Hemings" is fivefold at the least. First, it was predicated on the fact that the editors of the print edition of the *Papers of Thomas Jefferson* had already conducted significant research on the "former servant James," and determined through contextual information that the "James" mentioned in the letter was indeed James Hemings. Second, the editors made the decision to add a footnote to the letter in the print edition, indicating that the "former servant" referred to James Hemings. Third, those responsible for the editorial apparatus of the digital edition decided to include the footnotes from the print edition as "notes" visible to the viewer, as well as encode them as document metadata in the XML version of each letter on which *The Papers of Thomas Jefferson Digital Edition* is based. Fourth, the designers of the *Digital Edition* also decided to make the default scope of a keyword search include the notes on the

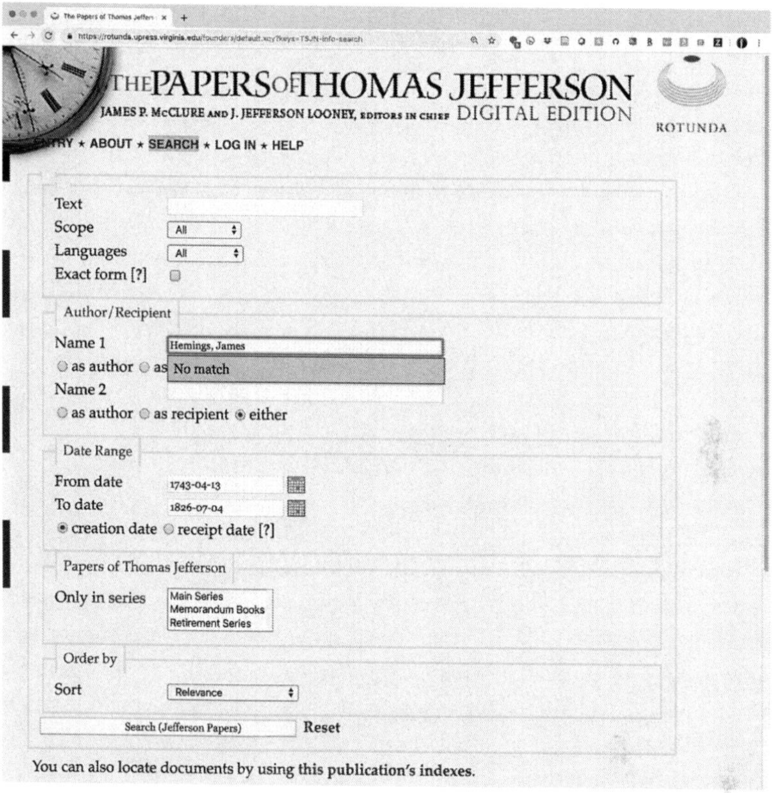

Figure 12. A "Name" search for James Hemings in The Papers of Thomas Jefferson Digital Edition, *displaying no results. Screen capture by the author.*

letters, as well as the letters themselves. Fifth, the search engine (or equivalent technology) that powers the search feature of the site was able—again, only seemingly effortlessly—to transform the phrase that I had entered into a string of text, enabling the query to be executed and the results returned.

When I typed the phrase "James Hemings" into the search box, however, I did not consider any of these constraints, at least not initially. From my perspective as a user of the site, the appearance of Evans's letter in the list of search results was simply fortuitous. Had I decided to begin my research instead, for example, with a more structured "Name" search for James Hemings—that is, a search for a person named "James Hemings" as either an author or recipient of a letter—I would have been returned no results. This remains true at the time of this writing, even as the contents of the *Digital Edition* have been expanded from the twenty-five thousand documents that I considered in my initial research, conducted in 2013, to include an additional sixteen thousand documents from Jefferson's later years.[10]

This striking instantiation of archival silence in digital form strongly demonstrates how simply having more information made available, or having that information made more easily accessible, does not necessarily lead to more knowledge. It also demonstrates how information, or the lack thereof, is not the only source of the silences that the archive encodes. Indeed, technologies both past and present impact our ability to preserve and access archival material, just as they also impact our ability to learn from whatever fragments remain. Throughout this book, I have explored a range of methods, and concomitant critical framings, that can help to account for some of these silences, lending the fragments that constitute the archive of eating additional narrative stability, political significance, and theoretical heft. In so doing, I have explored the power relations that underlie the relationships between the "founding fathers" such as Jefferson, or Washington, Madison, or Franklin—each of whom I have discussed at various points thus far—and the enslaved men and women who enabled each and every one of their celebrated (and less celebrated) acts. I have also considered methods for approaching the relationships between the enslaved and formerly enslaved people, such as Harriet Jacobs, who committed their thoughts to paper, and the group of mostly white reformers, such as Lydia Maria Child, who edited and published their works. I have also attempted to elaborate a set of techniques for identifying and extracting meaning from "underdetermined" documents such as cookbooks, including those authored by Malinda Russell, Amelia Simmons, and Mary Randolph (Parrish, 265). In the process, I have sought to show how the archive of eating overlaps both materially and conceptually with the archive of slavery in the early United States.

In explicitly shifting the focus from the archive of eating to the archive of slavery, an additional critical challenge comes into view: How does one pursue the silences in the archive without simultaneously reinforcing a *narrative* of silence? In other words, how does one avoid the damaging equation of silence in the archive with silence in life? For a book with absence at its center, this challenge is important to explicitly address. Those such as myself, who seek to study food and eating in the early

United States, might take heed of how those who study slavery in that same era have increasingly called for a shift away from identifying and recovering silences in the archive toward a new focus, instead, on animating the mysteries of the past. In conjuring a sense of these mysteries, scholars such as Saidiya Hartman and Marisa Fuentes, cited throughout this book, as well as Stephen Best, Avery Gordon, and Jeanette Bastian, among others, rely on a mixture of critical and creative methods.[11] But their methods are emphatically analog, as mine have also been thus far. To complement these aims, this chapter layers in an additional set of digital methods derived from the fields of computational linguistics and information visualization. In the work that follows, I show how digital methods might render visible certain absences in the archive of slavery, infusing these absences with additional meaning.

While the visualizations that I present in this chapter cannot counter what Hartman has characterized as the "irreparable violence of the Atlantic slave trade" ("Venus," 12), and they cannot redress what Best has identified as a consequence of chattel slavery—the fundamental "deformation" (151) of its archive—they can refocus our critical eye with respect to the contents that the archive of slavery *does* contain.[12] More specifically, they expose the pathways of connection between persons and among groups, as well as the networks of communication in which these men and women engaged, and the distributed impact of the labor they performed. Illuminating this movement through visualization contributes to a reframing of the archive of slavery as a site of action, rather than as a record of fixity or loss. This action, carried back to the archive of eating, is particularly helpful in acknowledging the lived experience and culinary expertise that contributed to the cultivation of republican taste, something we cannot ever access in full.

The Ghostly Presence of James Hemings

As indicated by Jefferson's request—to "send for" Hemings, and "tell him" he would be glad to receive him—Hemings was rarely, if ever, someone to whom Jefferson directly wrote. There are additional letters in *The Papers of Thomas Jefferson Digital Edition* that refer to Hemings, however, and these too can be identified by searching the archive's editorial notes as previously described. But the list of letters that results from such a search does little more than to reinscribe the absence of James Hemings in the Jefferson archive as a whole. The author or addressee of each letter appears in bold red type: "To Paul Bentalou, 25 August 1786," "From Philip Mazzei, 17 April 1787," while James Hemings, the subject of the search, is relegated to smaller type, often encased in brackets, for Hemings was most often referred to by first name alone, most likely, as Lucia Stanton points out, to "preserve conscience and principle by increasing the social distance between master and slave" (84). Rather than reveal his role in crafting Jefferson's notion of republican taste, a contribution that would clearly justify his presence in the Jefferson archive, the format of this list of search results reinforces the transactional nature of the system that placed him, like Harriet Jacobs, as discussed in chapter 4, outside the realm of humanity altogether.

But a rank-ordered list is not the only way in which search results can be presented. Consider, instead, a visualization of those same letters that I created, which dramatically shifts the archival frame. I see this shift as enabling a focus on the "surface of things" (Foucault, 58). This phrase, borrowed from Michel Foucault, is central to Stephen Best and Sharon Marcus's formulation of "surface reading," a set of critical practices that emphasizes attending to the materiality of the text and the structure of its language, as well as to our own affective or ethical response to the work. This perspective, Best and Marcus believe, can counter the symptomatic reading practices that insist on excavating deeper meaning and exhuming hidden truths. Surface reading, they explain, enables scholars to see shadows in the archive as "presences, not absences, and let ghosts be ghosts, instead of saying what they are ghosts *of*" (13). For Best and Marcus, as for many scholars of slavery, the ghost functions as an additional figure of absence. In its liminal status, it represents the condition of social death experienced by the enslaved. In its shadowy form, it captures a sense of what is palpable, yet cannot be fully grasped. In its lingering presence, it conjures a sense of the haunting of the present by the past. In its critical contribution, it gestures toward a textual plane that "insists on being looked *at* rather than [one that] we must train ourselves to see *through*" (9).

The figure of the ghost, like the notion of the surface—or, for that matter, like the illusory experience of eating that I have explored throughout this book—suggests something readily perceptible but not easily understood. Indeed, there are times when absences in the archive must linger, and the example of the absences associated with James Hemings's life, and his tragic death, is one such time. We cannot gain access to his

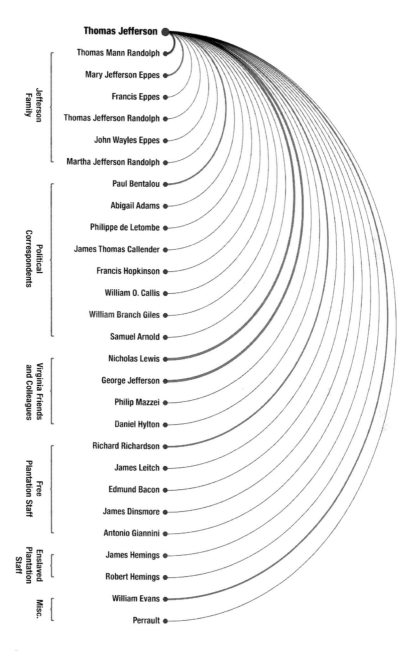

Figure 13. An arc diagram that visualizes Jefferson's correspondence concerning James Hemings. Image by the author.

inner life, nor should we necessarily continue to seek to do so. And while we might consider how his life might be reimagined in the present, as Colson Whitehead did for Harriet Jacobs, as discussed in chapter 4, we might learn more if we begin by asking not only *what*, but also *how* we have come to know.

The visualization in Figure 13 represents one way in which we might begin by asking how we have come to know. I created this image using Protovis, a JavaScript-based tool kit for data visualization developed by the Stanford Visualization Group.[13] Protovis facilitates a range of formats for visualizing social network data, including the arc diagram. Unlike the force-directed layouts more commonly employed to visualize network data, the arc diagram clearly identifies each individual, or "node," in the network, but foregrounds the connections between nodes—or "edges" in network terminology—through the arcs that dominate the image.[14] I generated the underlying data by searching the archive's content and editorial notes for letters that concerned James Hemings, using the expanded search features described earlier in this chapter. After compiling the search data in a spreadsheet, I then wrote a script in the Python programming language to convert the spreadsheet to the JavaScript Object Notation (JSON) format required by Protovis. This process involved identifying each correspondent that mentioned Hemings as a unique node; identifying each additional person with whom that individual had corresponded about Hemings; and then calculating the number of letters each pair of correspondents had exchanged. Even at this level, the level of the archive's surface, the process of enumerating the letters that mention Hemings begins to illuminate his presence in the archive, suggesting how correspondence networks such as these can provide a means of visually acknowledging the archive's ghosts.

One notable feature of the arc diagram is that it allows clusters of nodes to be arranged into groups. In this case, I grouped the people who corresponded about James Hemings according to their relationship to Jefferson. Reading from left to right, the diagram lists Jefferson and his family, his political correspondents, his Virginia friends and colleagues, his plantation overseers and free plantation staff, his enslaved plantation staff, and finally, people who do not fall into any of those categories, or about whom we have little or no biographical information. An arc connecting two names indicates correspondence between them, and the width of the arc indicates the frequency with which they corresponded.

Because this data is derived from Jefferson's personal archive, all of the arcs, as expected, connect to him. The widest arcs link Jefferson with Nicholas Lewis, Jefferson's neighbor in Virginia; George Jefferson, Thomas Jefferson's Virginia agent (although apparently not a close family relation); and Richard Richardson, who worked as a plantation overseer at Monticello. Presumably, Jefferson corresponded with each of these men about the materials and services required for Hemings to create his artful cookery for the plantation's residents and guests. In this way, the surface view of Jefferson's correspondence also acknowledges the reach of Hemings's cooking—centered in the kitchen, but extending across Monticello in the ingredients he purchased, the dinners he prepared, and the politics he subsequently influenced through the flavors of his food.[15]

However, the fourth wide arc in this diagram, the arc that connects Jefferson to Evans, cannot be linked to Hemings's culinary labor. This is an insight that the archive's surface view makes visible in a way that a listing of the same results does not. As previously noted, William Evans, by his location at the Indian Queen, served as a nodal point in the more material, and hence more easily preserved, network of print. For this reason, Evans's presence in the Jefferson archive is more readily discerned. In contrast to the return of a "Name" search for James Hemings, chillingly void, a "Name" search for William Evans yields a chain of correspondence through which additional details of Hemings's eventual fate can be discerned. An examination of this correspondence makes evident that Hemings had been involved in negotiations for employment with Jefferson well before Jefferson sought Evans's help. Having spent the first twenty-five years of his life in bondage, Hemings understood the importance of defining the terms of his employment in advance. As evinced by a letter written to Jefferson from another acquaintance, Francis Say, dated one day after Jefferson issued his request to Evans, Hemings had already requested that Jefferson "send him a few lines of engagement and on what conditions and what wages [Jefferson] would please to give him" (*Papers*, 33:53). Further specifying that the offer should be in Jefferson's "own hand wreiting [*sic*]," Hemings demonstrates his own awareness of the power of print—and, in particular, the power of Jefferson's personal hand, as president-elect—to stand in for the de jure agreement that his status as a black man, even free, precluded him from ever wielding to its full effect (*Papers,* 33:53).

For reasons unknown, Jefferson failed to comply with this request. The next letter in the archive is from Evans to Jefferson and suggests Hemings's confident tone. Although we do not know what Hemings actually said, Evans reports to Jefferson, "The answer he returned me, was, that he would not go [to Washington] untill [sic] you should write to himself" (*Papers,* 33:91). Here, we receive a powerful confirmation of Hemings's literacy, his business acumen, and his determined stance. Despite its importance, however, this letter does not appear in the results of a keyword search for James Hemings, as the editors have not added his name to the notes associated with this letter. Whether or not Evans influenced the outcome of this situation, the Jefferson archive also does not say. Hemings never became the chef at the White House. An eight-month gap in the correspondence between Jefferson and Evans ensues. The subsequent, and final, exchange in the archive, from November 1801, constitutes the entirety of the evidence that documents the circumstances of Hemings's suicide.

The ghost of James Hemings need not stand *for* something, as Best and Marcus caution. To be quite certain, the ghost of James Hemings means enough. And while we, as scholars, might seek to know more about Hemings's life, his story is one that is impossible to retrieve (Jefferson, *Papers,* 36:20). To recall the words of Hartman, every story that takes shape in the archive of slavery is "predicated upon impossibility— listening for the unsaid, translating misconstrued words, and refashioning disfigured lives—and intent on achieving an impossible goal: redressing the violence that produced numbers, ciphers, and fragments" (2–3). Thus even as we consider the information we might gain from the "numbers, ciphers, and fragments" in Jefferson's correspondence, transformed from absence into presence through computational means, we are reminded, with the foreknowledge of Hemings's suicide, of how little of his life— and not only his cooking—we will ever truly know.

Visualizing Absence in the Archive of Slavery

Is it possible to visualize the impossibility of retrieving knowledge about Hemings's life story? Even more fundamentally, is this a task that should be undertaken at all? As I have suggested throughout this book, I believe— following Hartman, Fuentes, and others—that the answer is, ultimately, yes. The stories of those like James Hemings are precisely what enable us to identify, in locations ranging from Jefferson's dinner table to the inn at the sign of the Indian Queen, the forms of cultural expression and of aesthetic taste that are too often underacknowledged in larger narratives of the nation's cultural foundation. More than that, the archival traces that document this sense of taste—precisely because of the impossibility of their full recovery, and the impossibility of complete redress—are what enable us to better comprehend the significance of the absences that structure the archive of slavery, as they do the archive of the United States as a whole.

But how, then, to pursue this task? The unlikely confluence of an archive always already deformed and a methodological school associated with the digital humanities that makes use of the term "deformative criticism" suggests one approach. In *Reading Machines,* Stephen Ramsay describes how the process of "deliberately and literally" altering the "graphic and semantic codes" of a text through computational means—what he calls the digital "deformance" of the text—results in a "critical self-consciousness that is difficult to achieve otherwise."[16] According to Ramsay, this "critical self-consciousness," by which he means a deliberate form of subjective engagement with the text, allows the "liberation of the potentialities of meaning."[17] In the case of James Hemings, however, this subjective engagement exposes the impossibilities of meaning. The result becomes, instead, an image that holds open the space of absence, enabling those who view it to contemplate, and make meaning from, what knowledge remains undisclosed.

In this image of absence, pictured on the next page, I sought to dismantle the letter as the unit of the archive. Rather than privilege the relationships between letter writers, I examined each word of content on an equal plane. To begin, I obtained the letters included in *The Papers of Thomas Jefferson Digital Edition* in XML form from the University of Virginia Press.[18] I then extracted the content of the letters from the XML files.[19] Next, I employed a technique from the field of computational linguistics called "named entity recognition" (NER), which is used to automatically identify, or "recognize," the words in a document, or set of documents, that represent the names of things, such as people or places. For instance, the mention of "James" in the phrase, "my former servant James" would be identified as a person, in contrast to how the editors of the *Digital Edition* only identified the people to whom Jefferson wrote letters, or from whom he received same. With the help of the NER software (I used the implementation included in the Stanford CoreNLP tool kit), I was

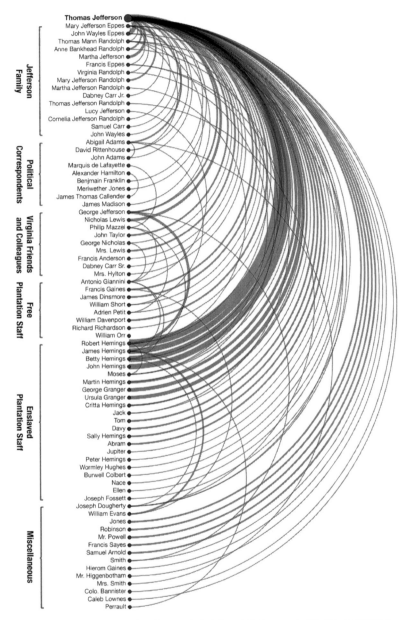

*Figure 14. An arc diagram that visualizes the network of relations within the corpus I call the "Hemings Papers."
Image by the author.*

able to automatically identify most of the references to people mentioned by name in the contents of the twenty-five thousand letters that had been digitized at the time I conducted the initial analysis for this project.

For the purposes of this visualization, however, I limited my scope to the fifty-one letters that the editors of *The Papers of Thomas Jefferson* identified as including references to Hemings or to a member of the Hemings family. To this more selective corpus, I added the seven letters I discovered through additional search techniques, including a letter that refers to what Jefferson came to call the "tragical end of James Hemmings" (*Papers,* 36:20).[20] I again employed NER to identify the people named in the letters, and then wrote a Python script to parse the output into human-readable form. The result was a list of names, which I then reviewed by hand in order to eliminate the discernable errors and duplicates, such as the fact that "Hemings" was sometimes spelled with one "m" and sometimes with two, as in the line quoted just above. The fact that Jefferson almost always used diminutives when referring to the men and women he enslaved also contributed to the complexity of the data under analysis. James Hemings, for example, was referred to as Jamey, Jim, and even Gimmé while in France.[21] After resolving such discrepancies to the best of my knowledge, I then wrote a second script, also in Python, in order to determine which names appeared together in the same letter. Finally, I formatted these relationships to be displayed in the arc diagram as shown.

Because this visualization shows the relationships among people mentioned *in* the letters, rather than the people to whom Jefferson wrote (or from whom he received letters), what emerges into view is evidence of the complexity of the relations among individuals, and across social groups. Significantly, the arcs that link Jefferson to the men and women he enslaved are much more prominent than those that link him to his family members and friends, suggesting the degree to which Jefferson relied on his enslaved plantation staff to implement his various directives. One can imagine that these directives included the purchase of provisions for his table, seeds for his farm and gardens, and other supplies that supported his project of producing republican taste. In this way, the visualization conjures a sense of the scope of Jefferson's dependence on the men and women he enslaved in order to advance this project, even as it cannot re-create what these people said in their conversations with Jefferson or with each other, where they went in order to conduct their required transactions, or how they truly lived their everyday lives.

The multiple, overlapping arcs that comprise this visualization also prompt further consideration about the multiple networks of power embedded in the Jefferson archive. There is evidence, of course, of the chokehold of slavery, that "encapsulation" of capitalism that, as Paul Gilroy has demonstrated, "provided the foundations for a distinctive network of economic, social, and political relations" that persist to this day (55). But the arcs that link Hemings and his family to the other enslaved men and women on the plantation also provide a visual marker of the economic, social, and political networks that were sustained through systems of communication that "passed below the radar," as Ivy Wilson has observed, and therefore are far more difficult to perceive in the archive today (29). In other words, because the relationships that are visualized are derived from the names mentioned in the letters, but do not correspond to any specific relationship beyond appearing together in the same letter, they are more abstract than, for instance, the correspondence network depicted in Figure 13, which shows the documented relationships among those who wrote to and received letters from Jefferson. After all, goods bartered or exchanged leave no financial record, news communicated orally leaves no written trace, and political rhetoric articulated in the vernacular leaves no tangible ideology, so these actions and ideas can never be as clearly documented in a textual archive as can writers and recipients of letters. This image thus helps to conjure a sense of the other powerful networks that are contained, if not explicitly documented, within *The Papers of Thomas Jefferson.*

To return to the documents in the archive with this image in view fundamentally shifts our focus. As confirmation, consider this letter from Jefferson to Evans, written on November 1, 1801, the first in the trail of correspondence to reveal his awareness of Hemings's death: "A report has come here through some connection of one of my servants that James Hemings my former cook has committed an act of suicide. As this whether true or founded will give uneasiness to his friends, will you be so good as to ascertain the truth & communicate it to me" (*Papers*, 35:542). This letter endures in the archive as an emblem of the "precarious lives which are visible only in the moment of their disappearance," as Hartman eloquently asserts (12). Notably, this letter, which is the first entry to appear in the results of a search for "James Hemings" in the *Digital Edition,* is one of only two documents in the archive that refer to Hemings by both first and last name. The letter is also significant for the oral "report" that it documents, the reference to the "connection" of one of Jefferson's "servants," and the mention of the "friends" who uneasily await confirmation of this news. Jefferson's language thus points to Wilson's below-the-radar networks of communication, as well as to the social networks that supported Hemings, and the circulation of subjects—Hemings once among them—who moved apart from the plantation world that Jefferson sought to control. To visualize this movement within the archive, rather than to represent the archive as static or fixed, resists what Best has described as the "logic and ethic of recovery" that reinscribes bodies and voices as lost (157). This image of absence, instead, challenges us as scholars to make the unrecorded stories that we detect—about eating as about life—expand with motion and meaning.

The Long Arc of Visual Display

At a time when the use of data visualization is becoming increasingly prevalent both in popular culture and in scholarly work, we must also, necessarily, recall the long, fraught history of visual display. It is not without irony to observe that this history passes directly through Jefferson and the way in which he utilized his own graphical displays of information, in the form of charts, lists, diagrams, and tables, to advance his empirical worldview. As I. Bernard Cohen explains, the "inductive" approach to knowledge favored by Jefferson and many others at the time "implied an experiential test of knowledge or of system, the same kind of criterion of truth that in the sciences had become Newton's 'Proof by Experiments,' or a reliance on critical observations."[22] This reliance on "critical observations" in turn derived from the Lockean belief that the creation of knowledge begins with sense perception, the same belief that undergirded the philosophy of taste. When applied to the sense of sight, this belief occasioned the emergence of additional ideologies, as well as a new form of scientific expression, a form that could more effectively convey the "factual" nature of the phenomena observed.

Jefferson forged his approach to visual knowledge-making at the College of William and Mary, where he studied with the Scottish mathematician and natural philosopher William Small. In his autobiography, Jefferson cites Small as his most significant mentor. "From his conversation," Jefferson recalls, "I got my first views of the expansion of science and of the system of things in which we are placed" (*Memoir*, 1:2). Jefferson also notes that Small returned to Europe, although he does not comment on Small's subsequent career. But only a decade later, in the 1770s, Small would go on to train the young William Playfair, the Scottish political economist now viewed as the leading progenitor of modern data visualization.[23] Playfair employed painstakingly composed charts and graphs—many the first of their kind—in order to advance his economic and political arguments about the British Empire. In "Exports & Imports to and from All North America," pictured in Figure 15, Playfair effectively demonstrates the impact of the American Revolution on Great Britain's balance of trade. Unlike Jefferson, he was not certain that revolution, at home or abroad, would result in any positive effect. As he explains in the preface to the third edition of *The Commercial and Political Atlas,* published in 1801, "A great change is now operating in Europe, and . . . it is impossible to guess in what it will most likely terminate" (iii–iv). Although he feared that the new century might be defined by "war and contention," he agreed with Jefferson about one thing: that the visual format of his charts and tables would ensure that the underlying data would be understood and remembered for generations to come (iv). "On inspecting any one of these charts attentively," he pronounces in the introduction, "a sufficiently distinct impression will be made, to remain unimpaired for a time, and the idea which does remain will be simple and complete" (xiv).

Jefferson demonstrates a similar desire to present an idea that remains "simple and complete" in his *Notes on the State of Virginia,* first discussed in chapter 1. The *Notes* constituted Jefferson's extended response to the Comte de Buffon's theory of New World inferiority, or "degeneration," as he termed it. Widely considered the most famous example of this form of scientific expression (and scientific racism) in the United States, the *Notes* includes, for example, tables comparing the size of animals in Europe and America, listings of indigenous American vegetables, and an extensive catalog of Virginian birds. As Bruce Dain observes, Jefferson's visual presentation of these "supposedly unvarnished facts," without recourse to analysis or explanation, was intended to "testif[y] that Buffon's idea of the inferiority of New World nature was absurd, an instance of prejudice and over-theoretical imagination running away with the facts" (28). In Jefferson's mind, as in Playfair's, the visual presentation of evidence aligned it more closely with an inductive methodology, and bolstered belief in the factual basis of what had been observed firsthand.

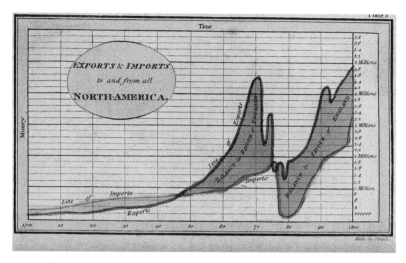

Figure 15. This time series chart, "Exports & Imports to and from All North-America," created by William Playfair, appears in The Commercial and Political Atlas, 3rd ed. (London: J. Wallis, 1801). Playfair is often cited as one of the early innovators of modern data visualization. Courtesy of the Library Company of Philadelphia.

The implications of the visual rhetoric of the *Notes* also extend from Jefferson's desire to assert the unequivocal nature of the evidence presented, to a parallel attempt—informed by the discourse of taste—to enforce a unanimity of response among the book's citizen readers. Christopher Looby, in his work on the political dimensions of taxonomic natural history, draws upon moral sense theory (if not the discourse of taste directly) in his argument about how the preponderance of "graphical, two-dimensional" modes of presentation in the *Notes* was deliberately "intended to foster" a "uniformity of sentiments and conceptions" among those who read the book (265). Because the nation's democratic governance relied upon the citizens themselves to make appropriate political decisions, it was of crucial importance to Jefferson, as we learned in chapter 1, that these citizens learn to cultivate a uniform set of behaviors and beliefs. Thus in his graphical mode of presentation, as in the table comparing the quadrupeds of Europe and America pictured in Figure 16, we see how Jefferson promotes a form of political control beyond the sense of taste; this is one enforced through his visual display.

But Jefferson had no public audience in mind when he traced the columns, rows, and rule lines in the small, leather-bound volume that he

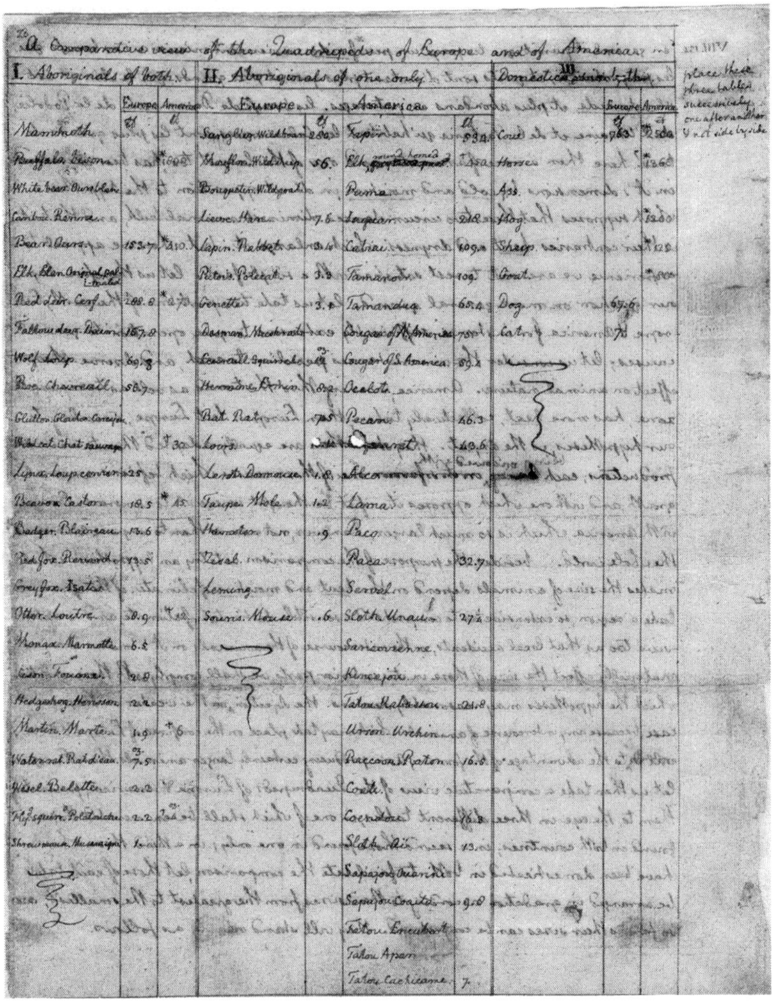

A Comparative view of the Quadrupeds of Europe and of America.

I. Aboriginals of both.

II. Aboriginals of one only.

Europe. America.

III. Domestic

place these three tables successively one after another & not side by side

Figure 16. The manuscript version of Thomas Jefferson's chart, "A Comparative View of the Quadrupeds of Europe and of America," which appears in Notes on the State of Virginia *(1781–85). Courtesy of the Massachusetts Historical Society.*

called his "Farm-book," pictured in Figure 17. In the Farm-book, Jefferson recorded the names, birth dates (when known), familial relationships, present locations, and countries of origin of the men, women, and children he enslaved. In the representation of this information about the people of Monticello in diagrams that resemble the charts and tables of the

Notes, Jefferson enacts a far more odious form of subjugation and control: his reduction of persons to objects, and stories to names. In contrast to the story of James Hemings, told through a combination of presences and absences in the Jefferson archive, the single line in the Farm-book that fixes James Hemings—"Jemmy. 1765."—serves as a reminder of the violence that can be enacted through visual display. "There is no bloodless data in slavery's archive," as Jessica Marie Johnson reminds us. "Data is the evidence of terror, and the idea of data as fundamental and objective . . . obscures rather than reveals the scene of the crime" (70). The "crime" to which Johnson refers is the first enunciative act of enslavement: of transforming a rich human life into salable property by recording that person's identifying information as data in a book. In this context, the data of James Hemings in the Farm-book conjures a cautionary tale of its own: a reminder to examine the underlying assumptions and biases embedded in the research methods, the technical structures, and the methods of presentation that we, as scholars of that archive, employ.

In a now canonical essay of the digital humanities, "Humanities Approaches to Graphical Display," Johanna Drucker cautions that scholars in the field must resist the "intellectual Trojan horse" of data visualization, in which "assumptions about what constitutes information . . . are cloaked in a rhetoric taken wholesale from the techniques of the empirical sciences that conceals their epistemological biases under a guise of familiarity" (para. 1). By these "techniques," Drucker refers to the panoply of line charts and bar charts that appear in contemporary scientific publications, which can be traced directly back to Thomas Jefferson, as we have just learned. But in the more specific case of how Jefferson records the life of James Hemings in his Farm-book, we should take heed to recall the "epistemological biases" of Enlightenment humanism itself. One by-product of the belief in the human capacity for reason—and, in particular, of the ability to transform sensory experience into knowledge—is the assumption that anything observable carries the status of a fact.[24] We see this very perversion of observational science in Jefferson's own lack of understanding of his range of scientific, social, and personal biases. By recording Hemings as "data" in his Farm-book, Jefferson supposed that Hemings might become an object of empirical knowledge, one not only controlled but also understood through visible, visualizable facts.

In this way, the Farm-book calls into question the positivist rhetoric so often associated with contemporary data visualization, rhetoric that

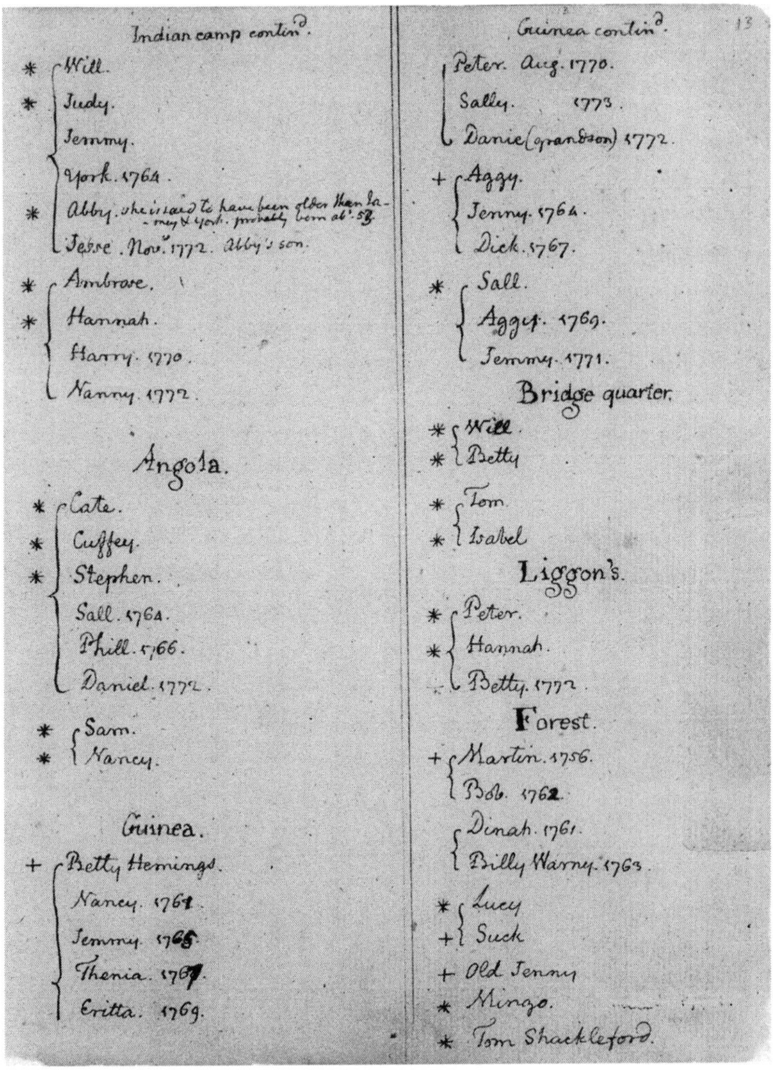

Indian camp contin.ᵈ

* ⎰ Will.
* ⎱ Judy.
    Jemmy.
    York. 1764.
*   Abby. she is said to have been elder than Ja-
       — my & York. probably born ab.ᵗ 58.
    Jesse. Nov.ᵣ 1772. Abby's son.
* ⎰ Ambrose.
* ⎱ Hannah.
    Harry. 1770.
    Nanny. 1772.

Angola.

* ⎰ Cate.
* ⎱ Cuffey.
*   Stephen.
    Sall. 1764.
    Phill. 1766.
    Daniel. 1772.

* ⎰ Sam.
* ⎱ Nancy.

Guinea.

+   Betty Hemings.
    Nancy. 1761.
    Jemmy. 1765.
    Thenia. 1767.
    Critta. 1769.

Guinea contin.ᵈ

    Peter. Aug. 1770.
    Sally. 1773.
    Danie (grandson) 1772.

+   Aggy.
    Jenny. 1764.
    Dick. 1767.

*   Sall.
    Aggy. 1769.
    Jemmy. 1771.

Bridge quarter.

* ⎰ Will.
* ⎱ Betty
* ⎰ Tom.
* ⎱ Isabel

Liggon's.

*   Peter.
*   Hannah.
    Betty. 1772.

Forest.

+   Martin. 1756.
    Bob. 1762.
    Dinah. 1761.
    Billy Warny. 1763.

*   Lucy
+   Suck
+   Old Jenny
*   Mingo.
*   Tom Shackleford.

Figure 17. The page in one of Thomas Jefferson's "Farm-books"—journals he kept from 1774 to 1824—that inscribes James Hemings's enslavement into the archive as "Jemmy. 1765." Courtesy of the Massachusetts Historical Society.

derives from Jefferson and his age. It is no coincidence that critics most often point to Jefferson's racial taxonomies, as articulated in the *Notes,* as evidence of the limits of his empirical science. Certainly, as Timothy Sweet has suggested, Jefferson's assessment that "the races of black and red men . . . have never yet been viewed by us as subjects of natural history" indicates how Jefferson fails to "reflect critically on his own process of data-gathering and inference, [and] on the larger implications of the paradigm in which he work[ed]" (110). Following Foucault, Sweet cites these lines as an instance of the epistemological "gap in the Enlightenment scientific paradigm" that prompted the emergence of the modern human sciences (110). Thus when Drucker contends, in her essay on visualization, that the "humanistic concept of knowledge depends upon the interplay between a situated and circumstantial viewer and the objects or experiences under examination and interpretation," we might more precisely identify the gap made manifest by Jefferson's unreflective scientific racism as the one that, heeding Drucker, we as scholars must seek to close.

Jefferson's epistemology of the visible—what I have defined as the tripartite relation that he posits between the observable, the visualizable, and the truth—also subtends his conception of race. Recall from chapter 1 how Jefferson understood black and white people as "distinct" racial groups (*Notes,* 270). Also recall from that chapter how Jefferson sought to reserve certain internal capabilities—namely, the capability to cultivate good taste—for white people alone. In his racial taxonomies, we can see an additional attempt to identify certain external features—visible features—that might allow him to continue to enforce his damaging racial divide.

The visualizations of James Hemings's traces in the archive that I have presented in this chapter seek to reveal the "grid of control" that consigned him first to social and then to corporeal death (Chun, 56).[25] They also seek to reveal a "lived social reality" rich with community, kinship, and support (57). In the context of an archive—and an ideology—that effaces these relations, I have sought to use what Wendy H. K. Chun describes as "the technology of race" against itself (40). By deforming the archive through computational and visual means, I have sought to reveal some of the possibilities of recognition that *The Papers of Thomas Jefferson* itself resists. I have also endeavored to expose the impossibilities of recognition—and of cognition—that remain essential to our understanding of the archive of slavery today.

Culinary Labor, Digital Work, and the Archive of the Early United States

Jefferson's "emancipation agreement" with James Hemings, introduced in chapter 1, is another document that, we now know, Jefferson penned in his special ink, encased in his imported paper, copied in his copying press, and then placed in his personal archive to preserve.[26] In that document, the second of the two in the entire Jefferson archive that refer to Hemings by his full name, Jefferson insists that Hemings train another person "to be a good cook" before he can be freed (*Papers*, 27:119). With this stipulation, Jefferson offers enduring textual evidence of Hemings's culinary expertise. The fact that Jefferson decided to preserve this document in his personal archive reveals how he was, at times, required to recognize—if not ever to redress—the flawed logic that suggested Hemings should be reduced to data in order for his labor to be seen. In sharp contrast to the entry for James Hemings in Jefferson's Farm-book, which is a distillation of stolen labor, and life, of the highest degree, the emancipation agreement with Hemings identifies his labor as an "art"— indeed as techne—the precise form of applied, experiential knowledge that Jefferson himself most esteemed.

As exemplified by the copying press that he not only utilized but also designed, Jefferson particularly admired the "mechanic arts," as technical knowledge was then described, and saw such arts as intimately related to his empirical worldview (Marx, 3). And yet, Jefferson's supposition that if Hemings were to simply train a replacement cook then his absence would not be felt at Monticello reveals an additional limitation of his observing eye: his lack of awareness that there were aspects of Heming's culinary work that he was unable to perceive. In the agreement, Jefferson does not acknowledge the intellectual aspects of Heming's cookery, such as his ability to select the particular foodstuffs that would represent Monticello's unique terroir or to combine flavors that would best please the palates of Jefferson and his guests. Neither does Jefferson register the affective impact of Heming's cooking—the work of influencing, through Hemings's specific methods of preparation and presentation, the development of Jefferson's own conception of republican taste. The condition of chattel slavery of course fundamentally precludes any equivalence between Hemings's culinary labor and work today. But it remains instructive to consider how the dimensions of Hemings's techne that transcend the visible might, in turn, help to illuminate the invisible aspects of digital labor in the present.

With this notion of invisible labor in mind, let us return to the Jefferson archive as we most often encounter it today, in *The Papers of Thomas Jefferson Digital Edition*. When we are reading a letter from that archive online, as I described with respect to Jefferson's letter to Evans that began this chapter, we see only the final result of the myriad forms of labor that led to the archive's digital instantiation. Like the "artful cookery" for which James Hemings was renowned, we must work backward from the finished product in order to identify the work—intellectual and affective as much as technical—that went into the archive's finished form.[27] More specifically, we must consider the processes that contribute to creating a digital archive, those that, like a single dish of Hemings's creation, involve much larger networks of people, resources, and ideas. There is, for example, the process of transcribing each letter in the Jefferson archive from his original handwriting to the structured XML that underlies the contents of the *Digital Edition*. This was likely a process that took place over decades, and was enacted by numerous people in multiple roles: first the editors of the print edition (or more likely, their research assistants), who transcribed the manuscripts into the text printed in each book; then those who took that text and transformed it from something like a Microsoft Word document into a plain text file, which could then be further manipulated as data; and then those who inserted the XML tags that would mark each section of each letter, and each notable feature, so that they could be formatted on the screen. Each of these portions of the process drew upon different sets of skills: first, the ability to decipher eighteenth-century penmanship; then, the capacity to translate machine-readable text across multiple file formats; and then, the knowledge of XML and related encoding standards, as well as the ability to contribute to a technical project team, to name only a few. Like the people and their skills who contributed to any single one of Hemings's culinary confections, we cannot know each of their names, or the details of the roles that they played. But a consideration of the processes that we know to have contributed to the final product, as well as the skills that were required for each phase, can do much to acknowledge the otherwise invisible labor that contributes to the information in the archive that we are able to see, and learn from, today.[28]

We are not able to see any of James Hemings's "artful cookery," of course. Nor can we ever hope to taste it. But there exists one artifact that gets us closer to the labor, both visible and invisible, that Hemings contributed

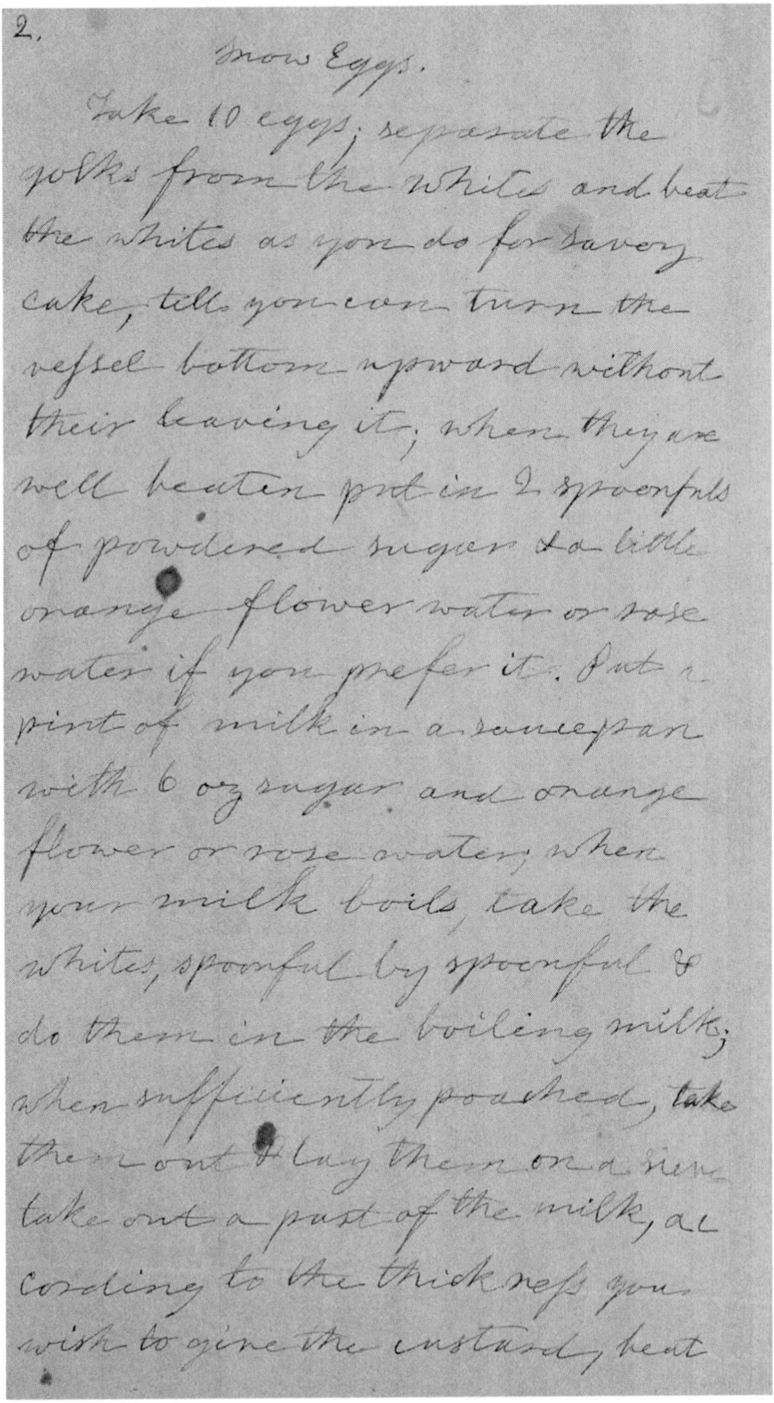

2.

Snow Eggs.

Take 10 eggs; separate the
yolks from the whites and beat
the whites as you do for savory
cake, till you can turn the
vessel bottom upward without
their leaving it; when they are
well beaten put in 2 spoonfuls
of powdered sugar & a little
orange flower water or rose
water if you prefer it. Put 1
pint of milk in a saucepan
with 6 oz sugar and orange
flower or rose water; when
your milk boils, take the
whites, spoonful by spoonful &
do them in the boiling milk;
when sufficiently poached, take
them out & lay them on a sieve
take out a part of the milk, ac
cording to the thickness you
wish to give the custard, beat

Figure 18. The only recipe explicitly attributed to James Hemings, for "Snow Eggs," can be found in the family recipe book of Thomas Jefferson's granddaughter, Virginia Jefferson Randolph Trist. Copyright Thomas Jefferson Foundation at Monticello.

up the yolks & stir them in
the remainder; as soon as it
thickens take the mixture
from the fire, strain it through
a sieve; dish up your whites
& pour the custard over them.
A little wine stirred in is a
great improvement.

James, cook at Monticello.

Chocolate cream.

Put on your milk, 1qt to 2
squares of chocolate; boil it away
one quarter; take it off, let it
cool, & sweeten it; lay a napkin
in a bowl, put 3 gizzards in the
napkin or a bowl & pass the cream
through it four times, as quick as
possible, one person rubbing the
gizzards with a spoon while another
pours. Put it in cups & set the cups
in cold water halfway up their
sides. Let the water on the fire,

to each dish that he put on Jefferson's table. It is a recipe that appears in a cookbook kept by Virginia Jefferson Randolph Trist, Thomas Jefferson's granddaughter; one of three hundred she transcribed from a wide range of sources. This particular recipe is labeled "Snow Eggs," and it describes the process of making an elaborate meringue. The meringue requires ten eggs, the yolks separated from the whites. The whites are whipped, infused with powdered sugar and an additional flavor—either orange flower or rose water "if you prefer." The mixture is then poached in a milk bath, "spoonful by spoonful," yielding a set of oval-shaped meringues that resemble the eggs from which they came. The remaining milk bath is then cooked down into a custard, "according to the thickness you wish to give" it. The custard—what we would call today a *sauce anglaise*—is then strained and poured over the meringues, which then rise to the top. "A little wine stirred in is a great improvement," we are told. The recipe concludes with a line of attribution, "James, cook at Monticello."

This "James" is, of course, James Hemings. While Jefferson himself transcribed several recipes for some of his (presumably) favorite dishes, some of which were likely dictated to him by Hemings, this is the only known recipe, in any archive, to be explicitly credited to Hemings himself.[29] That it exists not in the Jefferson archive, but in a set of papers housed at the University of Virginia Library that span the years 1825 to 1936, points to how Hemings's own culinary legacy, as much as the republican taste that his cuisine enabled, extended far beyond the end of his tragically abbreviated life. The number of advanced techniques involved in the recipe—the whipping of the egg whites into an airy cream; the poaching of the spoonfuls of cream back into egg shape; and the precision required in the cooking of the custard—each attest to the high degree of Hemings's culinary training and skill. In addition, the numerous references to choices that were required to be made in the midst of the cooking process—the flavor of the egg mixture, the texture of the custard, and the addition (or not) of wine—underscore the various forms of tacit knowledge, invisible to the eye, that Hemings also possessed to the highest degree.

There is something affirming about the circular yellow and brown stains that dot the recipe, suggesting that this particular cooking process was followed by Trist or someone in her kitchen, and therefore further suggesting that Hemings's influence could be experienced, to some degree, decades after the last meal that Hemings himself ever prepared. And yet the idea that Jefferson's granddaughter—and not any of Hemings's kin—

would be the one to perform this embodied incantation of Hemings's "artful cookery" produces an equal-but-opposite sense of unease. We do not have equivalent records that document the Hemings family, of course. But the affective dimensions of this lack, whether experienced as unease, or silence, or shadow, or absence—as I have named it in this chapter—also holds value. For it is through these unsettling absences that the most expansive version of the archive of the early United States emerges into view. This is an archive that encompasses impossibility, and that knowingly depends upon the interplay between scholar and text, as well as between archival technologies and archivists. An emphasis on eating offers one entry point into this expanded archive, but there exist many more. What unites these multiple points of access is an understanding of the archive—of the early United States, or of any other domain—not as a neutral repository of knowledge, but instead as a tool for exposing the limits of our knowledge. It is only by acknowledging these limits that we can, at last, begin to see.

Two Portraits of Taste

There are no extant recipes directly attributed to Hercules, the man whose "elegant" cookery elevated the kitchen at Mount Vernon—and later, the President's House in Philadelphia—to the highest level of haute cuisine. But there does exist one artifact that has been employed by scholars over the past several decades to conjure an image of the man who was once described as "one of the most finished and renowned dandies of the age," and whose physical appearance "entitle[d] him to be compared with his namesake of fabulous history" (Conkling, 151; Custis, 422). It is a painting long known as *Portrait of George Washington's Cook,* part of the permanent collection of the Museo Nacional Thyssen-Bornemisza, an art museum housed in a former palace in Madrid. Through at least the summer of 2017, it was installed in a gilded frame at one end of a long rectangular hall, one of two rooms in the museum dedicated to North American painting. [1] The wall text attributed the painting to Gilbert Stuart, the Rhode Island–born, British-trained painter most famous for the portrait of Washington that appears on the one-dollar bill. On the wall text, the date range given for the painting was 1795–97, a span that corresponds to the final years that Hercules spent cooking at the President's House.[2] In the painting, the sitter is depicted against a muted brown background in a style that was typical for the time. He is dressed in a white coat, white necktie, and in what appears to be white chef's toque; his hands are at his sides. His body is drawn at bust length, turned slightly to the side. His eyes probe the viewer; his facial expression hints at a smile.

I was never able to travel to the Thyssen-Bornemisza Museum, but I was able to determine these details about the painting because the museum decided to create a digital archive of high-resolution images of all of the artifacts in its permanent collection, made accessible to the public through a link on its website. In the summer of 2017, as I was completing the first full draft of this book, I went to the website, followed the link to the archive, searched for the painting, and downloaded an image of *Portrait of George Washington's Cook*. Seeking more information about how the painting was actually installed, I wrote to a colleague who was then living in Madrid, asking if he would not mind paying a visit to the museum and letting me know what he saw. He agreed, and several weeks later, he wrote back with detailed notes, a panoramic image of the gallery in which the painting was displayed, and scans of the various maps and guides provided to in-person visitors to the museum. I drafted the above description, corroborated the details with the materials that my colleague had compiled, and sent my book manuscript off for review.

In early 2019, in the process of securing permission to include an image of *Portrait of George Washington's Cook* in this Epilogue, I returned to the museum's website. I went through the same process that I had employed two years earlier. I clicked the link to the archive, typed in the name of the painting, and clicked "search." This time, however, the search yielded no results. It was not just that the image was unavailable; there was no record of the painting—nor of Washington, nor Hercules, nor even of Gilbert Stuart—in the catalog at all.

I had some idea as to what had happened. In the several years prior, art historians had begun to disagree as to whether the man shown in the portrait was Hercules, as well as to whether the portrait was in fact painted by Stuart. Proponents of the argument in favor of the sitter being Hercules cited his penchant for fashion as a possible reason for his trend-setting toque. (Culinary historians generally agree that it was not until the 1820s that the chef's toque was popularized, by one of Grimod de la Reynière's French inheritors, the chef Marie-Antoine Carême.)[3] They also cited the fact that Stuart was working on several portraits of Washington during the time when Hercules served in the President's House, and in all likelihood sampled his cooking.[4] But others, citing inconsistencies such as the style of the chef's hat, as well as the fact that the painting is excluded from all major studies of Stuart, advised caution when attributing much historical significance to the piece.[5]

Unbeknownst to me, however, that caution had already been converted into curatorial action on the part of the Thyssen-Bornemisza Museum. As a result of a two-year-long study, which began shortly after my colleague visited the museum, it was conclusively determined that the portrait was not painted by Stuart; nor was the subject of the painting even a chef. Analysis revealed that the brushstrokes used in the painting, its method of conveying light and shadow, and the level of detail involved in the sitter's clothing, were not consistent with Stuart's style. An ultraviolet light analysis of the lead content of the paint revealed that the painting did indeed date to the late 1700s, but that finding served only to confirm that the painting could not be of Hercules. Because the chef's toque would have needed to have been added to the painting in the nineteenth century—a retroactive insertion intended to better signal to contemporaneous viewers that the sitter was a chef—that area would have needed to show evidence of having been painted over. While the ultraviolet light analysis found some evidence of overpainting, there was none in the area of the hat.[6] The "tantalizing possibilities" that the portrait once offered for learning more about Hercules's life, as Craig LaBan, a restaurant critic for the *Philadelphia Inquirer* who has devoted significant coverage to the portrait, once described them, were transformed into "disappointment" ("Shock," n.p.; "Disappears," n.p.). The traces of Hercules in the archive had become, once again, scant.

But this disappointment, and even the study that served as its source, also serve to confirm just how much we hunger for eating in the archive. In this book, I have attempted to show how we might begin to access such instances of eating and invest them with philosophical significance. From the meals prepared by chefs like Hercules and James Hemings for the first commanders in chief, to the dining room service (among other forms of assistance) proffered by personal valets like Paul Jennings, I have argued for the preparation, presentation, and consumption of food as sites of embodied philosophical thinking. I have further argued that the bodies that prepare, present, and consume—along with others involved in acts of aesthetic expression—serve as additional sites through which the dominant discourse of taste can be tested, contested, and transformed. As the bodies of Benjamin Franklin, Grimod de la Reynière, and Phillis Wheatley help to show, the judgments of taste that are alternately invited (as in the case of Franklin and, at times, Grimod) or imposed upon them (as in the case of Wheatley and, at other times, Grimod) further strengthen an argument about how "aesthetics is born as a discourse of the body," as Terry Eagleton once memorably wrote, and how it finds expression in a range of embodied and sensory acts (328). And yet, the realm of eating—among the most sensory and immediate aspects of aesthetic experience, and the very "root" of aesthetic thought, to borrow another of Eagleton's phrasings—is precisely what is left

Figure 19. In 2019, an ultraviolet light analysis of the painting known as Portrait of George Washington's Cook, which had been attributed to Gilbert Stuart, revealed insufficient overpainting for it to be of Hercules. A related analysis rejected the claim that the artist was Stuart. Photo by Craig LaBan. Courtesy of Craig LaBan/The Philadelphia Inquirer.

unrecorded in the archive, if it was ever recordable at all (328).[7] In contrast to the tradition of formal aesthetic philosophy, which is not only easily archived, but also easily circulated in print and today even online, these embodied expressions and speculative theories continue to resist preservation and circulation, even in the advent of digital technologies.

By calling attention to the significance of these expressions and theories of taste, as well as to what they leave unexplained, this book has attempted to correct any assumption that we can consider matters of taste without the body, or without the archive. Indeed, the challenge of recovering accounts of eating in the archive—or, alternatively, the challenge of reimagining what, like the portrait of Hercules, no longer exists—reveals how certain philosophical abstractions are in fact quite preservable, even as the physical objects that they imbue with significance are highly perishable. Here, we might consider the example of Malinda Russell's cookbook and the theory of satisfaction that it sets forth, which only recently entered an institutional archive (even as it had been preserved in a private collection for years). While Russell herself ceased preparing her delectable dishes more than a century ago, her recipes remain as records of how her food once functioned as a means of furthering her liberatory aims. At the same time, for every portion of the past that is preserved, there are many more that are not. We know nothing beyond the name of Fannie Steward, the "colored cook of Virginia" whom Russell credits with teaching her her "trade" (5). We know even less about the women whom Mary Randolph enslaved, whose names remain unknown, even as they directly contributed to her own method of culinary and corporeal control. Their ephemeral acts of aesthetic production perished with the dishes that they prepared—those they prepared both according to and, perhaps even more deliciously, against Randolph's methodical plan.

In this way, the archive of eating and its particular methodological and theoretical challenges open up to engage other sites of archival silence relating to enslaved peoples, paid servants, farm laborers, and women—the subjects whose knowledge and labor built the cultural and actual foundation of the United States. Our archives typically record the contributions of these laborers in documents that attest to the work that they performed. These documents are often dry, and are at times actively dehumanizing, as the example of Jefferson's Farm-book makes plain. Among the results of such acts of inscriptive violence is that the inner lives and personal philosophies of these men and women are most often relegated to the shadows of archives, if they appear at all. What is needed in order to expand the significance of these archival traces is an array of methods, both critical and creative.

Colson Whitehead's *The Underground Railroad* offers one such example of methodological synthesis. Whitehead employs historical fiction as a means of infusing additional interiority into the otherwise fragmentary accounts of inner life that emerge from the personal narratives of the antebellum era, such as Harriet Jacobs's *Incidents in the Life of a Slave Girl.* We might also consider how digital techniques, such as those explored in this book's final chapter, can help to augment the significance of archival fragments in other ways. By employing the techniques of social network analysis and data visualization, combined with an informed historical account, we can hold open the space to acknowledge what resists interpretation, and what will forever remain unknown.

Our ability to expand upon our knowledge of the past, and to infuse fragmentary artifacts—as well as their absence—with new meaning, is not limited to text alone. Consider now a second portrait, *Scipio Moorhead, Portrait of Himself, 1776* (2007) by the contemporary artist Kerry James Marshall. Scipio Moorhead was the enslaved black artist who is credited with creating the frontispiece for Phillis Wheatley's *Poems on Various Subjects, Religious and Moral,* as discussed in chapter 2. A black painter himself, Marshall is most interested in giving visual form to Moorhead, about whom little is known. He depicts Moorhead in the act of art making in the same way that Moorhead once depicted Wheatley. The artist is shown standing in front of an easel, his brush poised in midstroke. His left hand holds the canvas to the easel, securing it as he paints. The title of Marshall's portrait, *Scipio Moorhead, Portrait of Himself, 1776,* offers the work to Moorhead as his own. That gesture is perhaps an acknowledgment that Moorhead's status as an enslaved man virtually ensured that any self-portraits he might have painted, should they ever have existed, would not have been preserved.[8] In fact, it is primarily because one of the poems in Wheatley's volume—"To S.M. a Young *African* Painter, on seeing his Works"—is thought to describe an earlier experience of seeing Moorhead's paintings, that Moorhead is able to be identified as the artist of Wheatley's portrait at all.[9]

There is much more to be said about the portrait of Moorhead and its significance for Marshall, especially as he positions this work as first in a series that moves on from this historical figure, albeit one shrouded in

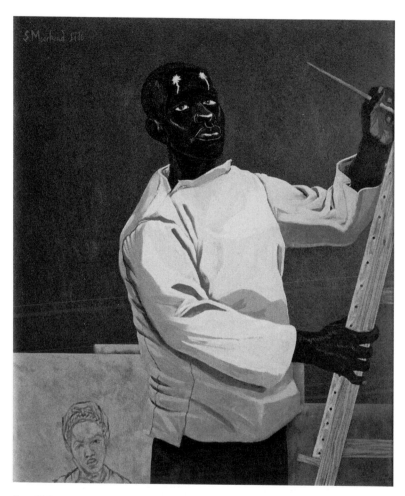

Figure 20. Kerry James Marshall, Scipio Moorhead, Portrait of Himself, 1776 (2007). Copyright Kerry James Marshall. Courtesy of the artist and Jack Shainman Gallery, New York.

uncertainty, to six additional portraits of black painters, all fictional, who are perhaps intended to stand for those who have been wholly lost to the historical record. (Each subsequent work is titled *Untitled [Painter].*)[10] But there is an additional portrait within this body of work, one that has gone largely unremarked upon. It is a portrait of Phillis Wheatley, which Marshall places on the ground, in the background of the scene of Moorhead at work. The portrait occupies the lower left corner of the Marshall's canvas, although only the top half is visible to the viewer. This portrait, also a work on canvas, is presumably a study for the painting of Moorhead's that we cannot see. The portrait of Wheatley borrows from Moorhead's original; Wheatley wears the same bonnet, and her hand is similarly cupping her chin. But there is one crucial difference: in this portrait, unlike the original, Wheatley is painted facing forward. Her contemplative gaze connects the viewer's place in the present to her own position in the past.

This is the contribution of Marshall as he imagines what Wheatley saw in her own time—the full gamut of life as an enslaved and then free black woman in the period surrounding the nation's founding—that was not captured by Moorhead's original work. We might further extend Marshall's line of inquiry to ask what Wheatley could see that her white contemporaries, like Franklin, could *not* see, not to mention ever hope to understand. We might additionally inquire as to what kind of kinship, real or imagined, she found with Moorhead, and with the "breathing figures" that, as she wrote to Moorhead in her poem, "learnt from thee to live" (l. 4). The answers to each of these questions remain outside the archive, even as we—like Wheatley, Moorhead, and Marshall all—attempt to animate their absence from the fragments that remain.

In closing, we might linger on the central subject of Marshall's painting: the "breathing figure" of Moorhead whom Marshall conjures to life. He looks directly at the viewer, probing us as much as we might probe him. His penetrating gaze is at once accentuated by the whites of his eyes, and diffused by the bluish-gray marks above them—a signature styling of Marshall's, who often employs this combination of starbursts and lines to convey the luminosity of the dark skin of his subjects, as well as, one could speculate, an anointed status bestowed by the artist, or by the divine. Moorhead wears a stiff white smock; the uniform of the artist at work. Its deep folds are what point to the fact that Moorhead has been captured in the act of painting—in the act of creating his art.

It is here that we might return to the portrait once believed to be of Hercules, and interpret it for what its viewers hoped to see: a portrait of an artist at work. Like Marshall's portrait of Moorhead, the man in the painting wears a white coat—a sign, to those hopeful viewers, of his participation in a process of not simply cooking but of art making.[11] For it was Hercules's food, as much as Moorhead's original painting or Wheatley's artful poetry, that directly contributed to shaping the tastes of the new nation. We may never be able to perceive Hercules's face, or Moorhead's; and we will certainly not be able to meet Wheatley's direct gaze. But it is my hope that by placing their range of forms of aesthetic expression alongside each other, as I have done throughout this book, we can expand our sense in the present of the richness of the aesthetic experiences of the past. Indeed, each of the artifacts discussed in this book carries with it a theory of taste: of how lived experience enters into cultural production, and how both shape and are shaped by political constraints. For the enslaved figures in this study, in particular, this expanded conception of taste opens up additional space for their contributions to aesthetic philosophy to be recognized as such. At the same time, this opening should not be viewed as any form of redress. Rather, it should be viewed as a call to action for us, as readers and scholars today, to continue to push against the boundaries of our knowledge, and to continue to push ourselves to find new meaning from the fragments of the past.

Notes

Introduction

1. Jefferson's plantation and the foodstuffs he cultivated are discussed in detail in chapter 1. For an extensive account of the Newtown Pippin, see Hatch, *The Fruits and Fruit Trees of Monticello,* 70–73.

2. Fraunces's biography, while outside the scope of this project, is also fascinating. He is most widely remembered as the owner/operator of Fraunces Tavern in New York during the Revolutionary War—the site, in fact, where Washington said farewell to his troops upon the conclusion of the war. Fraunces's personal history has also been a continued subject of interest. His nickname, "Black Sam," has suggested to some—including W. E. B. Du Bois—that Fraunces might have a mixed-race background worthy of additional investigation; he was likely born somewhere in the West Indies, lending some credence to that theory. But as other scholars have observed, that moniker was also often bestowed on white men with dark complexions, so it provides no conclusive evidence. In addition, Fraunces himself enslaved people; the 1790 census lists one enslaved person (no name or gender provided) as living in his house. See Blockson, "Black Samuel Fraunces."

3. Much has been written on the concept of "republican ideals" and the ideology of republicanism more generally. For two early theorizations, still referenced today, see Bailyn, *The Ideological Origins of the American Revolution,* and Wood, *The Creation of the American Republic, 1776–1787.* For an early account of the concept's scholarly use, see Shalhope, "Toward a Republican Synthesis." Rodgers, in "Republicanism," provides a relatively more recent historiographic assessment. As a recent example of how republicanism is discussed in relation to early American literature, see Drexler and White, "Secret Witness."

4. While I am hesitant to reinforce the narrative that credits these men, and these men alone, as responsible for providing the nation's intellectual foundation, I recognize that the term "founders" provides a useful and legible shorthand for referring to this group of figures. With my use of the term in quotation marks, I intend to designate both the group of men it commonly includes, as well as the common—and eminently valid—critique of its basis.

5. Korsmeyer, in *Making Sense of Taste,* provides the most thorough overview of the discourse of taste from a philosophical perspective. Gigante's *Taste* is responsible for introducing that discourse to literary scholars through an analysis of British literary texts ranging from Milton to the Romantic poets.

6. Here and throughout this book, I attempt to be precise in my use of the terms "United States" and "America." In general, I employ the term "United States" to refer to the country and to the archive that documents its foundation. When I employ the term "America," it is intended to indicate a broader temporal and/or geographic scope—the latter not necessarily limited to the North American continent. See Gruesz, "America."

7. The source for this description is a 1795 letter from Theophilus Bradbury, a one-term Massachusetts congressman, to his daughter, Harriet Hooper, which documents the "elegant variety of roast beef, veal, turkey, ducks, fowls, hams, &c; puddings, jellies, oranges, apples, nuts, almonds, figs, raisins, and a variety of wines and punches" that was served at one of Washington's weekly congressional dinners (qtd. in Adrian Miller, *President's Kitchen Cabinet,* 64).

8. In fact, it was not until 2009, when Mary V. Thompson, a historian at Mount Vernon, discovered a reference to Hercules's escape in one of Washington's weekly farm reports, that the date and circumstances of his escape were confirmed. For a summary of all that is currently known, see LaBan, "A Birthday Shock from Washington's Chef."

9. Gikandi, in *Slavery and the Culture of Taste,* has also done much to confirm the contributions of enslaved workers of African descent, in locations ranging from England to the Caribbean to the United States, to the dominant discourse of taste. Other works, referenced throughout this book, focus on the specifically culinary contributions of enslaved field hands and kitchen workers of African descent that were registered throughout the Atlantic world, although few of these studies connect these contributions to the discourse of taste.

10. Here I also build on a substantial body of work that has come up through the field of food studies, especially the scholarship that has focused on the Caribbean. See, for instance, Loichot, *The Tropics Bite Back,* and Simek, *Hunger and Irony in the French Caribbean.* In a colonial context, see Morton, *Cultures of Taste/Theories of Appetite,* along with his other works. In a modern European context, see Novero, *Antidiets of the Avant-Garde,* among others.

11. The scholarship on the imbrications of food and culture is vast. In addition to Bourdieu's *Distinction,* cited later in this chapter, Douglass, in *Purity and Danger,* pioneered this work. In a U.S. context, groundbreaking studies include Counihan, *Food in the USA;* Levenstein, *Revolution at the Table;* and Mintz, *Tasting Food, Tasting Freedom.* Mintz's *Sweetness and Power,* discussed in depth in chapter 2, also bears mention here for how it models scholarship that connects issues of food to issues of politics.

12. Issues of periodization in this project are complex. Among the primary audiences of this book are scholars of early American literature—a period that is generally thought to conclude by the early years of the Jacksonian era. But because the discourse of taste, which is primarily associated with the eighteenth century, took decades to travel to the United States, and longer still to proliferate—as will be discussed more fully below—the project focuses on texts from the tail end of the "early" American literary period, and includes some texts emphatically associated with the nineteenth century—a distinct scholarly field. Even as the scope of the texts under analysis extends into the antebellum era, I attempt to retain my central focus on the issues and concerns associated with early American literary scholarship, as I indicate above.

13. Parrish's primary focus, in this piece and in her work more generally, is on the biotic archives of the Columbian exchange. See Parrish, *American Curiosity*.

14. Margaret Cockburn Conkling (1814-90) was the author of thirteen books across a variety of genres, including fiction and biography, as well as conduct manuals. She was the daughter of a New York congressman; her two brothers also served in Congress. An obituary in *Publishers Weekly* credits her as "contribut[ing] often to current literature," although scant biographical details are known ("Obituary").

15. See Shields, *Southern Provisions*, for a polemical account of the meaning (and taste) that inheres in food.

16. See, for instance, Carney, *Black Rice*. Note, also, that Shields positions his study, which centers on the literal revitalization of historical foods, against projects such as Carney's that posit the "value of a cultivar or a dish" as residing "in its being a heritage marker, a survival from an originating culture previous to its uses in southern planting and cooking" (11). Shields also cites work by Gary Nabham and Karen Hess, in addition to Harris, *High on the Hog*.

17. See, for instance, Harris, *High on the Hog*. For a book that considers the more contemporary implications of this passage of foodstuffs, see Witt, *Black Hunger*.

18. On the multiple valences of consumption, see bell hooks, "Eating the Other: Desire and Resistance," in *Black Looks*, 21–41; Kyla Wazana Tompkins, *Racial Indigestion*; Githire, *Cannibal Writes*; and Zafar, *Recipes for Respect*.

19. For an assessment of these challenges from the perspective of a historian, see Haley, "The Nation before Taste."

20. In so doing, I place this study in the line of works prompted by Kyla Wazana Tompkins's call, in *Racial Indigestion*, to "shift to a framework we might call *critical eating studies,*" characterized by a "critique of the political beliefs and structures that underlie eating as a social practice" (2).

21. Critiques of brain-imaging studies center on the notion that visual similarity does not equate to cognitive sameness, even if that is what the images suggest. For this reason, I limit my claim to the visual similarity between these

two activities, and direct interested readers to consult the paper referenced in Kobayashi et al. "Functional Imaging of Gustatory Perception and Imagery."

22. See, for instance, Dickie, *The Century of Taste*. Korsmeyer, in *Making Sense of Taste,* confirms that the eighteenth century was the time when "the sense of taste [stood] right next to aesthetic Taste in philosophical writings" (40).

23. Korsmeyer summarizes: "In Baumgarten's 1750 work, *Aesthetica*, the term 'aesthetic' became particularly associated with beauty. In the *Critique of Pure Reason* (1781), Kant used 'aesthetic' to refer to sense perception; in the *Critique of Judgment* (1790) he employed it to refer to judgments of Taste, or the judgment that something is beautiful. The term 'aesthetic' was not used in English until the nineteenth century" (*Making Sense of Taste,* 42n10).

24. Scholars generally credit the work of Kant and Schiller, published in the 1790s, as the impetus for the term's more widespread adoption. See Korsmeyer, *Making Sense of Taste,* 54–60.

25. Joseph Addison, in his influential 1712 essay "On Taste," makes the case most clearly: "We may be sure this metaphor would not have been so general in all tongues had there not been a very great conformity between that mental taste which is the subject of this paper and that sensitive taste which gives us a relish of every different flavor that affects the palate" (qtd. in Mackie, *The Commerce of Everyday Life,* 383).

26. In this regard, the two-phase structure of the process of passing judgment closely adheres to the Lockean model of knowledge acquisition. But the taste philosophers extended Locke's original theory by emphasizing, first, the existence of an inner sense that guided individuals in their aesthetic judgments and, second, the fact that this sense—what they called the sense of taste—could be cultivated and refined.

27. For more on the philosophical basis of "civic virtue," see Shields, *Civil Tongues and Polite Letters in British America*; and Dillon, "Sentimental Aesthetics."

28. See Dillon, "Sentimental Aesthetics," and Cahill, *Liberty of the Imagination,* for more extended discussions of this relationship. Scholars of Enlightenment philosophy will also note that here and throughout the book I separate the discourse of taste from the discourse of sensibility. This is to retain a sharp focus on food and eating, which is central to the discourse of taste but peripheral to the larger discourse of sensibility. For a recent survey of this discourse as it relates to ideas about embodiment, see Lloyd, *The Discourse of Sensibility.*

29. Although Franklin attributes this "Position" to Kames, most scholars view Kames's moral philosophy as derivative of Hume's more rigorous theory. See Korsmeyer, *Making Sense of Taste,* as well as Dickie, *The Century of Taste.*

30. Wills, in *Inventing America,* provides a helpful overview of Scottish Enlightenment philosophy in relation to civic virtue. See note 28 for how literary scholars have incorporated this discourse into their work.

31. See Adrian Miller, *President's Kitchen Cabinet*, as well as DeWitt, *Founding Foodies*.

32. To be sure, there is more historical work that can be done. Dunbar's recent study, *Never Caught*, demonstrates how a compelling and informative narrative can be assembled from these scant sources. For additional information about the other enslaved residents of the President's House, see "Enslaved Persons of African Descent in the President's House."

33. Other influential theorists along these lines include Stoller, in *Along the Archival Grain*, and Best and Marcus, in "Surface Reading." The latter is discussed in detail in chapter 5. The reference to the "ghostly lives" of the enslaved is at once to Gordon's, *Ghostly Matters*, and Patterson's *Slavery and Social Death*.

34. For a thorough accounting of how power shapes the telling of history, see Trouillot, *Silencing the Past*.

35. For an account of the painting's deauthentication, see LaBan, "George Washington's Enslaved Chef" and "Behind the Story."

1. Taste

1. Historian Norman Risjord has gone so far as to suggest an interpretive compromise: "Either that the dinner Jefferson recalled took place earlier than anyone has supposed or that there was more than one political dinner. Or maybe both" ("The Compromise of 1790," 310).

2. On the notion of "republican ideals," see note 3 in the Introduction.

3. For a detailed account of the emergence of the French notion of *bon goût* and its relation to that country's larger food culture, see Spang, *The Invention of the Restaurant*. For a consideration of how French taste spread abroad, see Ferguson, *Accounting for Taste*. For an examination of the French Revolution in relation to the rise of modern French cuisine, see Pinkard, *A Revolution in Taste*. For an account of the United States' "culinary declaration of independence," as he terms it, see James McWilliams, *A Revolution in Eating*. For a consideration of how the next generation of writers, such as James Fenimore Cooper, Catharine Maria Sedgwick, and Lydia Maria Child, would imbue specific foods with republican significance, see Mark McWilliams, "Distant Tables." For a treatment of food and its significance in the earlier era of British America, see Eden, *The Early American Table*.

4. In the letter, penned to Nicholas Lewis, the friend whom Jefferson tasked (along with Francis Eppes) with running his Virginia plantation while he served in France, he describes growing "Indian corn . . . to eat green in our manner." In the same letter he also requests that Lewis send him "an ear of two of the drying corn from the Cherokee country, some best watermelon seeds, some fine Cantaloupe melon seeds, seeds of the common sweet potato . . . , an hundred or two acorns of

the willow oak and about a peck of acorns of the ground oak or dwarf oak." He further notes a former failed "attempt to send bacon hams," but remains undaunted: "I should think Mr. Donald could get them to me safely. A dozen or two would last me a year, would be better than any to be had on this side the Atlantic, which, inferior as they are, cost about a guinea apiece" (Jefferson, *Papers*, 12:135). In addition to letters like these, of which there are many, Jefferson also maintained formal journals, known as the Garden and Farm Books, for a large part of his life. These books date from 1766 to 1824 and contain detailed records of his many agricultural experiments at Monticello. Among his most successful experiments were the French fig and the Spanish almond. For a more detailed account of these journals, see Baron's introduction to Jefferson, *The Garden and Farm Books of Thomas Jefferson*.

5. As president, Jefferson would make waves across the Atlantic when he insisted on this style of seating at the dinner to welcome the British foreign minister, Anthony Merry. This "implementation of the ideals of republican egalitarianism," as Stagg explains in his introduction, was perceived as a personal affront, and it was compounded by Merry's subsequent experiences at Jefferson's distinctive table (Madison, *Papers*, Secretary of State Series, 6:xxvii).

6. This description of Jefferson's table is attributed to Daniel Webster, the Massachusetts senator, himself a great gastronome. For more on Webster's table, and his acclaimed cook Monica McCarty, see Elizabeth Dowling Taylor, *A Slave in the White House*, 144–58. It should also be noted that James Madison, while less known for his deliberate dining, also adhered to Jefferson's (and Webster's) view. In *A Revolution in Eating*, James McWilliams relates one anecdote of a meal served in Madison home: when Dolley Madison overheard a dinner-party guest describe the meal as "more like a harvest home supper than the entertainment of the Secretary of State," she immediately retorted that "the profusion of my table arises from the happy circumstances and abundance and prosperity in our country" (316). In another document, "Notes on an American Dinner," penned on July 4, 1798, Madison drew special attention to that meal as "a testimony of the American character" (Madison, *Papers*, Congressional Series [CS], 17:160). He commented on the "temperate but cheerful repast," observing that "there was not on the table a single dish that had a foreign ingredient in it. Even the liquors were the produce of our own happy soil climate ingenuity & industry."

7. In addition to Gigante, see Morton, *Cultures of Taste/Theories of Appetite*, as well as Morton's other works, including *The Poetics of Spice*.

8. Wills's *Inventing America* offers the foundational work on the subject. Numerous authors, including Lance Banning, Jay Fliegelman, Drew McCoy, Lori Merish, David Shi, David S. Shields, and Michael Warner, have taken up and refined this claim.

9. This quotation derives from a longer passage from the introduction to *American Literature's Aesthetic Dimensions,* in which Weinstein and Looby lay out their intent to "join in an effort to place aesthetics back on the critical agenda—and not in a fixed subordinate position either, but in a dynamic and unpredictable relationship to the social and political and ideological matters that have dominated our conversations for a good while now" (29).

10. In fact, in a more recent essay, "The Atlantic World, the Senses, and the Arts," Shields identifies—although does not resolve—the "historical dilemma" illuminated by the cultural encounters that took place in the eighteenth-century Atlantic world. On the one hand, the sensory pleasures offered by the non-Western cultures of the Atlantic world "suggest the reality of a human *sensus communis.*" On the other, the "cultural relativism" that allowed such positive judgments of taste to take place would seem to preclude such universal standards. This dilemma, Shields concludes, points to the existence of "multiple communities of sense that did not map neatly upon each other, yet coincided sufficiently to permit trade and the sharing of pleasure and pain" (145).

11. See *Early American Literature* 47, no. 2 (2012) for a colloquy that discusses this important work.

12. For a more extended discussion of Heming's culinary knowledge and labor, see chapter 5.

13. Arguments that excuse Jefferson's contradictory behavior on the grounds of his personal failings have thankfully fallen out of style. For an example of this type of defense, see John Chester Miller, *The Wolf by the Ears.* Not without irony, a work of young adult historical fiction that imagines the life of Harriet Hemings, believed to be the daughter of Jefferson and Sally Hemings, borrows this title for its own; see Rinaldi, *Wolf by the Ears.*

14. It is tempting to interpret this passage as a reflection of Jefferson's awareness of the negative impact of slavery on the nation's ideological underpinnings and, in so doing, resolve—at least in part—the contradiction between Jefferson's political philosophy and his ideas about racial difference. In fact, John Chester Miller argues convincingly that the passage reveals a conviction that slavery "created an atmosphere deadly to the kind of public and private virtue without which a republican form of government could not survive" (*The Wolf by the Ears,* 41). To be sure, Jefferson viewed slavery as damaging to republican virtue, but it is this virtue, predicated upon his highly developed sense of taste, that allows him to condone the continued existence of slavery in the United States.

15. According to the teachings of John Calvin, "temperance must prevent excess and luxury; otherwise man's passions would promote a selfish materialism and social strife," as Shi, in *The Simple Life,* helpfully summarizes (11). Cotton Mather would take up and at times challenge these original teachings, advocating

for a "Puritan ethic that demanded both diligence and temperance" (21). At the time of the Revolution, John Adams opined that Americans must be "preserved from the effects of intemperance" by the "force of severe manners" (67). Opinions like this would persist throughout the eighteenth century, into the nineteenth century, and through the present, as evidenced by the various waves of temperance movements targeted at alcohol but driven by very similar ideological beliefs.

16. Summarizing this main argument, Korsmeyer explains that taste "does not furnish significant information about the external world; it delivers only bodily pleasures; and hence it offers temptations that without strict control can lead to gluttony and intemperance" ("Tastes and Pleasures," para. 8).

17. The image of "sucking . . . mother's milk" would have carried tremendous cultural resonance at the time; most people believed that breastfeeding conveyed social attributes as well as nutritional value. See Golden, *A Social History of Wet Nursing in America*.

18. While Jefferson makes sure to state that taste is "not even a branch of morality," he continues to analogize the moral sense to the sense of taste throughout his letter. His discussion is largely influenced by Kames, although he concludes his discussion with reference to the "moral instinct"—a phrase that derives not from Kames but from the work of Dugald Stewart, whom Jefferson met in Paris, as Hafertepe observes in "An Inquiry into Thomas Jefferson's Ideas of Beauty."

19. See McCoy, *The Last of the Fathers*, 232, and Elizabeth Dowling Taylor, 6. Sweet's *American Georgics* offers analyses of other instances of Jefferson's allusions to slavery.

20. This sentiment echoes across the work of contemporary farmer, essayist, and poet Wendell Berry. In "Renewing Husbandry," a recent essay against the incursion of industrial farming, for example, Berry argues that "the effort of husbandry is partly scientific but it is entirely cultural." Like Madison and Jefferson, he also sees "colleges of agriculture" as playing a large role in initiating "a new legitimacy, intellectual rigor, scientific respectability, and responsible teaching" of farming.

21. For an extensive treatment of Jefferson and architecture, see Faherty, *Remodeling the Nation*.

22. In fact, in a letter composed in August of that same year, Madison would make special note of the "pleasure excited [in him] by the growing taste for agricultural improvements" (*Papers*, Retirement Series [RS], 4:343).

23. Several sentences later, when Madison and Jefferson contrast their belief in the benefits of formal education with the Indians' desire for a "return to the days of eating acorns and roots," they confirm that the "Native stock" they seek to refine does not include Native Americans either (Madison, *Papers*, RS, 1:330).

24. McCoy observes that visitors often called upon Madison and Jefferson in close succession, since they lived so near to each other in Virginia. This resulted

in many firsthand accounts that directly compared the two men (*The Last of the Fathers*, 33–35).

25. It might also be noted that Jacques Brissot, mentioned above, had the occasion to dine with Madison during his time in the United States. In his *New Travels in the United States* (1791), Brissot observed of Madison: "His look announces a censor; his conversation discovers the man of learning; and his reserve was that of a man conscious of his talents and his duties" (101).

26. Elizabeth Dowling Taylor cites a letter from Dolley which read, "His hands and fingers are still so swelled and sore as to be nearly useless, but I lend him mine," but Taylor comments that "it was more likely Jennings's hands that cut Madison's food" (*A Slave in the White House*, 118).

27. Bertelsen describes a general "atmosphere of burgeoning consumption" during which discussions of taste "became the vogue" (*The Nonsense Club*, 45). Also see Breen's influential "'Baubles of Britain.'"

28. For a discussion of Madison's conception of control and its relation to the body, see Shapiro, "'Man to Man I Need Not Dread His Encounter.'" For an extended treatment of Madison's conception of control and its relation to aesthetics, including a detailed reading of the *Federalist Papers*, see chapter 1 of Cahill's *Liberty of the Imagination*.

29. Some have argued that by selling Gardner within Philadelphia Madison intended to take advantage of a state law that declared that individuals could be enslaved for no more than seven years. The fact remains, however, that Madison did not choose to emancipate Gardner on his own accord.

30. This possibility is more than hypothetical. In his *Appeal to the Coloured Citizens of the World, but in Particular, and Very Expressly, to Those of the United States of America* (1828), David Walker suggested that "each of [his] brethren . . . buy a copy of Mr. Jefferson's 'Notes on Virginia,' and put it in the hand of his son," in order to encourage that generation to refute Jefferson's "charges" in their own terms (17). For an extended discussion of Walker's *Appeal*, see Jarrett, "'To Refute Mr. Jefferson's Arguments Respecting Us.'"

31. See Elizabeth Dowling Taylor, *A Slave in the White House*, 162, for an account of what is known about the context for this image.

32. Jefferson came to extol the younger Hemings's culinary abilities, albeit not as much as his older brother's French techniques. In 1802, he wrote to his daughter, "Pray enable yourself to direct us here how to make muffins in Peter's method. My cook here cannot succeed at all in them, and they are a great luxury to me" (*Family Letters*, 238). But because Jefferson was unwilling to relinquish his taste for the "great luxury" of Peter's muffins, he refused to allow that cook to ever negotiate his freedom. Consequently, Peter Hemings remained in servitude, and was among the enslaved people sold at the time of Jefferson's death in order to settle the debts of his estate.

33. See Matthewson, "Jefferson and Haiti," and Newman, "American Political Culture and the French and Haitian Revolutions."

34. Louis-André Pichon, a French diplomat in Washington at the time, reported to Talleyrand that Jefferson had assured him that "nothing would be easier than to furnish your army and fleet with everything and to reduce Toussaint to starvation" (qtd. in Lachance, "Repercussions of the Haitian Revolution in Louisiana," 210).

2. Appetite

1. Writing in 1913, Elizabeth Robins Pennell, whose cookbook collection is held in the Library of Congress, described Grimod as "the first great master" of the "new writers" on food. Gigante confirms that "Grimod's work was enormously influential in nineteenth-century Europe. It was adapted and, in some cases, transported wholesale into English, influencing the development of haute cuisine beyond the borders of France and into England and America. In the Paris of his day, Grimod was a minor celebrity, dining with everyone from dignitaries down to actresses (not at this period the cultural elite) and supporting the rise of the restaurant in post-revolutionary France" (*Gusto*, 1–2).

2. Very little of Grimod's *Almanach* has been translated into English. Gigante's *Gusto* contains several excerpts. Except when indicated, passages from the text are from the contemporary French edition (Menu Fretin, 2012) and translations are my own.

3. Attendees were also served drinks in "Electrified bumpers," which would administer a slight shock "if the Party be close shaved, and does not breathe on the Liquor" (Franklin, *Memoirs*, 2:254).

4. See Riskin, "Poor Richard's Leyden Jar," and her later monograph, *Science in the Age of Sensibility*.

5. This line can be found in a letter to John Adams that is rife with the language of food. Alluding to the reports of his luxurious lifestyle that dogged Franklin throughout his tenure as Ambassador, he "commend[s]" the "Readers of Connecticut Newspapers" for their sense of "Oeconomy," and vows to "imitate it by diminishing" his own "Expence." He then declares that his "Countrymen" shall no longer "be troubled with any more Accounts of our Extravagance," vowing that the Connecticut readers "must be contented for the future, as I am, with plain Beef and Pudding." He concludes, "For my own part, if I could sit down to Dinner on a Piece of their excellent Salt Pork and Pumpkin, I would not give a Farthing for all the Luxuries of Paris" (Franklin, *Papers*, 42:101).

6. Plato understood reason as the natural ruler over the passions, and other aspects of the mind. Aristotle took this idea further, defining human beings as rational animals; see *The Nicomachean Ethics*.

7. See Fred D. Miller, "The Rule of Reason."

8. Thomas Hobbes's *Leviathan* (1651) is the landmark text in this regard, but the Earl of Shaftesbury and his interlocutor, Bernard Mandeville, together popularized this debate in the early eighteenth century. For a discussion of this intellectual climate, of which Franklin was a part, see Douglas Anderson, *The Radical Enlightenments of Benjamin Franklin.*

9. "Civility is hard-wired into the eighteenth-century political discourse out of which the American state is constituted," writes Jenny Davidson, in *Hypocrisy and the Politics of Politeness,* 11.

10. In this regard, I align myself with Roy's use of the body in *Alimentary Tracts,* in which, as explicated by Holland et al., "the text *is* the body's alimentary tract, and the work is not to think of inside and outside but to think of the impossibility of separation between self and other, body and text, tongue and bowel" (393).

11. While this chapter treats Grimod's representation of his body through his public performances, and subsequently links this self-representation to his writing, I attempt to do so while remaining attentive to the critiques of certain forms of disability studies scholarship that further objectify and/or pathologize their subjects under analysis, rather than contribute to a more capacious field. For a recent distillation of this critique, see Minich, "Enabling Whom?"

12. For an impressively rich account of Wheatley's final years, see Carretta, *Phillis Wheatley,* 172–96.

13. "You philosophers are sages in your maxims, and fools in your conduct," the Gout admonishes, reminding Franklin of the advice about an abstemious diet that he dispensed not only in the *Autobiography,* but also in *Poor Richard's Almanack,* which he published annually between 1732 and 1758 (*Memoirs,* 3:258).

14. For an encapsulation of the ideas at the center of this debate, see Lundblad, "From Animal to Animality Studies."

15. Despite Franklin's characterization of Keimer as a "vainglorious bumbler," he also lived a fascinating life (Frasca, *Benjamin Franklin's Printing Network,* 10). See Frasca's work for biographical detail.

16. An earlier episode in the *Autobiography* suggests how Franklin was already quite prepared to consider to how eating might expose certain affinities between humans and animals. Describing his apprenticeship in his brother's print shop, Franklin recalls an influential text he encountered there: Thomas Tryon's 1691 volume, *The Way to Health, Long Life, and Happiness; Or, a Discourse of Temperance, and the Particular Nature of All Things Requisite for the Life of Man.* Tryon's text argued for the extended benefits of "the Vegetable Diet," and included, according to Waldstreicher, "not only recipes but impromptu speeches by cows, sheep, birds, and horses, against their oppression" (*Runaway America,* 99). Waldstreicher suggests that Franklin, then indentured to his brother, may

have been drawn to Tryon's doctrines because of a sense of sameness with the animals he would eat. Franklin affirms his adherence to this view in the fried cod episode, explaining how he had long "considere'd with [his] Master Tryon, the taking every Fish as a kind of unprovok'd Murder" (*Autobiography,* 87). But upon conjuring the image of a gutted fish with a smaller fish inside its stomach, Franklin revises his initial formulation. The relation he perceives with this particular aquatic creature is not any that asserts their shared humanity. Rather, it appears instead to be how closely Franklin, as an eating animal—guided not by taste but by appetite—resembles an eating fish.

17. For a detailed accounting of the significance of this trip, see Douglas Anderson, *The Radical Enlightenments of Benjamin Franklin.*

18. The progenitor of moral sense philosophy, Anthony Ashley Cooper, third earl of Shaftesbury, in all probability would have responded to Mandeville's charges directly, but he had died several years before.

19. Perhaps for this reason, Franklin devoted considerable attention in *Poor Richard's Almanack* to advocating in plain language for the importance of subjecting appetite to reason. In the first volume, Franklin intones, "Eat to live, and not live to eat" (*Poor Richard,* 7). He reinforces this position over many years, with multiple aphorisms about the importance of eating to satisfy hunger, rather than to indulge in superfluous desire. In fact, in the introduction to the 1742 volume, Franklin provides explicit confirmation of this view. Speaking in the voice of the god-fearing Poor Richard, Franklin asks: "Woudst though enjoy a long Life, a healthy Body, and a vigorous Mind, and be acquainted also with the wonderful Works of God? Labor in the first place to bring thy Appetite into Subjection to Reason" (100–101).

20. Some recent philosophical investigations of eating include Hird, *The Origins of Sociable Life*; Bennett, *Vibrant Matter*; and Elizabeth Wilson, *Gut Feminism.*

21. The only extant meeting notes of the Junto, the "Club for mutual Improvement" that Franklin founded upon his return to Philadelphia, in 1727, record a discussion about "Whether it is worth a Rational Man's While to forego the Pleasure arising from the present Luxury of the Age in Eating and Drinking and artful Cookery" (Franklin, *Papers,* 1:259). The manuscript reveals how Franklin inserted the word "rational" after the fact, indicating his own instinct not to bind "man" to that quality as a matter of course. In the next line, Franklin offers another illumining addition, clarifying that the goal of "a healthy old age" should be recorded as a more specific process of "studying to gratify the appetite" so that such health can be achieved. Here again, Franklin indicates his awareness of the extent of the effort required in order to transform appetite into a cultivated sense of taste. And while Franklin fails to register the Junto's conclusion on the matter—in marked contrast to the notes associated with all other

discussion questions, which are followed by short summaries of the ensuing conversation—he continued to probe the relationship between appetite and reason in his own experiences of eating.

22. And Franklin was indeed a fan: he first tasted the sweetened treat at the Café Procope in Paris, in the late 1770s, while serving as Minister to France; and it was rumored (although almost certainly untrue) that he had a batch whipped up during the Constitutional Convention of 1787 in order to literally cool the hotter heads. In truth, it is Washington who enters the record as the first of the founders to import an ice cream maker to the United States; in May 1784, he paid one pound, thirteen shillings, and three pence for a "Cream Machine for Ice" (Thompson, "Ice Cream," para. 1).

23. Benjamin Franklin's "On the Slave Trade," published just three weeks before his death, confirmed what abolitionists had long believed: that the "founding father" was, in fact, against slavery. In a satire—Franklin's characteristic literary mode—he attempted to underscore the absurdity of trafficking in people. If Franklin had a deeper, philosophical objection to the slave trade, however, it went with him to his grave. In fact, most scholars agree that Franklin came to his antislavery stance not because of any moral objection, but as an extension of his anger toward Britain. He identified a proximate relation between Britain's enslaving of the colonies and the colonists' enslavement of African and African American people. Franklin himself held several slaves at his home in Philadelphia, and he readily accepted advertisements for the sale of slaves in his various publications.

24. Here and throughout, my account derives from Rebecca Spang's extensive research on the dinner.

25. This description was also the result of the event's invitations, which were styled as elaborate burial announcements. See Spang, *The Invention of the Restaurant*, 88.

26. In *Gusto,* Gigante also describes the dinner. Two biographies of Grimod also exist: Rival's *Grimod de la Reynière* and MacDonough's *A Palate in Revolution.* MacDonough strongly faults Rival's research methodologies, which are for the most part undocumented, although neither are scholarly texts.

27. Although not a focus of this chapter, historians of science have theorized Grimod's prostheses to profound effect. See, for instance, Benhamou, "The Artificial Limb in Preindustrial France," and Riskin, "Eighteenth-Century Wetware."

28. Gigante reproduces this anecdote in *Gusto,* 2.

29. See Downie, *A Taste of Paris.*

30. See Garland-Thompson, *Extraordinary Bodies.*

31. In a later essay, "On Savoir-Vivre," Grimod articulates an even more concise encapsulation of this idea, in which "one must enlist intelligence in the service of appetite" (qtd. in Gigante, *Gusto,* 29).

32. Further corroborating this exchange, the majority of the subsequent frontispieces iterate on the same general concept: a gourmand in his library-cum-dining room. See Grimod, *Almanach*, vols. 2, 4, 7, and 8.

33. The idea was prompted by Grimod's experience, decades before, as a member of the *Societé des mercredis*. That group met every Wednesday—the *mercredi* of the society's name—at one of the finest restaurants in Paris, where they were served a full dinner and then discussed its culinary merits. See Gigante, *Gusto*, 1–2.

34. In extolling the Jury's first president, one Doctor Gastaldy, Grimod similarly comments upon his "grand art of the maw" as much as his ability to pronounce his eloquent opinions (555).

35. For more on Grimod in the context of Napoleonic France, and his "picture of Paris purged of the momentous events of the 1790s," see Spang, *The Invention of the Restaurant*, 154–63. For more on slavery and its abolition in France, see Sue Peabody, *"There Are No Slaves in France."*

36. His satirical essay, "On the Slave Trade," published in 1790, at last confirmed what abolitionists had long wanted to believe: that Benjamin Franklin was indeed against slavery. See note 23 above.

37. See Carretta, *Phillis Wheatley*, 117–18.

38. A 1779 proposal for a second volume of poems, published in the *Boston Evening Post and General Advertiser,* described "a Volume of Poems and Letters on Various Subjects, Dedicated to the Right Honourable Benjamin Franklin Esq: One of the Ambassadors of the United States at the Court of France" (Wheatley, *Complete Writings,* 167). Wheatley also confirms this encounter in a letter to David Worcester, mentioning a visit to "Benjamin Franklin Esqr. F.R.S." in a list of distinguished figures she met while abroad (146).

39. See Gates, "Mister Jefferson and the Trials of Phillis Wheatley."

40. I am not the first to assert that the appetite for black "flesh," as Hortense Spillers has famously theorized the captive subject position, undergirded the Enlightenment project as a whole ("Mama's Baby, Papa's Maybe," 67). In addition, Weheliye, mentioned earlier in the chapter, directly connects Spillers's theorization to Enlightenment humanism in his *Habeas Viscus*. In the area of food studies, Kyla Wazana Tompkins's *Racial Indigestion* and Woodard's *The Delectable Negro* directly engage this topic.

41. See Joseph Addison, "The Pleasures of the Imagination," in Gigante, *The Great Age of the English Essay*. Franklin also, famously, cites the *Spectator* as a major influence on his writing. In the *Autobiography,* Franklin even claims to have committed the third volume of the *Spectator* to memory as he attempted to refine his own writing style.

42. Carretta quotes Mason, who edited an early twentieth-century edition of Wheatley's poetry, in asserting that "certainly she cooperated in its conception and contents" (*Phillis Wheatley*, 80).

43. Carretta states that "Wheatley's modern reading was rather eclectic, but apparently it was fairly limited to works published in the early eighteenth century" (*Phillis Wheatley,* 51).

44. I thank Natalia Cecire for suggesting that I elaborate this line of inquiry.

45. For a more explicit elaboration of the intersection, often grotesque, between black bodies and sugar cane, see James Grainger's four-book georgic, *The Sugar-Cane* (1764). Dillon, in "The Cost of Sugar: Narratives of Loss and Limb," has interpreted Grainger's poem along these lines.

46. This line comes from a letter written to Susanna Wheatley; Calef did not write to Phillis Wheatley directly.

47. Slauter, "Looking for Scipio Moorhead." On the frontispiece, also see Shaw, "'On Deathless Glories Fix Thine Ardent View.'"

48. For a helpful encapsulation, see Jain, "The Prosthetic Imagination."

49. Note that there is no evidence that King George read the poem, although several of Wheatley's other works were published in the prestigious *London Magazine,* an indication of her international readership. See Carretta, *Phillis Wheatley,* 78–108.

3. Satisfaction

1. Russell writes of her son: "I am still a widow, with one child, a son, who is crippled; he has the use of but one hand" (*A Domestic Cookbook,* 3).

2. Until 2001, when the University of Michigan's William L. Clements Library acquired Russell's cookbook, Abby Fisher's *What Mrs. Fischer Knows about Old Southern Cooking* (1881) was believed to be the first African American–authored cookbook. See the online collection *Feeding America: The Historic American Cookbook Project* (https://d.lib.msu.edu/fa) for an introduction to that volume, as well as a digitized version of the first edition. Here it should also be noted that there are many other important "firsts" in cookbook history, including Lafcadio Hearne's *La Cuisine Creole: A Collection of Culinary Recipes from Leading Chefs and Noted Creole Housewives, Who Have Made New Orleans Famous for Its Cuisine* (ca. 1885), considered to be the first creole cookbook; and Caroline Sullivan's *Classic Jamaican Cooking: Traditional Recipes and Herbal Remedies* (1893), considered to be the first Caribbean cookbook. Tipton-Martin's *The Jemima Code* offers short entries on over 150 black-authored cookbooks from Roberts to the present. (Many of these are also available in digitized form on the *Feeding America* website.)

3. A large body of work considers the consolidation of the cookbook as a women's genre that took place in the late eighteenth and early nineteenth centuries. For a survey of recent books on the subject, see Le Dantec-Lowry, "Reading Women's Lives in Cookbooks and Other Culinary Writings."

4. The term "speculative aesthetics" has also been provisionally theorized by Hayles, among others, as a "partner" in the project of speculative realism—what she takes to mean the investigation of objecthood and the status and relations, both knowable and unknowable, among "non-human" objects and other living things ("Speculative Aesthetics and Object-Oriented Inquiry (OOI)," 175). But this concept and its associated methods require significant revision when set against the backdrop of early America. As the site that served as the principal proving ground for Enlightenment ideas about humanity, personhood, and objecthood, as well as about aesthetics, the contested terrain of early America underscores how theories such as speculative realism that seek to destabilize these restrictive categories cannot help but reinforce the same distinctions as the basis for any revised view. See Mackay et al., *Speculative Aesthetics,* for additional perspectives. I discuss the relationship between this notion of speculative aesthetics and early American literature in more detail in "Speculative Aesthetics."

5. In addition to the Kazanjian cited above, see Moten on "improvisation" ("Knowledge of Freedom," 275) and Ivy Wilson on the "vernacular" (*Specters of Democracy,* 13). Although framed in terms of creolization rather than speculation, Simek makes a similar case for how irony, as it is expressed across a range of cultural registers, including eating, functions as a creolized form of capital-T Theory—what she terms "epistemological justice" (*Hunger and Irony in the French Caribbean,* 4).

6. An additional valence worthy of note is how Russell's vision for her new life in Liberia itself remained speculative, in that she never arrived at her destination. I thank one of the anonymous reviewers of this book for this observation.

7. See the Introduction for an overview of this history.

8. The notion of the "mental sense" can be traced to Shaftesbury's *Characteristics of Men, Manners, Opinions, Times* (1711).

9. Recall that Alexander Baumgarten's landmark *Aesthetica,* which is generally credited with introducing the term, was published in 1750—nearly a full century before Peabody issued her remarks.

10. It might seem, to the careful reader, that the notion of speculative aesthetics is redundant, since my argument is that, in the early United States, any use of the term "aesthetic" carried with it an element of speculation. I have chosen to risk redundancy in my nomenclature because of how this speculative dimension of aesthetic theory remains for the most part unacknowledged, even today.

11. See Ridley for an account of *American Cookery* as the "first" American cookbook ("The First American Cookbook," 114). See Hess's introduction to *The Virginia House-Wife* for an argument in favor of its status as the "earliest full-blown American cookbook" (ix). See Longone's introduction to *A Domestic*

Cookbook for evidence of its status as the "first cookbook authored by an African American" (vii).

12. Food writer Molly O'Neill, who documented Longone's research for the *New York Times,* describes how she was unable to find conclusive evidence of any "Malinda, Mylinda, Melinda and Russel, Rusell, [or] Russell" living in any small town in Tennessee, Virginia, or North Carolina ("A 19th-Century Cookbook Gives New Twist to 'Soul Food'").

13. As Eagleton explains in "The Ideology of the Aesthetic," the eighteenth-century discourse of taste concerned itself with "reconstructing the human subject from the inside, informing its subtlest affections and bodily response with this law that is not a law" (330).

14. For a discussion of these social and intersubjective processes of cultivation, see, for instance, Shields, *Civil Tongues.*

15. This view is confirmed throughout the text. Later, Roberts writes: "Therefore, my young friends, when you hire yourself to a lady or gentleman, your time or your ability is no longer your own, but your employer's; therefore they have a claim on them whenever they choose to call for them and my sincere advice to you is, always to study to give general satisfaction to your employers, and by so doing you are sure to gain credit for yourself" (*The House Servant's Directory,* x).

16. For a discussion that touches on the taste philosophers' consideration of satisfaction, see Korsmeyer, *Making Sense of Taste,* 46–51.

17. In *Racial Indigestion,* Kyla Wazana Tompkins provides a detailed reading of the "Jim Crow" cookie in terms of cannibalism, slavery, and orality. See the section on "Modernity's Cannibals: Hawthorne's *House of the Seven Gables*" (93–104).

18. On the rise of liberal capitalism and its relationship to republicanism, see Appleby, *Capitalism and a New Social Order,* and Appleby, *Liberal and Republicanism in the Historical Imagination,* as well as Prindle, *The Paradox of Democratic Capitalism.*

19. See Zafar, *Recipes for Respect,* 19–28. It is also well documented how, for black Americans in the era of slavery, entrepreneurial success took the place of political expression as a primary means of asserting national belonging. In his analysis of *The Interesting Narrative of the Life of Olaudah Equiano, or Gustavus Vassa, the African* (1789), for example, Jaros observes how Equiano's numerous accounts of his entrepreneurial efforts demonstrate his ability to successfully engage in the (then emergent) structures of liberal capitalism, while also "drawing attention to the unavailability of economic and legal rights to slaves and ex-slaves" (5). It might be said that Russell, similarly, performs her participation in the national economy, enlisting the evidence of her entrepreneurial success so as to mount critique of liberal capitalism at the same time that she participates in it.

20. That Russell would seek to make a political intervention through her cookbook is unsurprising. In fact, the handful of scholars who have explored

Russell's work to date have each focused on elaborating her subtle yet significant expressions of political opinion. Zafar, in *Recipes for Respect*, finds evidence of a clear antislavery stance in Russell's rhetorical choice to infuse elements of the genre of the slave narrative into her cookbook's introduction (20). Fretwell compares Russell's recipes to those of Emily Dickinson, reading their shared interest in sweetness—Dickinson's as a metaphor of race, and Russell's as a synecdoche for pleasure—as "an experiment in poetical freedom and political freedom, respectively" ("Emily Dickinson in Domingo," 74).

21. This quotation and all those in this paragraph come from the introduction to Simmons's cookbook, which was published by Hudson and Goodwin in 1796.

22. In her introduction to the volume, Hess writes: "So, again, what makes *American Cookery* so very American? It is precisely in the bringing together of certain native American products and English culinary traditions" (xv).

23. For a complete account of *American Cookery*'s publication history, including the plagiarized editions, see Hess's introduction, xii.

24. No biographical information about Simmons has been found. See Eden, "About That Recipe," for a survey of scholarship on Simmons to date. See Pazicky, *Cultural Orphans in America*, for an in-depth exploration of the trope of orphanhood in the Revolutionary and post-Revolutionary periods.

25. Simmons's philosophy closely adheres to the ideology of republican motherhood, which has itself been proven to be deeply influenced by British aesthetic philosophy. See Kerber, "The Republican Mother."

26. For an example of how literary scholars have theorized the improvisation associated with the recipe genre, see Kyla Wazana Tompkins, "Consider the Recipe."

27. The recipe, which is one of nine distinct recipes for "Pastes" that appears in the book, reads as follows: "Rub one third of one pound of butter, and one pound of lard into two pound of flour, wet with four whites well beaten; water as much as necessary: to make a paste, roll in the residue of shortening in ten or twelve rollings—bake quick" (Simmons, *American Cookery*, 38).

28. In his study of Charleston caterers, Shields confirms what any aspiring pastry cook knows to be true: that the "mastery of dough" is among the most difficult of culinary techniques, and earned nineteenth-century pastry cooks the distinction as the "most skilled and valuable" type of cook (*Southern Provisions*, 122).

29. For a discussion of Russell's intent in aligning herself with these "first families," see Zafar, *Recipes for Respect*, 21.

30. After Randolph's husband was dismissed from his post as Virginia's federal marshal, a blow which coincided with the drop in tobacco prices that triggered the recession of 1800–1802, the Randolph family experienced increasing

amounts of financial distress. After selling their custom-designed Richmond manse, Moldavia, they moved to a more modest home, which became the site of the boardinghouse they ran between 1808 and 1819.

31. In another context, Williams-Forson, in *Building Houses Out of Chicken Legs,* has argued for how enslaved cooks should be credited for making food taste good *in spite of* the attempts of the mistress of the house to control the process.

32. The full passage is as follows: "The prosperity and happiness of a family depend greatly on the order and regularity established in it" (xii). Compare this to Madison's pronouncement, discussed in chapter 1, that "the class of citizens who provide at once their own food and their own raiment may be viewed as the most truly independent and happy" (Madison, *Papers,* CS, 14:246).

33. See Williams-Forson's discussion of the culinary implications of "gender malpractice," in *Building Houses Out of Chicken Legs,* 165–85.

34. How cookbooks often enact a transfer of culinary knowledge is the subject of one of the earliest and most canonical essays in the field of food studies, Appadurai's "How to Make a National Cuisine."

35. See Shields, *Southern Provisions,* for an extended discussion of the importance of acknowledging regional differences in southern cuisine.

36. Longone, in her introduction to *A Domestic Cookbook,* describes the difficulties of locating Steward in the archive.

37. The name Moldavia was created by combining the names of "Molly" (as Mary was known to her friends) and "David." After the Randolphs' economic decline, the manse was sold to the adoptive parents of Edgar Allan Poe, who memorialized the two-story home in "The Fall of the House of Usher" (1839).

38. See Egerton, *Gabriel's Rebellion,* 69–79, for an account of the unraveling of the plan.

39. For more on Harland's two cookbooks, *Common Sense in the Household: A Manual of Practical Housewifery* (1873) and *Breakfast, Luncheon and Tea* (1875), and to explore digitized versions of each, see the entry on "Marion Harland" at the *Feeding America* site: http://digital.lib.msu.edu/projects/cookbooks/html/authors/author_harland.html.

40. The anecdote is most closely traced to Harland's novel. In the second chapter of what Egerton describes as an "astonishingly racist epic," the titular grandmother, whose narration strains to advance the plot, recalls Gabriel's plans as follows: "When the white folks were all dead, [Gabriel] was to be crowned 'King of Virginia.' Richmond was chosen as his capital, and Mrs. Marcia Randolph, a beautiful widow, for his queen" (Egerton, *Gabriel's Rebellion,* 180; Harland, *Judith,* 22–23). Because the name and circumstances differed slightly from the actual person, Harland, in the voice of Judith, adds: "You may have seen her cookery-book, 'The Virginia Housewife'" (23). This episode was soon merged

back into the original testimony, and transformed into fact. For instance, Stanard reports that "Gabriel was quoted as having declared that he would save Mrs. David Meade Randolph and make her his queen because she knew so much about cooking" (*Richmond, Its People and Its Story,* 83). This appears to be the source for Daniels's account; he quotes it (without attribution) in its entirety. It is a case of fact and fiction being conflated: Randolph was known as "Queen Molly" in her own time, not for any relation to Gabriel, "King of Richmond," but instead for her (seemingly) gracious rule over her home. See Sterling P. Anderson, "'Queen Molly' and *The Virginia Housewife.*"

41. The history of barbecue is complicated, as Warnes explores in *Savage Barbecue.* While emphasizing that barbecue, in the United States, is an "invented tradition," he acknowledges how the enslaved "and their descendants revitalized this invented tradition and made it their own" (116).

42. Many works on the origin of soul food cite the meals prepared and consumed on "free Sundays" as a major source of the Sunday supper that has become a cornerstone of contemporary African American culinary practice. See, for instance, Adrian Miller, *Soul Food.* However, in "The Unbearable Taste," Twitty cautions that "soul food has a spice that enslaved food did not. The average enslaved person would only intermittently enjoyed elements of the classic 'Sunday dinner' of soul tradition," and even then their pleasure was fundamentally circumscribed by their condition of enslavement (n.p.). For a detailed history of "free Sundays," see Berlin, *Generations of Captivity.* Berlin also provides an account of the slave codes that in some states (but not Virginia) prohibited worship and large gatherings. Foner's *Give Me Liberty!* also discusses the Virginia slave codes in more detail.

43. D. Bellegarde, *Histoire du people haïtien (1492–1952)* (Port-au-Prince: n.p., 1953), trans. by and qtd. in Geggus, *Haitian Revolutionary Studies,* 81, 85. Geggus has also documented how the meal almost certainly involved the ritual sacrifice of a pig, although he does not find evidence to corroborate the claim that it was subsequently cooked and consumed (81–92). I thank one of the anonymous peer reviewers of the manuscript for the suggestion to explore this connection.

44. For the origins of the moniker, see Sterling P. Anderson, "'Queen Molly' and *The Virginia Housewife.*"

45. See Rucker, *The River Flows On,* for a more recent critique of Egerton's account.

4. Imagination

1. The distinction between Harriet Jacobs, the author, and Linda Brent, the name Jacobs gives her narrator/protagonist, has long presented a challenge to critics; Blackwood, in ""Fugitive Obscura," aptly describes the difficulty of distinguishing between the author and her fictionalized persona as "narrative twi-

light" (109). With this acknowledgment of the impossibility of perfect attribution, I nevertheless attempt to refer to assertions made by the author as "Jacobs," and observations made by (or about) the protagonist as "Brent." I similarly employ the characters' real names when making arguments about their actual life circumstances, but use their fictional names when describing events in the book.

2. See, for example, Nudelman, "Harriet Jacobs and the Sentimental Politics of Female Suffering" (discussed later in this chapter); Emsley, "Harriet Jacobs and the Language of Autobiography"; and, more recently, Pratt, "'These Things Took the Shape of Mystery.'"

3. For an interpretation of this scene as evidence of a larger "genealogy of human consumption" that is recorded in *Incidents*, see Woodard, *The Delectable Negro*, 26.

4. My interest in these narrative representations builds on the extensive critical bibliography about sentimentalism and its relation to slavery by connecting it to the discourse of taste. Among the foundational works in this area are, of course, Douglas, *The Feminization of American Culture*, and Jane Tompkins, *Sensational Designs*. Extending that initial body of work are studies including Brown, *Domestic Individualism*; Samuels, *The Culture of Sentiment*; and Sánchez-Eppler, *Touching Liberty*. In the early 2000s, works including Merish, *Sentimental Materialism*; Hendler, *Public Sentiments*; and Noble, *The Masochistic Pleasures of Sentimental Literature* extended this inquiry into more focused directions. More recently, works including Luciano, *Arranging Grief*; Coviello, *Tomorrow's Parties*; and Schuller, *The Biopolitics of Feeling* have translated the insights of sentimentalism into more contemporary conceptual configurations.

5. See the Introduction for this discussion. In the context of fiction writing, it is also worth invoking Toni Morrison's account of her creative process as "trying to fill in the blanks that the slave narratives left" ("Sites of Memory," 93).

6. For contemporary work on the subject of the relationship between Jacobs and Child, see Foreman, *Activist Sentiments*, and Tricomi, "Harriet Jacobs's Autobiography and the Voice of Lydia Maria Child"; on the subject of white editors, see Sekora's enduring essay, "Black Message/White Envelope."

7. Child dedicates her volume "To those who are not ashamed of economy," and explains in the introduction that she has deliberately "written for the poor" (*The Frugal Housewife*, 7). She leaves no doubt as to the broader implications of the exercise of economical taste for her readership, asserting that "living beyond [one's] income" is "wrong—morally wrong, so far as the individual is concerned; and injurious beyond calculation to the interest of our country" (6). In the recipes that follow, she adheres to this view, emphasizing how certain foods considered luxurious do not in fact taste as good, or provide as much satisfaction, as other, less refined dishes, and vice versa. For a detailed account of the *Housewife*, see Karcher, *The First Woman of the Republic*, 126–50.

8. Child prefaces *The Frugal Housewife* with an epigraph from Benjamin Franklin. And in the second issue of the *Juvenile Miscellany,* she includes a biography of Franklin as an example of the virtues of "industry and integrity" (18). Reminiscent of how Jefferson instructed his grandson to "imitate Franklin," Child urges her readers to model their lives after "this extraordinary man" (13). Consistent with an argument about her sustained attention to eating, Child concludes her account with an example of Franklin's virtuous taste: "If the laugh of the gay and fashionable, should ever make industry and economy appear like contemptible virtues, let them remember that Benjamin Franklin, a poor, hardworking mechanic, became, by means of these very virtues, a philosopher, whose discoveries were useful and celebrated throughout Europe. If they grow weary of application, and despise frugality; let them think of a dirty, printer boy, eating his roll of dry bread, in the streets of Philadelphia, afterwards ambassador to the Court of France; welcomed to the most splendid of Parisian saloons; and his grey hairs crowned with a wreath of laurel, by the young and fair of that enthusiastic nation" (22–23).

9. I offer this summary for those unfamiliar with the major developments in American literary history. It is of course reductive, as no single trajectory could define the rise of a national literature, nor should the idea of a national literature be considered as a single unified entity.

10. "The dreams of an America of complete food security . . . proved elusive in the early years of settlement," Eden explains (*The Early American Table,* 49). Also see Herrmann, "The 'Tragicall Historie.'"

11. Child prided herself on her deep archival research. Karcher documents how Child sought out relevant histories, narratives, journals, and other sources for each of her major projects (*The First Woman of the Republic,* 176).

12. It is also worth noting how Child envelops the description of the breakfast table in a larger scene redolent of sensory pleasure. The narrator observes how Mary Conant's eyes "sparkled as brightly, and the rich tones of her voice were as merry, as they could have been when her little aerial foot danced along the marble saloon of her grandmother" (*Hobomok,* 9). Child replaces the high-toned environment of the "marble saloon" with the rustic breakfast table, laden with indigenous foods, suggesting that the pleasures experienced while dancing— evident in the "sparkle" of Mary's eyes and the "rich tones" of her voice—might be similarly found in the sensory experience of eating. In addition, she perhaps underscores the relation between gustatory and aesthetic taste.

13. In contemporaneous works, "Catharine Beecher, Harriet E. Wilson, and Domestic Discomfort at the Northern Table," Drews similarly observes how the dinner table functioned as a potent symbol of democratic promise: Frederick Douglass, in *My Bondage and My Freedom* (1855), "used his own inclusion at the table to illustrate the promising character of the North"; Hannah Crafts, in *The*

Bondwoman's Narrative (ca. 1850), "illustrates a scene of welcome and human interaction at a shared table"; and Harriet Wilson, in *Our Nig* (1859), employs the dinner table to "illustrate the inconsistencies of Northern practices at the local level" (93, 95, 90). The Thanksgiving scene in "Willie Wharton" supports Drews's analysis. But as *Hobomok* makes plain, Child was already attuned to the symbolism of a shared table many years before these particular representations of food.

14. See Fielder, "'Those People Must Have Loved Her Very Dearly.'"

15. There is more subtle work to be done in unpacking Child's cultural colonialism. A recent essay by Kauanui, "'A Structure, Not an Event,'" points to some possible avenues of entry.

16. In constructing her larger argument about the meaning of the woman's sphere, Kaplan focuses on the dual meaning of domesticity—not simply as the home, but also as a process of domestication, "which entails conquering and taming the wild, the natural, and the alien" ("Manifest Domesticity," 184). "Domestic in this sense," Kaplan explains, "is related to the imperial process of civilizing, and the conditions of domesticity often become markers that distinguish civilization from savagery. Through the process of domestication, the home contains within itself those wild or foreign elements that must be tamed; domesticity not only monitors the orders between the civilized and the savage but also regulates the traces of the savage within itself" (184).

17. In fact, important work has explored this contradiction in *Hobomok*, as well as in other of Child's works. See Sorisio, "The Spectacle of the Body," and Samuels, "Women, Blood, and Contract."

18. See Tricomi, "Harriet Jacobs's Autobiography and the Voice of Lydia Maria Child," for the most recent analysis of Child's impact (or lack thereof) on the text.

19. As Fabian explains, "Like so much else in cultural life of the United States before the Civil War, the art of storytelling and the rules that governed the truth and fiction of stories were sharply shaped by slavery and by race. When fugitive narrators told their stories, they often found themselves labeled as either virtuous truth tellers or dangerous liars. Imagined fiction was not really an option" ("Hannah Crafts, Novelist," 44).

20. Indeed, in the narrative, Jacobs notes that her grandmother's "business proved profitable, and each year she laid by a little, which was saved for a fund to purchase her children" (*Incidents*, 6). (All biographical information derives from the account provided by Jean Fagen Yellin in her introduction to *Incidents*.)

21. Olney, in "'I Was Born,'" offers an early attempt to atomize the features of the slave narrative as a genre. The accounting of violence, in particular, is treated with much more nuance in later scholarship, including works by Hartman and Nudelman.

22. Vizenor's notion of an "aesthetics of survivance" is relevant here. Developed in relation to indigenous cultures, Vizenor describes an aesthetic that

elaborates its claims through "practice and consciousness" rather than direct assertion (*Native Liberty*, 18).

23. With "inhumanity of the enslaved," I reference what Hartman has described—drawing explicitly from the example of Harriet Jacobs—as the "restricted scope of black humanity" brought about by the institution of slavery (*Scenes*, 102).

24. In his analysis of Hannah Crafts's 1850s novel, *The Bondwoman's Narrative*, the first black-authored fictionalized account of slavery presently known, Castronovo observes that the "privilege of inhabiting an abstract plane above the material realm of the everyday was reserved for whiteness" ("The Art of Ghost-Writing," 196). Indeed, the opposition between that era's formal aesthetic philosophies and what Castronovo describes as the "embodied materiality" of everyday life was split along the racialized lines of slavery. Put simply: white bodies were free to imagine; black bodies were not.

25. Peter Gwinn, the slaver who captured Wheatley, began his mission in Senegal, although Carretta thinks "the odds are very low" that Wheatley was purchased in either Fort Lewis or Fort James (*Phillis Wheatley*, 8). More likely, Carretta writes, Gwinn continued down the west coast of Africa and captured Wheatley "either around Sierre Leone" or "further down the Windward Coast" (8).

5. Absence

1. The inn would later become known as the Indian Queen Hotel, when it was purchased by John Gadsby, a leading hotelier, upon Evans's death in 1808. Before that, it was described as the inn "at the sign of the Indian Queen," as in *The New Baltimore Directory, and Annual Register; for 1800 and 1801*, per the note included in the letter to Evans in *The Papers of Thomas Jefferson*.

2. In a journal that documents her stay at the Indian Queen Hotel in June 1815, Harriott Pinckney Horry, of South Carolina, describes the hotel as "a very large establishment," with "between 70 & 80 plates laid at the common Table (which they said was not sufficient) besides many private tables handsomely served." It also boasted a state-of-the-art kitchen, in which, according to Horry, "All the boiling is done by Steam and the roasting at large open fire places and the spits turned by smoke Jacks. The Coffee roaster which is a very large cylinder that I imagine will hold 20 or 30 < . . . > of Coffee is also turn'd by the Smoke Jack. a large patent oven and a number of stoves set in brick work are also in the kitchen" (1815 Journal, June 8, 1815, in Schulz, *The Papers of Eliza Lucas Pinckney and Harriott Pinckney Horry Digital Edition*).

3. My account of the operation of the copying press derives primarily from the process described by Titus et al. in "The Copying Press Process."

4. Bedini remarks upon the "preoccupation with recordkeeping" that Jefferson manifested since his college days (*Thomas Jefferson and His Copying Machines*, 3). Cogliano argues, more specifically, that Jefferson "carefully edited and preserved his massive collection of personal papers" out of an awareness of the "importance of primary sources as the basis of historical writing," and for this reason, he can be said to have demonstrated a calculated attempt to "shape the history of his life and times" (*Thomas Jefferson*, 10–11).

5. In the highly influential essay "Archive Fever: A Freudian Impression," Derrida explains that the French phrase *"en mal de"* (translated as "fever") can "mean something else than to suffer from a sickness." It can also mean "to burn with a passion," or "never to rest" (57). In the context of the archive, this manifests as a "compulsive, repetitive, and nostalgic desire for the archive" on the part of the scholar or—in the case of Jefferson—creator (57). In "The Archive, the Native American, and Jefferson's Convulsions," in which the quoted passage appears, Elmer analyzes *Notes on the State of Virginia* through the lens of Derrida's notion of archive fever, although he does not mention Jefferson's own archiving practice involving his copying press.

6. The quoted passage can be found on the home page of *The Papers of Thomas Jefferson* website (https://jeffersonpapers.princeton.edu/).

7. For a survey of these uses, see Carter, "Of Things Said and Unsaid."

8. For a detailed treatment of Thomas Jefferson's relationship to this particular technology, see Bedini, *Thomas Jefferson and His Copying Machines*.

9. On search, see Underwood, "Theorizing Research Practices We Forgot to Theorize Twenty Years Ago."

10. It is worth a note to pay respect to the incredible amount of human labor involved in this expansion. Each document from each new volume of the print edition—each of which itself takes at least a year to compile, annotate, and edit—would have needed to be translated from typeset copy (or an earlier editable digital format) into the XML format that underlies the digital edition. Even if the process were automated (and I suspect, but am not certain, that it was), the digital version of each document would need to have been proofread for any formatting errors, and then hand-corrected if any were found. In addition, any indices to the *Papers* would have had to be updated, as well as any contextual information provided on the website. With the number of documents increased by more than 50 percent, the underlying search algorithms would likely have had to be reoptimized, and additional storage space would likely have had to be secured. Each of these processes relies on people with specific forms of expertise, yet, like the search technologies themselves, we rarely stop to think about their essential contributions.

11. Hartman, "Venus in Two Acts"; Fuentes, *Dispossessed Lives*; Best, "Neither Lost nor Found"; Gordon, *Ghostly Matters*; and Bastian, "Whispers in the Archives."

12. Hartman, "Venus in Two Acts," 12; Best, "Neither Lost nor Found," 151. It is also worth noting that the field of postcolonial studies has also taken up the challenge of the fundamental incompleteness of its archive. In *Event, Metaphor, Memory,* for example, Amin attempts to "chart the distance that separates" subaltern voices from the judicial discourse that inscribes them into the archival record (118). As another example, Ghosh, in "The Slave of MS. H.6," anticipates Hartman in his use of narrative so as to dilate upon the numbers, names, and ancillary records that constitute the archive of the enslaved; see Ghosh, *The Imam and the Indian,* 169–242.

13. For more information about Protovis, see http://mbostock.github.io /protovis/. For information about its successor, D3.js, see http://d3js.org/.

14. The too-often inscrutable structure of network diagrams has increasingly become a subject of critique, from the fields of both data visualization and media studies. For an edifying critique of current network visualization techniques from the former, see Krzywinski et al., "Hive Plots." For a more media-critical perspective on the problem of the so-called hairball, see Galloway, *The Interface Effect,* 78–100.

15. In her work on antebellum food culture, Harris has described the Big House kitchen as "one of the centers of power" during that period. From the kitchen, she explains, "the cook, solo or in conjunction with the mistress of the house, fed the master's family and often oversaw the feeding on all the plantation. At some of the loftier plantations there could be twenty or more guests to dinner every evening" (*High on the Hog,* 102).

16. "Deformance" is a term first employed by McGann and Samuels, *Radiant Textuality,* 105–35; see also Ramsay, *Machines,* 33, 34.

17. Ramsay, *Machines,* 57.

18. I would like to thank David Sewell, editorial and technical manager of the Rotunda imprint of the University of Virginia Press, for granting me access to the XML files of *The Papers of Thomas Jefferson Digital Edition.* This generous act enabled the analysis described in this section.

19. XML is what is known as a "markup language," a set of agreed-upon standards that allow individuals to annotate a document in a way that can be later read—or "parsed"—by a computer. Many archival documents are encoded in XML so that key information such as author, recipient, or date of composition can be easily extracted and then manipulated and/or displayed. In this case, I received *The Papers of Thomas Jefferson* in XML form, but was required to extract the content of the letters for use with the Stanford Named Entity Recognizer. (I kept track of the additional information associated with each letter in a separate file.) Since the Stanford Named Entity Recognizer returns its output in XML form, I was required to write a second script to extract that information, which I then merged back into the file that contained the letters' original meta-

data. For more information on the Stanford Named Entity Recognizer, and the related set of CoreNLP tools, see http://nlp.stanford.edu/software/.

20. Note that in this letter, "Hemings" is spelled here with two "m's" rather than one. There is also no editorial note that indicates that James Hemmings and James Hemings are the same person. For these two reasons, the letter does not appear in a keyword search on "Hemings."

21. Gordon-Reed, *The Hemingses of Monticello*, 553.

22. Cohen, *Science and the Founding Fathers*, 58.

23. For more on the life of William Playfair, see Wainer and Spence's introduction to the modern edition of Playfair's *Commercial and Political Atlas and Statistical Breviary*. For more on the history of data visualization, see Tufte, *The Visual Display of Quantitative Information*, 13–52.

24. On the history of the fact and its relationship to data, see Rosenberg, "Data before the Fact."

25. I gloss Chun's notion of race as technology above, but it is worth additional discussion. She arrives at her formulation by positing that we understand race as a "mapping tool," one designed to associate visible "traces of the body" with "allegedly innate invisible characteristics" ("Race and/as Technology," 40). While acknowledging the violent history of how this "mapping tool" has been deployed, Chun asserts that the technology of race can, in very specific circumstances, be wielded to generative ends precisely because it "problematizes the usual modes of visualization and revelation" (56). She concludes that "race as technology is both the imposition of a grid of control and a lived social reality in which kinship with technology can be embraced. Importantly, it displaces ontological questions of race—debates of what race really is and is not, focused on separating ideology from truth—with ethical questions: what relations does race set up? As Jennifer Gonzalez has argued, race is fundamentally a question of relation, of an encounter, a recognition, that enables certain actions and bars others. The formulation of race as technology also opens up the possibility that, although the idea and the experience of race have been used for racist ends, the best way to fight racism might not be to deny the existence of race, but to make race do different things" (56–57). I take inspiration from Chun here in attempting to make the Jefferson archive "do different things" with its contents, in full view of its repressive force.

26. See chapter 1 for an image of the document as well as a complete transcription.

27. This approach of working backward to identify the labor (and tools) employed is exemplified by Posner in "How Did They Make That?"

28. For an extended consideration of digital labor, and the implications for human rights, ethics, and history, among other themes, see Scholz, *Digital Labor*. On labor as it applies to data work, see D'Ignazio and Klein, *Data Feminism*.

29. For a list of all known recipes recorded by Jefferson and his close family members, including several that perhaps originated with Hemings, see "Jefferson Family Recipe Sources."

Epilogue

1. Thanks to Christopher Farrish for providing me with a photo of the wall text as it was then displayed, and to Mark Sample for providing additional details of the painting's installation.

2. As described in the Introduction, it is now known that Hercules escaped from bondage in early 1797, after being sent back to Mount Vernon estate by Washington, who did so in order to avoid a law in place in Pennsylvania at the time that granted freedom to any enslaved person who had lived in Pennsylvania for six continuous months. By sending Hercules back to Virginia every six months, as Washington did for each of the men and women he enslaved, he would restart what Adrian Miller calls Hercules's "freedom clock" (65).

3. On Carême, see Kelly, *Cooking for Kings*.

4. Adrian Miller also discusses this possibility; see *President's Kitchen Cabinet*, 66–70.

5. For a roundup of these assessments, see LaBan, "A Birthday Shock from Washington's Chef."

6. Fascinatingly, the conclusion of the art historians assembled to analyze the image was that the hat—and, therefore, the sitter—was likely from the Caribbean. LaBan describes the hat as "a Caribbean headdress like the ones seen in paintings by Agostino Brunias of Dominican Creoles in that era" ("Behind the Story," n.p.). An alternate epilogue could have probed the significance of this finding to the depth it deserves.

7. In the full quote from which this sentiment is taken, Eagleton even more directly connects the history of aesthetic thought to eating. He writes: "It is as though philosophy suddenly wakes up to the fact that there is a dense, swarming territory beyond its own mental enclave, threatening to fall utterly outside its sway. That territory is nothing less than the whole of our sensate life—the business of affections and aversions, of how the world strikes the body on its sensory surfaces, of what takes root in the guts and the gaze and all that arises from our most banal, biological insertion into the world" ("The Ideology of the Aesthetic," 327–28).

8. The date specified in the title—that of the Declaration of Independence— underscores Moorhead's enslaved status; while figures such as Benjamin Franklin, Thomas Jefferson, and James Madison were asserting their autonomy, Moorhead remained enslaved.

9. Wheatley is believed to have commissioned the original portrait to accompany the publication of her book, as she was asked to include a portrait of

herself to confirm that she was, in fact, an enslaved black woman. She met Moorhead in Boston, where she lived near him for a time. In addition to her complimentary poem, art historians often point to the similarities between the portrait and those of the Boston-based artist John Singleton Copley, whose work Moorhead would have likely seen, as well as to the fact that a white artist would have been unlikely to take a commission to paint a black woman, as evidence for Moorhead as the artist. That the original portrait does not survive has made further authentication difficult. See Slauter, "Looking for Scipio Moorhead," for more on this background.

10. Erikson, in "Posing the Black Painter," suggests that the painters depicted in the subsequent portraits are wholly "fictional" (43).

11. Recall, once again, the nineteenth-century characterization of Hercules as a "celebrated *artiste*" (Custis, *Recollections and Private Memoirs of Washington,* 422).

Bibliography

Adams, Rachel. "'A Mixture of Delicious and Freak': The Queer Fiction of Carson McCullers." *American Literature* 71, no. 3 (1999): 551–83.

Addison, Joseph. "The Pleasures of the Imagination." In *The Great Age of the English Essay: An Anthology,* edited by Denise Gigante, 78–81. New Haven, Conn.: Yale University Press, 2008.

Allewaert, Monique. *Ariel's Ecology: Plantations, Personhood, and Colonialism in the American Tropics.* Minneapolis: University of Minnesota Press, 2013.

Amin, Shahid. *Event, Metaphor, Memory: Chauri Chaura, 1922–1992.* Berkeley: University of California Press, 1995.

Anderson, Douglas. *The Radical Enlightenments of Benjamin Franklin.* Baltimore: Johns Hopkins University Press, 1997.

Anderson, Sterling P. "'Queen Molly' and *The Virginia Housewife.*" *Virginia Cavalcade* 20 (Spring 1971): 28–35.

Appadurai, Arjun. "How to Make a National Cuisine: Cookbooks in Contemporary India." *Comparative Studies in Society and History* 30, no. 1 (January 1988): 3–24.

Appleby, Joyce. *Capitalism and a New Social Order: The Republican Vision of the 1790s.* New York: New York University Press, 1984.

Appleby, Joyce. *Liberal and Republicanism in the Historical Imagination.* Cambridge, Mass.: Harvard University Press, 1992.

Aristotle. *The Nicomachean Ethics.* Edited by Lesley Brown and translated by David Ross. New York: Oxford University Press, 2009.

Bailyn, Bernard. *The Ideological Origins of the American Revolution.* Cambridge, Mass.: Harvard University Press, 1967.

Barthes, Roland. "Towards a Psychosociology of Contemporary Food Consumption." In *Food and Culture: A Reader.* 3rd ed., edited by Carole Counihan and Penny Van Esterik, 23–50. New York: Routledge, 2012.

Bastian, Jeannette. "Whispers in the Archives: Finding the Voices of the Colonized in Records of the Colonizer." In *Political Pressure and the Archival Record,* edited by Margaret Proctor et al., 25–43. Chicago: Society of American Archivists, 2005.

Bedini, Silvio A. *Thomas Jefferson and His Copying Machines.* Charlottesville: University of Virginia Press, 1984.

Benhamou, Reed. "The Artificial Limb in Preindustrial France." *Technology and Culture* 35, no. 4 (October 1994): 835–45.

Bennett, Jane. *Vibrant Matter: A Political Ecology of Things.* Durham, N.C.: Duke University Press, 2010.

Berlant, Lauren, and Jordan Alexander Stein. "Cruising Veganism." *GLQ: A Journal of Lesbian and Gay Studies* 21, no. 1 (January 2015): 18–23.

Berlin, Ira. *Generations of Captivity: A History of African American Slaves.* Cambridge, Mass.: Harvard University Press, 2004.

Bernstein, Robin. *Racial Innocence: Performing American Childhood from Slavery to Civil Rights.* New York: New York University Press, 2011.

Berry, Wendell. "Renewing Husbandry." *Orion Magazine* (2005). https://orion magazine.org/article/renewing-husbandry/.

Bertelsen, Lance. *The Nonsense Club: Literature and Popular Culture, 1749–1764.* New York: Oxford University Press, 1986.

Best, Stephen. "Neither Lost nor Found: Slavery and the Visual Archive." *Representations* 113 (Winter 2011): 150–63.

Best, Stephen, and Sharon Marcus. "Surface Reading: An Introduction." *Representations* 108 (Fall 2009): 1–21.

Blackwood, Sarah. "Fugitive Obscura: Runaway Slave Portraiture and Early Photographic Technology." *American Literature* 81, no. 1 (March 2009): 93–125.

Blockson, Charles. "Black Samuel Fraunces: Patriot, White House Steward, and Restaurateur Par Excellence." *Temple University Libraries.* https://library.temple .edu/collections/blockson/fraunces.

Bourdieu, Pierre. *Distinction: A Social Critique of the Judgment of Taste.* New York: Routledge, 2013 [1979].

Brant, Irving. *James Madison: The Nationalist, 1780–1787.* Indianapolis: Bobbs-Merrill, 1948.

Breen, T. H. "'Baubles of Britain': The American and Consumer Revolutions of the Eighteenth Century." *Past & Present* 119 (May 1988): 73–104.

Brennan, Teresa. *The Transmission of Affect.* Ithaca, N.Y.: Cornell University Press, 2004.

Brillat-Savarin, Jean Anthelme. *The Physiology of Taste: Or, Meditations on Transcendental Gastronomy.* Translated by M. F. K. Fisher. Washington, D.C.: Counterpoint, 1999 [1835].

Brissot de Warville, Jacques-Pierre. *New Travels in the United States.* Bowling Green, Ohio: Historical Publications, 1919 [1791].

Brown, Gillian. *Domestic Individualism: Imagining Self in Nineteenth-Century America.* Berkeley: University of California Press, 1990.

Buck-Morss, Susan. "Aesthetics and Anaesthetics: Walter Benjamin's Artwork Essay Reconsidered." *October* 62 (Autumn 1992): 3–41.

Buck-Morss, Susan. "Hegel and Haiti." *Critical Inquiry* 26, no. 4 (Summer 2000): 821–65.

Bynum, Tara. "Phillis Wheatley's Pleasures." *Common-Place: The Interactive Journal of Early American Life* 11, no. 1 (October 2010). http://www.common -place-archives.org/vol-11/no-01/bynum/.

Cahill, Edward. *Liberty of the Imagination: Aesthetic Theory, Literary Form, and Politics in the Early United States.* Philadelphia: University of Pennsylvania Press, 2012.

Cahill, Edward, and Edward Larkin. "Aesthetics, Feeling, and Form in Early American Literary Studies." *Early American Literature* 51, no. 2 (2016): 235–54.

Carney, Judith Ann. *Black Rice: The African Origins of Rice Cultivation in the Americas.* Cambridge, Mass.: Harvard University Press, 2001.

Carretta, Vincent. *Phillis Wheatley: Biography of a Genius in Bondage.* Athens: University of Georgia Press, 2011.

Carter, Rodney G. S. "Of Things Said and Unsaid: Power, Archival Silences, and Power in Silence." *Archivaria* 61 (Spring 2006): 215–33.

Castiglia, Christopher. *Interior States: Institutional Consciousness and the Inner Life of Democracy in the Antebellum United States.* Durham, N.C.: Duke University Press, 2008.

Castiglia, Christopher. "Revolution Is a Fiction: The Way We Read (Early American) Literature Now." *Early American Literature* 51, no. 2 (2016): 397–418.

Castronovo, Russ. "The Art of Ghost-Writing: Memory, Materiality, and Slave Aesthetics." In *In Search of Hannah Crafts: Critical Essays on* The Bondwoman's Narrative, edited by Henry Louis Gates Jr. and Hollis Robbins, 195–212. New York: Basic Civitas Books, 2004.

Cecire, Natalia. "Introduction: Theory and the Virtues of Digital Humanities." *Journal of Digital Humanities* 1, no. 1 (Winter 2011). http://journalofdigital humanities.org/1-1/introduction-theory-and-the-virtues-of-digital-humanities -by-natalia-cecire/.

Child, Lydia Maria. *An Appeal in Favor of That Class of Americans Called Africans.* Boston: Allen and Ticknor, 1833.

Child, Lydia Maria. "Benjamin Franklin." *Juvenile Miscellany* 2 (March 1827): 18–23.

Child, Lydia Maria. "Farewell." *National Anti-Slavery Standard,* 4 May 1843, 190.

Child, Lydia Maria. *The Freedmen's Book.* Boston: Ticknor and Fields, 1866.

Child, Lydia Maria. *The Frugal Housewife: Dedicated to Those Who Are Not Ashamed of Economy.* Boston: Carter and Hendee, 1830 [1829].

Child, Lydia Maria. *Hobomok and Other Writings on Indians.* Edited by Carolyn L. Karcher. New Brunswick, N.J.: Rutgers University Press, 1986.

Chun, Wendy H. K. "Race and/as Technology, or How to Do Things to Race." In *Race after the Internet,* edited by Lisa Nakamura and Peter Chow-White, 1–23. New York: Routledge, 2012.

Cogliano, Francis. *Thomas Jefferson: Reputation and Legacy.* Charlottesville: University of Virginia Press, 2008.

Cohen, I. Bernard. *Science and the Founding Fathers: Science in the Political Thought of Jefferson, Franklin, Adams, and Madison.* New York: Norton, 1997.

Conkling, Margaret. *Memoirs of the Mother and Wife of Washington.* Auburn, N.Y.: Derby, Miller, 1850.

Cooke, Jacob. "The Compromise of 1790." *William and Mary Quarterly,* 3rd. ser., 27, no. 4 (October 1970): 523–45.

Counihan, Carole, ed. *Food in the USA.* New York: Routledge, 2002.

Coviello, Peter. *Tomorrow's Parties: Sex and the Untimely in Nineteenth-Century America.* New York: New York University Press, 2013.

Custis, George Washington Park. *Recollections and Private Memoirs of Washington.* Philadelphia: J. W. Bradley, 1861 [1860].

Dain, Bruce. *Hideous Monster of the Mind: American Race Theory in the Early Republic.* Cambridge, Mass.: Harvard University Press, 2002.

Daniels, Jonathan. *The Randolphs of Virginia: America's Foremost Family.* New York: Doubleday, 1972.

Davidson, Jenny. *Hypocrisy and the Politics of Politeness: Manners and Morals from Locke to Austin.* New York: Cambridge University Press, 2007.

Davidson, Michael. *Concerto for the Left Hand: Disability and the Defamiliar Body.* Ann Arbor: University of Michigan Press, 2008.

Derrida, Jacques. "Archive Fever: A Freudian Impression." Translated by Eric Prenowitz. *Diacritics* 25, no. 2 (Summer 1995): 9–63.

DeWitt, Dave. *Founding Foodies: How Washington, Jefferson, and Franklin Revolutionized American Cuisine.* Chicago: Sourcebooks, 2010.

Dickie, George. *The Century of Taste: The Philosophical Odyssey of Taste in the Eighteenth Century.* New York: Oxford University Press, 1996.

D'Ignazio, Catherine, and Lauren F. Klein. *Data Feminism.* Cambridge, Mass.: MIT Press, 2020.

Dillon, Elizabeth Maddock. "Sentimental Aesthetics." *American Literature* 76, no. 3 (September 2004): 495–523.

Douglas, Ann. *The Feminization of American Culture.* New York: Avon, 1977.

Douglass, Mary. *Purity and Danger: An Analysis of the Concepts of Pollution and Taboo.* New York: Routledge, 2000.

Drews, Marie. "Catharine Beecher, Harriet E. Wilson, and Domestic Discomfort at the Northern Table." In *Culinary Aesthetics and Practices in Nineteenth-Century American Literature,* edited by Monika Elbert and Marie Drews, 89–105. New York: Palgrave Macmillan, 2009.

Drexler, Michael J., and Ed White. "Secret Witness; Or, the Fantasy Structure of Republicanism." *Early American Literature* 44, no. 9 (2009): 333–63.

Drucker, Johanna. "Humanities Approaches to Graphical Display." *Digital Humanities Quarterly* 5 (Winter 2011). http://digitalhumanities.org:8081/dhq/vol/5/1/000091/000091.html.

Dubey, Madhu. "Speculative Fictions of Slavery." *American Literature* 82, no. 4 (December 2010): 779–805.

Dunbar, Erica Armstrong. *A Fragile Freedom: African American Women and Emancipation in the Antebellum City.* New Haven, Conn.: Yale University Press, 2008.

Dunbar, Erica Armstrong. *Never Caught: The Washingtons' Relentless Pursuit of Their Runaway Slave, Ona Judge.* New York: Simon and Schuster, 2017.

Eagleton, Terry. "The Ideology of the Aesthetic." *Poetics Today* 9, no. 2 (1988): 327–38.

Eden, Trudy. "About That Recipe." *Common-Place: The Interactive Journal of Early American Life* 11, no. 3 (April 2011). http://www.common-place-archives.org/vol-11/no-03/eden/.

Eden, Trudy. *The Early American Table: Food and Society in the New World.* DeKalb: Northern Illinois University Press, 2010.

Egerton, Douglas R. *Gabriel's Rebellion: The Virginia Slave Conspiracies of 1800 and 1802.* Chapel Hill: University of North Carolina Press, 1993.

Elmer, Jonathan. "The Archive, the Native American, and Jefferson's Convulsions." *Diacritics* 28 (Winter 1998): 5–24.

Emsley, Sarah. "Harriet Jacobs and the Language of Autobiography." *Canadian Journal of American Studies* 28, no. 2 (Summer 1998): 145–62.

"Enslaved Persons of African Descent in the President's House." *UShistory.org.* http://www.ushistory.org/presidentshouse/slaves/index.php.

Erikson, Peter. "Posing the Black Painter: Kerry James Marshall's Portraits of Artists' Self-Portraits." *Nka: Journal of Contemporary African Art* 38–39 (November 2016): 40–51.

Erkkila, Betsy. "Franklin and the Revolutionary Body." *ELH* 67, no. 3 (Fall 2000): 717–41.

Fabian, Ann. "Hannah Crafts, Novelist; or, How a Silent Observer Became a 'Dabster at Innovation.'" In *In Search of Hannah Crafts: Critical Essays on The Bondwoman's Narrative,* edited by Henry Louis Gates Jr. and Hollis Robbins, 43–52. New York: Basic Civitas Books, 2004.

Faherty, Duncan. *Remodeling the Nation: The Architecture of American Identity, 1776–1858.* Hanover: University of New Hampshire Press, 2007.

Farrish, Christopher. "Theft, Food Labor, and Culinary Insurrection in the Virginia Plantation Yard." In *Dethroning the Deceitful Pork Chop: African American*

Foodways from Slavery to Obama, edited by Jennifer Jensen Wallach, 178–91. Fayetteville: University of Arkansas Press, 2015.

Ferguson, Priscilla Parkhurst. *Accounting for Taste: The Triumph of French Cuisine.* Chicago: University of Chicago Press, 2006.

Ferris, Marcie Cohen. *The Edible South: The Power of Food and the Making of an American Region.* Chapel Hill: University of North Carolina Press, 2014.

Fielder, Brigitte. "'Those People Must Have Loved Her Very Dearly': Interracial Adoption and Radical Love in Antislavery Children's Literature." *Early American Studies* 14, no. 4 (Fall 2016): 749–80.

Fischer, Sibylle. *Modernity Disavowed: Haiti and the Cultures of Slavery in the Age of Revolution.* Durham, N.C.: Duke University Press, 2004.

Fisher, Abby. *What Mrs. Fischer Knows about Old Southern Cooking.* San Francisco: Women's Co-Op Printing Office, 1881.

Fliegelman, Jay. *Prodigals and Pilgrims: The American Revolution against Patriarchal Authority, 1750–1800.* New York: Cambridge University Press, 1982.

Folsom, Ed. "Database as Genre: The Epic Transformation of Archives." *PMLA* 122, no. 5 (October 2007): 1571–79.

Foner, Eric. *Give Me Liberty! An American History.* New York: Norton, 2009.

Foreman, Pier Gabrielle. *Activist Sentiments: Reading Black Women in the Nineteenth Century.* Champaign-Urbana: University of Illinois Press, 2009.

Foucault, Michel. *Foucault Live: Interviews, 1961–84.* Edited by Sylvere Lotringer and translated by John Johnston. New York: Semiotext(e), 1996 [1989].

Fowler, Damon Lee, ed. *Dining at Monticello: In Good Taste and Abundance.* Chapel Hill: University of North Carolina Press, 2005.

Franklin, Benjamin. *The Autobiography of Benjamin Franklin.* Edited by Leonard Labaree, Ralph Ketcham, Helen Boatfield, and Helene Fineman. New Haven, Conn.: Yale University Press, 2003.

Franklin, Benjamin. *Memoirs of the Life and Writings of Benjamin Franklin.* Edited by William Temple Franklin. 3 vols. London: Henry Colburn, 1818.

Franklin, Benjamin. *The Papers of Benjamin Franklin Digital Edition.* Edited by Leonard W. Larabee et al. Packard Humanities Institute, Yale University. https://franklinpapers.org/digital.jsp.

Franklin, Benjamin. *Poor Richard: The Almanacks for the Years 1733–1758.* Edited by Van Wyck Brooks. New York: Bonanza, 1976.

Frasca, Ralph. *Benjamin Franklin's Printing Network: Disseminating Virtue in Early America.* Columbia: University of Missouri Press, 2016.

Fretwell, Erica. "Emily Dickinson in Domingo." *J19: The Journal of Nineteenth-Century Americanists* 1, no. 1 (Spring 2013): 71–96.

Fuentes, Marisa J. *Dispossessed Lives: Enslaved Women, Violence, and the Archive.* Philadelphia: University of Pennsylvania Press, 2016.

Galloway, Alexander R. *The Interface Effect.* Malden, Mass.: Polity Press, 2012.

Garland-Thomson, Rosemarie. *Extraordinary Bodies: Figuring Physical Disability in American Culture and Literature.* New York: Columbia University Press, 1997.

Garrison, William Lloyd. "Mrs. Child." *Genius of Universal Emancipation,* 20 November 1829, 85.

Gates Jr., Henry Louis. "Mister Jefferson and the Trials of Phillis Wheatley." Jefferson Lecture, National Endowment for the Humanities, 2002. https://www.neh.gov/about/awards/jefferson-lecture/henry-louis-gates-jr-biography.

Geggus, David Patrick. *Haitian Revolutionary Studies.* Bloomington: Indiana University Press, 2002.

Ghosh, Amitav. *The Imam and the Indian: Prose Pieces.* Delhi: Ravi Dayal, 2002.

Gigante, Denise. *Gusto: Essential Writings in Nineteenth-Century Gastronomy.* New York: Routledge, 2005.

Gigante, Denise. *Taste: A Literary History.* New Haven, Conn.: Yale University Press, 2005.

Gikandi, Simon. *Slavery and the Culture of Taste.* Princeton, N.J.: Princeton University Press, 2011.

Gilroy, Paul. *The Black Atlantic: Modernity and Double Consciousness.* Cambridge, Mass.: Harvard University Press, 1993.

Githire, Njeri. *Cannibal Writes: Eating Others in Caribbean and Indian Ocean Women's Writing.* Champaign: University of Illinois Press, 2014.

Golden, Janet. *A Social History of Wet Nursing in America: From Breast to Bottle.* New York: Cambridge University Press, 1996.

Gordon, Avery. *Ghostly Matters: Haunting and the Sociological Imagination.* Minneapolis: University of Minnesota Press, 2008 [1996].

Gordon-Reed, Annette. *The Hemingses of Monticello: An American Family.* New York: Norton, 2008.

Gordon-Reed, Annette. "The Resonance of Minds: Thomas Jefferson and James Madison in the Republic of Letters." In *The Cambridge Companion to Thomas Jefferson,* edited by Frank Shuffelton, 179–92. New York: Cambridge University Press, 2009.

Grainger, James. *The Sugar-Cane: A Poem. In Four Books. With Notes.* London: R. and J. Dodsley, 1764.

Grimod de la Reynière, Alexandre Balthazar. *L'almanach des gourmands.* Edited by Jean-Claude Bonnet. Paris: Menu Fretin, 2012.

Grosz, Elizabeth. *Volatile Bodies: Toward a Corporeal Feminism.* Indianapolis: University of Indiana Press, 1994.

Gruesz, Kristen Silva. "America." In *Keywords for American Cultural Studies,* edited by Glenn Hendler and Bruce Burgett, 16–21. New York: New York University Press, 2007.

Hafertepe, Kenneth. "An Inquiry into Thomas Jefferson's Ideas of Beauty." *Journal of the Society of Architectural Historians* 59, no. 2 (June 2000): 216–31.

Haley, Andrew P. "The Nation before Taste: The Challenges of American Culinary History." *The Public Historian* 34, no. 2 (May 2012): 53–78.

Harland, Marion. *Breakfast, Luncheon and Tea.* New York: Scribner, Armstrong, 1875.

Harland, Marion. *Common Sense in the Household: A Manual of Practical Housewifery.* New York: Scribner, Armstrong, 1873.

Harland, Marion. *Judith: A Chronicle of Old Virginia.* Philadelphia: Our Continent, 1883.

Harris, Jessica. *High on the Hog: A Culinary Journey from Africa to America.* New York: Bloomsbury, 2011.

Hartman, Saidiya. *Scenes of Subjection: Terror, Slavery, and Self-Making in Nineteenth-Century America.* New York: Oxford University Press, 1997.

Hartman, Saidiya. "Venus in Two Acts." *Small Axe* 26 (June 2008): 1–14.

Hatch, Peter J. *The Fruits and Fruit Trees of Monticello.* Charlottesville: University of Virginia Press, 1998.

Hawthorne, Nathaniel. *The House of the Seven Gables.* Edited by Milton Stern. New York: Penguin, 1981.

Hayles, N. Katherine. "Speculative Aesthetics and Object-Oriented Inquiry (OOI)." *Speculations: A Journal of Speculative Realism* 5 (2014): 158–79.

Hearne, Lafcadio. *La Cuisine Creole: A Collection of Culinary Recipes from Leading Chefs and Noted Creole Housewives, Who Have Made New Orleans Famous for Its Cuisine.* New Orleans: F. F. Hansell, ca. 1885.

Hendler, Glenn. *Public Sentiments: Structures of Feeling in Nineteenth-Century American Literature.* Chapel Hill: University of North Carolina Press, 2001.

Herrmann, Rachel B. "The 'Tragicall Historie': Cannibalism and Abundance in Colonial Jamestown." *William and Mary Quarterly,* 3rd. ser., 68, no. 1 (January 2011): 47–74.

Higginson, Thomas Wentworth. "Lydia Maria Child." In *Eminent Women of the Age; Being Narratives of the Lives and Deeds of the Most Prominent Women of the Present Generation,* edited by James Parton et al., 38–65. Hartford, Conn.: S. M. Betts, 1868.

Hird, Myra. *The Origins of Sociable Life: Evolution after Science Studies.* London: Palgrave Macmillan, 2009.

Holland, Sharon, Marcia Ochoa, and Kyla Wazana Tompkins. "On the Visceral." *GLQ: A Journal of Lesbian and Gay Studies* 20, no. 4 (2014): 391–406.

hooks, bell. *Black Looks: Race and Representation.* Cambridge, Mass.: South End Press, 1999.

Jacobs, Harriet. *Incidents in the Life of a Slave Girl, Written by Herself.* Edited by Jean Fagin Yellen. Cambridge, Mass.: Harvard University Press, 1987.

Jain, Sarah S. "The Prosthetic Imagination: Enabling and Disabling the Prosthesis Trope." *Science, Technology, & Human Values* 24, no. 1 (Winter 1999): 31–54.

James, C. L. R. *The Black Jacobins: Toussaint L'Ouverture and the San Domingo Revolution*. 2nd ed. New York: Vintage, 1963.

Jaros, Peter. "Good Names: Olaudah Equiano or Gustavus Vassa." *The Eighteenth Century* 41, no. 1 (Spring 2013): 1–24.

Jarrett, Gene Andrew. "'To Refute Mr. Jefferson's Arguments Respecting Us': Thomas Jefferson, David Walker, and the Politics of Early African American Literature." *Early American Literature* 46, no. 2 (2011): 291–318.

"Jefferson Family Recipe Sources." *The Thomas Jefferson Encyclopedia*. https://www.monticello.org/site/research-and-collections/jefferson-family-recipe-sources.

Jefferson, Thomas. *The Family Letters of Thomas Jefferson*. Edited by Edwin Morris Betts and James Adam Bear Jr. Charlottesville: University of Virginia Press, 1986.

Jefferson, Thomas. *The Garden and the Farm Books of Thomas Jefferson*. Edited by Robert C. Baron. Golden, Colo.: Fulcrum, 1987.

Jefferson, Thomas. *Letters, 1760–1826*. Edited by Merrill D. Peterson. New York: Literary Classics of the United States/Viking, 1985.

Jefferson, Thomas. "Letter to Mary Randolph," 30 March 1825. *Founders Online*, National Archives. https://founders.archives.gov/documents/Jefferson/98-01-02-5093.

Jefferson, Thomas. *Memoir, Correspondence, and Miscellanies from the Papers of Thomas Jefferson*. 4 vols. Edited by Thomas Jefferson Randolph. Boston: Gray and Bowen, 1830.

Jefferson, Thomas. *Notes on the State of Virginia*. Edited by Merrill D. Peterson. New York: Library of America, 1984 [1785].

Jefferson, Thomas. *The Papers of Thomas Jefferson Digital Edition*. Edited by Barbara Oberg and J. Jefferson Looney. Charlottesville: University of Virginia Press, 2008. https://www.upress.virginia.edu/content/papers-thomas-jefferson-digital-edition.

Jefferson, Thomas. *The Writings of Thomas Jefferson*. 19 vols. Edited by Albert Ellery Bergh. Washington, D.C.: Thomas Jefferson Memorial Association, 1905–7.

Jennings, Paul. *A Colored Man's Reminiscences of James Madison*. Brooklyn: George C. Beadle, 1865 [1863].

Jockers, Matthew. *Macroanalysis: Digital Methods and Literary History*. Champaign: University of Illinois Press, 2013.

Johnson, Jessica Marie. "Markup Bodies: Black [Life] Studies and Slavery [Death] Studies at the Digital Crossroads." *Social Text* 36, no. 4 (December 2018): 57–79.

Johnson, Walter. "On Agency." *Journal of Social History* 37, no. 1 (Fall 2003): 113–24.

Kaplan, Amy. "Manifest Domesticity." In *No More Separate Spheres! A Next Wave American Studies Reader,* edited by Cathy N. Davidson and Jessamyn Hatcher, 183–208. Durham, N.C.: Duke University Press, 2002.

Karcher, Carolyn L. *The First Woman of the Republic: A Cultural Biography of Lydia Maria Child.* Durham, N.C.: Duke University Press, 1994.

Kauanui, J. Kehaulani. "'A Structure, Not an Event: Settler Colonialism and Enduring Indigeneity.'" *Lateral: Journal of the Cultural Studies Association* 5, no. 1 (Spring 2016). https://csalateral.org/issue/5-1/forum-alt-humanities-settler-colonialism-enduring-indigeneity-kauanui/.

Kaufman, Cathy. "The Claw at the Table: The Gastronomic Criticism of Grimod de la Reynière." *Vintage Magazine* 2 (2010): 88–94.

Kazanjian, David. *The Colonizing Trick: National Culture and Imperial Citizenship in Early America.* Minneapolis: University of Minnesota Press, 2003.

Kazanjian, David. "Scenes of Speculation." *Social Text* 33, no. 4 (2015): 77–84.

Kazanjian, David. "The Speculative Freedom of Colonial Liberia." *American Quarterly* 63, no. 4 (December 2011): 863–93.

Kelly, Ian. *Cooking for Kings: The Life of Antonin Carême, the First Celebrity Chef.* New York: Walker Books, 2004.

Kerber, Linda. "The Republican Mother: Women and the Enlightenment—An American Perspective." *American Quarterly* 28, no. 2 (Summer 1976): 187–205.

Ketchum, Ralph Louis. *James Madison: A Biography.* Charlottesville: University of Virginia Press, 1990.

Kierner, Cynthia A. "'The Dark and Dense Cloud Perpetually Lowering over Us': Gender and the Decline of the Gentry in Postrevolutionary Virginia." *Journal of the Early Republic* 20, no. 2 (Summer 2000): 185–217.

Klein, Lauren F. "Dinner-Table Bargains: Thomas Jefferson, James Madison, and the Senses of Taste." *Early American Literature* 49, no. 2 (Spring 2014): 403–33.

Klein, Lauren F. "The Image of Absence: Archival Silence, Data Visualization, and James Hemings." *American Literature* 85, no. 4 (Winter 2013): 661–88.

Klein, Lauren F. "The Matter of Early American Taste." In *The Cambridge Companion to Food and Literature,* edited by J. Michelle Coghlan, 58–72. New York: Cambridge University Press, 2020.

Klein, Lauren F. "Speculative Aesthetics." *Early American Literature* 51, no. 2 (Spring 2016): 439–47.

Kobayashi, Masayuki, et al. "Functional Imaging of Gustatory Perception and Imagery: 'Top-Down' Processing of Gustatory Signals." *NeuroImage* 23 (2004): 1271–82.

Korsmeyer, Carolyn. *Making Sense of Taste: Food and Philosophy.* Ithaca, N.Y.: Cornell University Press, 2002.

Korsmeyer, Carolyn. "Tastes and Pleasures." *Romantic Circles* (January 2007). https://romantic-circles.org/praxis/gastronomy/korsmeyer/korsmeyer_essay.html.

Krzywinski, Martin, Inanc Birol, Steven J. M. Jones, and Marco A. Marra. "Hive Plots—Rational Approach to Visualizing Networks." *Briefings in Bioinformatics* 13, no. 5 (September 2012): 627–44.

LaBan, Craig. "Behind the Story: How Experts Knew the Painting Wasn't Hercules and Wasn't a Gilbert Stuart." *Philadelphia Inquirer and Daily News*, 6 March 2019. https://www.inquirer.com/food/craig-laban/george-washington -gilbert-stuart-portrait-hercules-slave-chef-craig-laban-20190306.html.

LaBan, Craig. "A Birthday Shock from Washington's Chef." *Philadelphia Inquirer and Daily News*, 22 February 2010. https://www.inquirer.com/philly/food /restaurants/20100222_A_birthday_shock_from_Washington_s_chef.html.

LaBan, Craig. "George Washington's Enslaved Chef, Who Cooked in Philadelphia, Disappears from Painting, but May Have Reappeared in New York." *Philadelphia Inquirer and Daily News*, 1 March 2019. https://www.inquirer .com/food/craig-laban/george-washington-slave-chef-cook-hercules-gilbert -stuart-painting-wrong-20190301.html.

Lachance, Paul. "Repercussions of the Haitian Revolution in Louisiana." In *The Impact of the Haitian Revolution in the Atlantic World*, edited by David P. Geggus, 209–30. Columbia: University of South Carolina Press, 2001.

Larkin, Edward. *The American School of Empire*. New York: Cambridge University Press, 2016.

Le Dantec-Lowry, Hélène. "Reading Women's Lives in Cookbooks and Other Culinary Writings: A Critical Essay." *Revue Française d'études Américaines* 116, no. 2 (2008): 99–122.

Lee, Jean Butenhoff, ed. *Experiencing Mount Vernon: Eyewitness Accounts, 1784– 1865*. Charlottesville: University of Virginia Press, 2006.

Lepore, Jill. *The Name of War: King Philip's War and the Origins of American Identity*. New York: Knopf, 1998.

Levenstein, Harvey. *Revolution at the Table: The Transformation of the American Diet*. Berkeley: University of California Press, 1988.

Liu, Alan. "Where Is Cultural Criticism in the Digital Humanities?" In *Debates in the Digital Humanities*, edited by Matthew K. Gold, 490–506. Minneapolis: University of Minnesota Press, 2012.

Lloyd, Henry Martyn, ed. *The Discourse of Sensibility: The Knowing Body in the Enlightenment*. Cham, Switzerland: Springer, 2013.

Loichot, Valérie. *The Tropics Bite Back: Culinary Coups in Caribbean Literature*. Minneapolis: University of Minnesota Press, 2013.

Looby, Christopher. "The Constitution of Nature: Taxonomy as Politics in Jefferson, Peale, and Bartram." *Early American Literature* 22 (Winter 1987): 252–73.

Love, Heather. *Feeling Backward: Loss and the Politics of Queer History*. Cambridge, Mass.: Harvard University Press, 2009.

Luciano, Dana. *Arranging Grief: Sacred Time and the Body in Nineteenth-Century America*. New York: New York University Press, 2007.

Lundblad, Michael. "From Animal to Animality Studies." *PMLA* 124, no. 2 (2009): 496–502.

MacDonough, Giles. *A Palate in Revolution: Grimod de La Reynière's Almanach des Gourmands*. London: Robin Clark, 1987.

Mackay, Robin, Luke Pendrell, and James Trafford, eds. *Speculative Aesthetics*. Windsor Quarry, U.K.: Urbanomic, 2014.

Mackie, Erin. *The Commerce of Everyday Life: Selections from* The Tatler *and* The Spectator. New York: Bedford-St. Martin's, 1998.

Maclay, William. *Journal of William Maclay: United States Senator from Pennsylvania, 1789–1791*. Edited by Edgar Stanton Maclay. New York: D. Appleton, 1890.

Madison, Dolley. *The Papers of Dolley Madison Digital Edition*. Edited by Holly C. Shulman. Charlottesville: University of Virginia Press, 2008. https://rotunda.upress.virginia.edu/dmde/.

Madison, James. *Letters and Other Writings of James Madison*. Philadelphia: J. B. Lippincott, 1865.

Madison, James. "Letter to Mary Randolph," 26 March 1825. *Founders Online*. National Archives. https://founders.archives.gov/documents/Madison/04-03-02-0505.

Madison, James. *The Papers of James Madison Digital Edition*. Edited by J. C. A. Stagg. Charlottesville: University of Virginia Press, 2010. https://rotunda.upress.virginia.edu/founders/JSMN.html.

"Marion Harland." *Feeding America*. Michigan State University. https://fedcom4a.lib.msu.edu/content/biographies?author_name=Harland%2C+Marion%2C+1830-1922.

Marx, Leo. "What Is Technology?" In *Major Problems in the History of American Technology*, edited by Merritt Roe Smith and Gregory Clancey, 2–7. New York: Houghton Mifflin, 1997.

Matthewson, Tim. "Jefferson and Haiti." *Journal of Southern History* 61, no. 2 (May 1995): 209–48.

Max, D. T. "A Man of Taste: A Chef with Cancer Fights to Save His Tongue." *New Yorker*, 12 May 2008, 83–93.

May, Cedrick. "Phillis Wheatley's Poetics of Liberation: Backgrounds and Contexts." *Early American Literature* 45, no. 3 (2010): 724–27.

McCoy, Drew. *The Last of the Fathers: James Madison and the Republican Legacy*. New York: Cambridge University Press, 1989.

McGann, Jerome, and Lisa Samuels. *Radiant Textuality: Literature after the World Wide Web*. New York: Palgrave, 2001.

McLuhan, Marshall. *Understanding Media: The Extensions of Man.* Edited by W. Terrence Gordon. Corte Madera, Calif.: Gingko Press, 2003 [1964].

McWilliams, James E. *A Revolution in Eating: How the Quest for Food Shaped America.* New York: Columbia University Press, 2005.

McWilliams, Mark. "Distant Tables: Food and the Novel in Early America." *Early American Literature* 38, no. 3 (2003): 365–93.

Merish, Lori. *Sentimental Materialism: Gender, Commodity Culture, and Nineteenth Century American Literature.* Durham, N.C.: Duke University Press, 2000.

Miller, Adrian. *The President's Kitchen Cabinet: The Story of the African American Who Have Fed Our First Families from the Washingtons to the Obamas.* Chapel Hill: University of North Carolina Press, 2017.

Miller, Adrian. *Soul Food: The Surprising Story of an American Cuisine, One Plate at a Time.* Chapel Hill: University of North Carolina Press, 2013.

Miller, Fred D. "The Rule of Reason." In *The Cambridge Companion to Aristotle's Politics,* edited by Marguerite Deslauriers and Pierre Destrée, 38–66. Cambridge: Cambridge University Press, 2013.

Miller, John Chester. *The Wolf by the Ears: Thomas Jefferson and Slavery.* Charlottesville: University of Virginia Press, 1991.

Minich, Julie Avril. "Enabling Whom? Critical Disability Studies Now." *Lateral: Journal of the Cultural Studies Association* 5, no. 1 (Spring 2016). https://csalateral .org/issue/5-1/forum-alt-humanities-critical-disability-studies-now-minich/.

Mintz, Sidney. *Sweetness and Power: The Place of Sugar in Modern History.* New York: Penguin, 1986.

Mintz, Sidney. *Tasting Food, Tasting Freedom: Exercises into Eating, Culture, and the Past.* Boston: Beacon Press, 1997.

Mitchell, David T., and Sharon L. Snyder, *Narrative Prosthesis: Disability and the Dependencies of Discourse.* Ann Arbor: University of Michigan Press, 2001.

Moretti, Franco. *Graphs, Maps, Trees: Abstract Models for Literary History.* New York: Verso, 2007.

Morrison, Toni. "The Site of Memory." In *Inventing the Truth: The Art and Crat of Memoir.* 2nd ed., edited by William Zinsser, 83–102. New York: Houghton-Mifflin, 1995.

Morton, Timothy. "Blood Sugar." In *Romanticism and Colonialism: Writing and Empire, 1780-1830,* edited by Tim Fulford and Peter J. Kitson, 87–106. Cambridge: Cambridge University Press, 1998.

Morton, Timothy. *Cultures of Taste/Theories of Appetite: Eating and Romanticism.* New York: Palgrave Macmillan, 2004.

Morton, Timothy. *The Poetics of Spice: Romantic Consumerism and the Exotic.* New York: Cambridge University Press, 2006.

Moten, Fred. "Knowledge of Freedom." *New Centennial Review* 4, no. 2 (Fall 2004): 269–310.

Neuhaus, Jessamyn. *Manly Meals and Mom's Home Cooking: Cookbooks and Gender in Modern America*. Baltimore: Johns Hopkins University Press, 2012.

Newman, Simon. "American Political Culture and the French and Haitian Revolutions: Nathaniel Cutting and the Jeffersonian Republicans." In *The Impact of the Haitian Revolution on the Atlantic World*, edited by David P. Geggus, 72–92. Columbia: University of South Carolina Press, 2001.

Noble, Marianne. *The Masochistic Pleasures of Sentimental Literature*. Princeton, N.J.: Princeton University Press, 2000.

Nolan, J. Bennett. *Benjamin Franklin in Scotland and Ireland, 1759 and 1771*. Philadelphia: University of Pennsylvania Press, 1956.

Novero, Cecilia. *Antidiets of the Avant-Garde: From Futurist Cooking to Eat Art*. Minneapolis: University of Minnesota Press, 2009.

Nudelman, Franny. "Harriet Jacobs and the Sentimental Politics of Female Suffering." *ELH* 59, no. 4 (Winter 1992): 939–64.

"Obituary: Mrs. Margaret Cockburn Conkling Steele." *Publishers' Weekly* 966 (2 August 1890): 168.

Olney, James. "'I Was Born': Slave Narratives, Their Status as Autobiography and as Literature." *Callaloo* 20 (Winter 1984): 46–73.

O'Neill, Molly. "A 19th-Century Cookbook Gives New Twist to 'Soul Food.'" *New York Times*, November 22, 2007. https://www.nytimes.com/2007/11/22/arts/22iht-cookbook.1.8431779.html.

Onuf, Peter. "'To Declare Them a Free and Independent People': Race, Slavery, and National Identity in Jefferson's Thought." *Journal of the Early Republic* 18, no. 1 (Spring 1998): 1–46.

Parrish, Susan Scott. *American Curiosity: Cultures of Natural History in the Colonial British Atlantic World*. Chapel Hill: University of North Carolina Press, 2006.

Parrish, Susan Scott. "Rummaging/In and Out of Holds." *Early American Literature* 45 (Spring 2010): 261–74.

Pasanek, Brad. *Metaphors of the Mind: An Eighteenth-Century Dictionary*. Baltimore: Johns Hopkins University Press, 2015.

Patterson, Orlando. *Slavery and Social Death: A Comparative Study*. Cambridge, Mass.: Harvard University Press, 1985.

Pazicky, Diana Loercher. *Cultural Orphans in America*. Jackson: University of Mississippi Press, 1998.

Peabody, Elizabeth Palmer. "The Word 'Aesthetic.'" In *Aesthetic Papers*, edited by Elizabeth Palmer Peabody, 1–4. New York: G. P. Putnam, 1849.

Peabody, Sue. *"There Are No Slaves in France": The Political Culture of Race and Slavery in the Ancien Régime*. New York: Oxford University Press, 2002.

Pellien, Jessica. "Rotunda Launches a Digital Edition of *The Papers of Thomas Jefferson.*" *Princeton University Press Blog,* 9 April 2009. http://blog.press .princeton.edu/2009/04/06/rotunda-launches-a-digital-edition-of-the-papers -of-thomas-jefferson/.

Pennell, Elizabeth Robbins. *My Cookery Books.* New York: Houghton Mifflin, 1903.

Pinkard, Susan. *A Revolution in Taste: The Rise of French Cuisine.* New York: Cambridge University Press, 2009.

Plasa, Carl. *Slaves to Sweetness: British and Caribbean Literatures of Sugar.* Liverpool: Liverpool University Press, 2009.

Playfair, William. *Commercial and Political Atlas and Statistical Breviary.* Edited by Howard Wainer and Ian Spence. New York: Cambridge University Press, 2005.

Pollan, Michael. *The Omnivore's Dilemma: A Natural History of Four Meals.* New York: Penguin, 2007.

Posner, Miriam. "How Did They Make That?" *UCLA Digital Humanities Boot Camp,* 28 August 2013. http://dhbasecamp.humanities.ucla.edu/bootcamp/ 2013/08/28/how-did-they-make-that/.

Pratt, Casey. "'These Things Took the Shape of Mystery': Incidents in the Life of a Slave Girl as American Romance." *African American Review* 47, no. 1 (Spring 2014): 69–81.

Prindle, David. *The Paradox of Democratic Capitalism: Politics and Economics in American Thought.* Baltimore: Johns Hopkins University Press, 2006.

Proust, Marcel. *Remembrance of Things Past.* Vol. 1, *Swann's Way* and *Within a Budding Grove.* Translated by C. K. Scott Moncrieff and Terence Kilmartin. New York: Vintage, 1982 [1919].

Ramsay, Stephen. *Reading Machines: Toward and Algorithmic Criticism.* Champaign: University of Illinois Press, 2011.

Randolph, Mary. *The Virginia House-Wife.* Edited by Karen Hess. Columbia: University of South Carolina Press, 1984 [1824].

Ridley, Glynis. "The First American Cookbook." *Eighteenth-Century Life* 23, no. 2 (May 1999): 114–23.

Rinaldi, Ann. *Wolf by the Ears.* New York: Scholastic, 1991.

Risjord, Norman. "The Compromise of 1790: New Evidence on the Dinner Table Bargain." *William and Mary Quarterly,* 3rd. ser., 33, no. 2 (April 1976): 309–14.

Riskin, Jessica. "Eighteenth-Century Wetware." *Representations* 83 (Summer 2003): 97–125.

Riskin, Jessica. "Poor Richard's Leyden Jar: Electricity and Economy in Franklinist France." *Historical Studies in the Physical and Biological Sciences* 28, no. 2 (1998): 301–36.

Riskin, Jessica. *Science in the Age of Sensibility: The Sentimental Empiricists of the French Enlightenment.* Chicago: University of Chicago Press, 2002.

Rival, Ned. *Grimod de la Reynière: Le gourmand gentilhomme.* Paris: Le Pré aux Clercs, 1983.

Roberts, Robert. *The House Servant's Directory, or A Monitor for Private Families: Comprising Hints on the Arrangement and Performance of Servants' Work.* Boston: Munroe and Francis, 1827.

Rodgers, Daniel T. "Republicanism: The Career of a Concept." *Journal of American History* 79, no. 1 (1992): 11–38.

Rosenberg, Daniel. "Data before the Fact." In *Raw Data Is an Oxymoron,* edited by Lisa Gitelman, 15–40. New York: New York University Press, 2013.

Rowlandson, Mary. *The Sovereignty and Goodness of God.* In *American Captivity Narratives,* edited by Gordon Sayers, 137–76. New York: Houghton Mifflin, 2000.

Roy, Parama. *Alimentary Tracts: Appetites, Aversions, and the Postcolonial.* Durham, N.C.: Duke University Press, 2010.

Rucker, Walter. *The River Flows On: Black Resistance, Culture, and Identity Formation in Early America.* Baton Rouge: Louisiana State University Press, 2008.

Russell, Malinda. *A Domestic Cookbook: Containing A Careful Selection of Useful Receipts for the Kitchen.* Introduced by Janice Bluestein Longone. Ann Arbor: William L. Clements Library, 2007 [1866].

Samuels, Shirley, ed. *The Culture of Sentiment: Race, Gender, and Sentimentality in Nineteenth-Century America.* New York: Oxford University Press, 1992.

Samuels, Shirley. "Women, Blood, and Contract." *American Literary History* 20, nos. 1–2 (Spring–Summer 2008): 57–75.

Sánchez-Eppler, Karen. *Touching Liberty: Abolition, Feminism, and the Politics of the Body.* Berkeley: University of California Press, 1993.

Scheinfeldt, Tom. "Where's the Beef? Does Digital Humanities Have to Answer Questions?" In *Debates in the Digital Humanities,* edited by Matthew K. Gold, 56–60. Minneapolis: University of Minnesota Press, 2012.

Schiff, Stacy. *A Great Improvisation: Franklin, France, and the Birth of America.* New York: Holt, 2006.

Scholz, Trebor, ed. *Digital Labor: The Internet as Playground and Factory.* New York: Routledge, 2012.

Schuller, Kyla. *The Biopolitics of Feeling: Race, Sex, and Science in the Nineteenth Century.* Durham, N.C.: Duke University Press, 2017.

Schulz, Constance, ed. *The Papers of Eliza Lucas Pinckney and Harriott Pinckney Horry Digital Edition.* Charlottesville: University of Virginia Press, Rotunda, 2012. https://rotunda.upress.virginia.edu/PinckneyHorry/.

Scofield, Merry Ellen. "The Fatigues of His Table: The Politics of Presidential Dining during the Jefferson Administration." *Journal of the Early Republic* 26 (Fall 2006): 449–69.

Sekora, John. "Black Message/White Envelope: Genre, Authenticity, and Authority in the Antebellum Slave Narrative." *Callaloo* 32 (Summer 1987): 482–515.

Shalhope, Robert E. "Toward a Republican Synthesis: The Emergence of an Understanding of Republicanism in American Historiography." *William and Mary Quarterly,* 3rd. ser., 29 (January 1972): 49–80.

Shapiro, Steven. "'Man to Man I Need Not Dread His Encounter': *Edgar Huntly*'s End of Erotic Pessimism." In *Revising Charles Brockden Brown: Culture, Politics, and Sexuality in the Early Republic,* edited by Philip Barnard, Mark L. Kamrath, and Stephen Shapiro, 216–53. Knoxville: University of Tennessee Press, 2004.

Sharpe, Christina. *In the Wake: On Blackness and Being.* Durham, N.C.: Duke University Press, 2016.

Shaw, Gwendolyn DuBois. *Portraits of a People: Picturing African Americans in the Nineteenth Century.* Seattle: University of Washington Press, 2006.

Shi, David. *The Simple Life: Plain Living and High Thinking in American Culture.* Athens: University of Georgia Press, 2007.

Shields, David S. "The Atlantic World, the Senses, and the Arts." In *The Oxford Handbook of the Atlantic World: 1450–1850,* edited by Nicholas Canny and Philip Morgan, 130–45. New York: Oxford University Press, 2011.

Shields, David S. *Civil Tongues and Polite Letters in British America.* Chapel Hill: University of North Carolina Press, 1997.

Shields, David S. *Southern Provisions: The Creation and Revival of a Cuisine.* Chicago: University of Chicago Press, 2016.

Simek, Nicole. *Hunger and Irony in the French Caribbean: Literature, Theory, and Public Life.* London: Palgrave Macmillan, 2016.

Simmons, Amelia. *American Cookery, or the Art of Dressing Viands, Fish, Poultry, and Vegetables, and the Best Modes of Making Pastes, Puffs, Pies, Tarts, Puddings, Custards, and Preserves, and All Kinds of Cakes, from the Imperial Plum to Plain Cake: Adapted to This Country, and All Grades of Life.* 2nd ed. Edited by Karen Hess. Bedford, Mass.: Applewood, 1996 [1798].

Slauter, Eric. "Looking for Scipio Moorhead: An 'African Painter' in Revolutionary North America." In *Slave Portraiture in the Atlantic World,* edited by Agnes Lugo-Ortiz, 89–116. Cambridge: Cambridge University Press, 2013.

Sorisio, Carolyn. "The Spectacle of the Body: Torture in the Antislavery Writing of Lydia Maria Child and Frances E. W. Harper." *Modern Language Studies* 30, no. 1 (Spring 2000): 45–66.

Spang, Rebecca L. *The Invention of the Restaurant: Paris and Modern Gastronomic Culture.* Cambridge, Mass.: Harvard University Press, 2000.

Spillers, Hortense. "Mama's Baby, Papa's Maybe: An American Grammar Book." *Diacritics* 17, no. 2 (Summer 1987): 64–81.

Stanard, Mary Newton. *Richmond, Its People and Its Story*. Philadelphia: J. B. Lippincott, 1923.

Stanton, Lucia. "Jefferson's People: Slavery at Monticello." In *The Cambridge Companion to Thomas Jefferson*, edited by Frank Shuffelton, 83–100. New York: Cambridge University Press, 2009.

Stoller, Laura Ann. *Along the Archival Grain: Epistemic Anxieties and Colonial Common Sense*. Princeton, N.J.: Princeton University Press, 2010.

Sullivan, Caroline. *Classic Jamaican Cooking: Traditional Recipes and Herbal Remedies*. Edited by Christie MacKie. London: Serif, 2003 [1893].

Sundquist, Eric J. *To Wake the Nations: Race in the Making of American Literature*. Cambridge, Mass.: Harvard University Press, 1993.

Sweet, Timothy. *American Georgics: Economy and Environment in Early American Literature*. Philadelphia: University of Pennsylvania Press, 2002.

Sweet, Timothy. "Jefferson, Science, and the Enlightenment." In *The Cambridge Companion to Thomas Jefferson*, edited by Frank Shuffelton, 101–13. New York: Cambridge University Press, 2009.

Taylor, Diana. *The Archive and the Repertoire: Performing Cultural Memory in the Americas*. Durham, N.C.: Duke University Press, 2003.

Taylor, Elizabeth Dowling. *A Slave in the White House: Paul Jennings and the Madisons*. New York: Palgrave Macmillan, 2012.

"Testimony in the Trial of Gabriel, 6 October 1800." *Library of Virginia*. http://www.lva.virginia.gov/exhibits/DeathLiberty/gabriel/gabtrial17.htm.

Thompson, Mary V. "Ice Cream." *The Digital Encyclopedia of George Washington*. George Washington Presidential Library. https://www.mountvernon.org/library/digitalhistory/digital-encyclopedia/article/ice-cream/.

Tillet, Salamishah. *Sites of Slavery: Citizenship and Racial Democracy in the Post-Civil Rights Imagination*. Durham, N.C.: Duke University Press, 2012.

Tipton-Martin, Toni. *The Jemima Code: Two Centuries of African American Cookbooks*. Austin: University of Texas Press, 2015.

Titus, Sonja, Regina Schneller, and Gerhard Banik. "The Copying Press Process: History and Technology, Part 1." *Restaurator* 27 (June 2006): 90–102.

Tompkins, Jane. *Sensational Designs: The Cultural Work of American Fiction, 1790–1860*. New York: Oxford University Press, 1985.

Tompkins, Kyla Wazana. "Consider the Recipe." *J19: The Journal of Nineteenth-Century Americanists* 1, no. 2 (Fall 2013): 439–45.

Tompkins, Kyla Wazana. *Racial Indigestion: Eating Bodies in the Nineteenth Century*. New York: New York University Press, 2012.

Tricomi, Albert. "Harriet Jacobs's Autobiography and the Voice of Lydia Maria Child." *ESQ: A Journal of the American Renaissance* 53, no. 3 (2007): 216–52.

Trouillot, Michel-Rolph. *Silencing the Past: Power and the Production of History*. Boston: Beacon, 1997.

Tufte, Edward. *The Visual Display of Quantitative Information*. 2nd ed. Cheshire, Conn.: Graphics Press, 2001.

Twitty, Michael W. "The Unbearable Taste: Early African American Foodways." *Common-Place: The Interactive Journal of Early American Life* 11, no. 3 (April 2011) http://www.common-place-archives.org/vol-11/no-03/twitty/.

Underwood, Ted. "Theorizing Research Practices We Forgot to Theorize Twenty Years Ago." *Representations* 127, no. 1 (Summer 2014): 64–72.

Vizenor, George. *Native Liberty: Natural Reason and Cultural Survivance*. Lincoln: University of Nebraska Press, 2009.

Wagoner, Jennifer. *Jefferson and Education*. Charlottesville: University of Virginia Press, 2004.

Waldstreicher, David. "Benjamin Franklin, Slavery, and the Founders: On the Dangers of Reading Backwards." *Common-Place: The Journal of Early American Life* 4, no. 4 (July 2004). http://common-place.org/book/benjamin-franklin-slavery-and-the-founders-on-the-dangers-of-reading-backwards/.

Waldstreicher, David. *Runaway America: Benjamin Franklin, Slavery, and the American Revolution*. New York: Hill and Wang, 2004.

Walker, David. *Appeal to the Coloured Citizens of the World, but in Particular, and Very Expressly, to Those of the United States of America*. Rev. ed. Boston, 1830 [1829].

Warner, Michael. *The Letters of the Republic: Publication and the Public Sphere in Eighteenth-Century America*. Cambridge, Mass.: Harvard University Press, 1990.

Warnes, Andrew. *Savage Barbecue: Race, Culture, and the Invention of America's First Food*. Athens: University of Georgia Press, 2008.

Washington, George. *The Papers of George Washington: Retirement Series*. Vol. 1, *March–December 1797*. Edited by W. W. Abbot. Charlottesville: University Press of Virginia, 1998. *Founders Online,* National Archives. https://founders.archives.gov/volumes/Washington/06-01.

Weheliye, Alexander. *Habeas Viscus: Racializing Assemblages, Biopolitics, and Black Feminist Theories of the Human*. Durham, N.C.: Duke University Press, 2014.

Weinstein, Cindy, and Christopher Looby, eds. *American Literature's Aesthetic Dimensions*. New York: Columbia University Press, 2012.

Wheatley, Phillis. *Complete Writings*. Edited by Vincent Carretta. New York: Penguin, 2001.

Whitehead, Colson. *The Underground Railroad*. New York: Doubleday, 2016.

Williams-Forson, Psyche. *Building Houses Out of Chicken Legs: Black Women, Food, and Power*. Chapel Hill: University of North Carolina Press, 2006.

Wills, Garry. *Inventing America: Jefferson's Declaration of Independence*. New York: Mariner-Houghton Mifflin, 2002.

Wilson, Elizabeth. *Gut Feminism*. Durham, N.C.: Duke University Press, 2015.

Wilson, Ivy. *Specters of Democracy: Blackness and the Aesthetics of Politics in the Antebellum U.S.* New York: Oxford University Press, 2011.

Witt, Doris. *Black Hunger: Soul Food and America*. Minneapolis: University of Minnesota Press, 2004.

Wolfe, Cary. *What Is Posthumanism?* Minneapolis: University of Minnesota Press, 2009.

Wood, Gordon S. *The Creation of the American Republic, 1776–1787.* Chapel Hill: University of North Carolina Press, 1969.

Woodard, Vincent. *The Delectable Negro: Human Consumption and Homoeroticism within US Slave Culture.* Edited by Justin Joyce and Dwight McBride. New York: New York University Press, 2014.

Zafar, Rafia. *Recipes for Respect: African American Meals and Meaning.* Athens: University of Georgia Press, 2019.

Zafar, Rafia. *We Wear the Mask: African Americans Write American Literature, 1760–1870.* New York: Columbia University Press, 1997.

Index

Page numbers in italics refer to illustrations.

LAUREN F. KLEIN is associate professor in the departments of English and Quantitative Theory and Methods at Emory University. She is coauthor of *Data Feminism* and coeditor of *Debates in the Digital Humanities 2016* (Minnesota, 2016) and *Debates in the Digital Humanities 2019* (Minnesota, 2019).